WITHDRAWN

"A Thing Divided"

"A Thing Divided"

Representation in the Late Novels of Henry James

John Landau

Madison • Teaneck
Fairleigh Dickinson University Press
London: Associated University Presses

Associated University Presses
440 Forsgate Drive
Cranbury, NJ 08512

Associated University Presses
16 Barter Street
London WC1A 2AH, England

Associated University Presses
P.O. Box 338, Port Credit
Mississauga, Ontario
Canada L5G 4L8

The paper used in this publication meets the requirements
of the American National Standard for Permanence of Paper
for Printed Library Materials Z39.48-1984.

Library of Congress Cataloging-in-Publication Data

Landau, John, 1948–
    A thing divided : representation in the late novels of Henry James
/ John Landau.
        p.   cm.
    Includes bibliographical references and index.
    ISBN 0-8386-3626-8 (alk. paper)
    1. James, Henry, 1843–1916—Criticism and interpretation.
2. Mimesis in literature. I. Title.
PS2127.M55L36 1996
813'.4—dc20   95-53134
                                                              CIP

PRINTED IN THE UNITED STATES OF AMERICA

to Naomi

". . . as a thing divided and contested."

—James, *The Golden Bowl*

Contents

Acknowledgments

I want to begin by saying thank you. To all those who helped me in the long process of writing this book. The conventional "slot" of acknowledgments cannot do justice to my sense of gratitude. More people than I can mention had a share in the making of this book.

My first contact with Henry James was in a class taught by Baruch Hochman. Without Baruch, good friend, colleague, and later doctoral supervisor, this book would not have been written. I hope that the influence of Baruch's acuity finds some expression here. His generosity and warmth have been unending as he helped me "chew my cud." I can only *begin* to express my thanks. Thanks to Barbara Hochman who listened and listened again to my endless formulations, read and reread. Her patience and friendship have been untiring. Barbara's invitation to participate on a panel on artist/audience relations was instrumental in helping me write the chapter on *The Tragic Muse*.

With Elizabeth Freund, Josh Wilner, Ruth Nevo, Rael Meyerowitz, and occasional visitors I participated in an informal reading group that nurtured the intellectual and moral inspiration for this book. More recently I have benefited from similar conversation with Judy Levy and Daphne Leighton. I thank them.

I think of all those whose ears I have bent over the years trying to sort out my thoughts. Elizabeth Freund, colleague and friend, has consistently been an intellectual touchstone. Without her ear I would be deaf. In no particular order, I thank Ron Kuzar, Doron Narkiss, and Deganit Schocken for hours of argument and support. Doron and Ron, as well as Gil Freund also provided invaluable technical assistance. My friend Lindsay Talmud was particularly helpful in talking me through the chapter on *The Wings of the Dove*.

In the final stages of preparing this manuscript Batya Stein's editorial skills and critical intelligence helped to sharpen my thoughts and my sentences. She fleshed out my ideas and gave them body. Her enthusiasm—for James and for my work—and her unstinting assistance gave me confidence in this task at a dark hour. I thank her deeply.

I am grateful for the support of the Wolfson Foundation whose post-doctoral scholarship allowed me to spend a year at the University of California at Berkeley where I benefited from the company of Alex Zwerdling, Alex Gelley, and Charles Altieri. I spent long hours talking about my work with Leo Lowenthal, whose wisdom was always great and whose memory I cherish. In Berkeley I met David Heyd, a Jerusalem colleague who has since become a close friend. He was especially useful in helping me formulate the introductory chapter.

In the acknowledgments to his book my friend Steve Aschheim thanked me for enduring his bleatings; I want to return the favor, express my sense that our long friendship transcends the tit for tat, and remind him that I have the tentative last word in one-upmanship . . . until his next book.

I would like to thank the people at Fairleigh Dickinson University Press and at Associated University Presses for all their assistance. Special thanks to Chris Owen whose careful editing has, I believe, improved this book.

This book grew out of a doctoral dissertation written in the English Department at the Hebrew University of Jerusalem, which has been home to me since the beginning of my university education. The department has consistently provided a warm and stimulating environment for which I am grateful. Bill Daleski, Ruth Nevo and Shlomith Rimmon-Kenan have always been available with assistance and advice.

Above all, thanks to my wife Naomi and my children, David and Yael. They have suffered with me, borne with me, and given me more than I can say.

"A Thing Divided"

1

Representation in the Late Novels

Since Dorothea Krook used James's description of Milly, the heroine of *The Wings of the Dove,* as the title for her book,[1] James's phrase "the ordeal of consciousness" has become synonymous with what many critics of James take to be his central concern, namely, representing the unfurling of individual consciousness in its struggle to define a self in the context of the pressures, tangible and intangible, of life in society.[2]

In the following study, I too understand James as concerned with the question of how to live in the world, that is, as engaging essentially ethical issues. In this sense, I understand James's work in the context of the traditional concerns of the novel. He projects a world where the problems faced by his lifelike characters have to do with marriages and money; success and failure; frustrated and fulfilled love; problems of loss, absence and death—the concrete issues that center traditional fiction in the nineteenth century.

Many critics have focused on the moral dimensions of the "ordeal of consciousness."[3] In this book, however, I show how, in addition, and on a different level, James's fiction dramatizes the project of representation itself as the "ordeal of consciousness." The difficulties attendant on the challenge of representing life in literature are seen to entail elements of the experience that his characters undergo in their own struggle to apprehend themselves and perceive others. The much noted self-reflective dimension of James's late fiction—the way in which the text directs attention to itself and to its own strategies of representing experience—reflects not only the writer's difficulty in creating fictional worlds, but the existential problem experienced by the characters as they represent themselves to themselves and to each other.

There are grounds that would indicate the felicity of discussing James's late work in terms of the themes, motifs, structures, and problems that unify it and tend to be repeated and explored from novel to novel. In this study, however, I have chosen not to organize my discussion in terms of these separate issues, but to read the individual novels as discrete works of art. There are two reasons for this choice.

The lesser of these has to do with a sense that, in his late novels, James himself is working through a series of problems. Considering the books together is, therefore, to shortcut, and thus short-circuit, a sense of process and, I will argue, of progress in James's own working out of the problems he engages. Although the novels deal with a series of related issues, from novel to novel the handling of these issues tends to develop. In this work, then, I trace James's attempt to create a form of fiction able to deal with his concerns about the nature of art and its relationship with reality.

The primary consideration dictating the particular form of this study, however, has to do with a sense of the integrity of James's work, not as a metaphysical treatise or an exploration of philosophical problems, but as a series of separate, discrete works of literature.[4] Although the novels center on and circulate common issues, each of them projects a fictitious world which creates its own peculiar, albeit related, excitement. These novels, although sharing much in common besides a common author, generate independent aesthetic experiences. To treat the late James's ouvre as a unified, undifferentiated corpus is to highlight the common concerns, but also to distort the artistic achievement of each separate book; it is to reduce the experience of reading to an exercise in thinking, and the experience of participation in a specific world to an intellectual challenge. In treating each novel separately, I would like to maintain the tension prevailing in James's late work between the mimetic project and the problems it raises.

In the many studies focusing on James, in line with prevalent schools of thought, critics have used structuralist and rhetorical strategies. These were followed by post-structuralist studies that understand James as a pioneer of modernism, with some critics suggesting that James is a forerunner of postmodernism. Recently, there have been studies dealing specifically with more contemporary issues in James's work, such as feminism; even more recently, there have been works influenced by the new historicism, which both use and counter rhetorical criticism by attempting to contextualize James in the market for which he wrote.

In a mode that shares much with the close reading of the new critics, I use some of the strategies of rhetorical criticism to shed light on how James manages in his late works to bridge the gap between what earlier critics took for granted, namely, the ethical problems implicit in the theme of the ordeal of consciousness and in the novel of manners, and the epistemological and ontological problems that have been the focus of the more recent criticism informed by a postmodernist perspective. James's late works dramatize, in aesthetic terms, many of the problems that are important in the discourse of contemporary literary theory. This retrospective view will illuminate the *weltanschauung* shared by these different critics.

My claim is that the world James projects in his late novels can be best described from the vantage point provided by the concepts that post-structuralist rhetorical criticism has made available.[5] The inevitable question is whether James's work lends itself to this kind of analysis, or whether I am retrospectively imposing my own critical sensibility on James's work by relying on this set of critical terms. Since to renounce bias is, in my own terms, impossible, let me "simply state"—with an awareness that such statements can never be simple—that I believe that the interpenetration of James's works and postmodernist rhetorical theory will illuminate aspects of both.

I do not see myself as deconstructing James but as using the strategies of a deconstructionist reading to show how James's late work reconciles an awareness of the problematic of rhetoric with the problematic of the traditional nineteenth-century mimetic novel. The problem is how to represent a fictional world in which characters struggle to crystallize selves, and find ways to fulfill those selves through expression and action in a world involving relationships with other characters, that is, in a world that, because it is social, is irreducibly and impossibly ethical.[6]

In the novels of the major phase, James creates worlds in which consciousness struggles to constitute itself in the very world that makes self-constitution difficult. The self experiences the difficulty of distinguishing representation from reality as a critical element in the endeavor to orient and ground itself. Due to the inability to do so with any degree of certitude, the project of constituting the self may come to be felt as almost impossible. The world of James's fiction thus reflects the tentative and porous nature of the boundary between representation and reality, or fiction and reality. The Jamesian self thus has to struggle to separate its own representations of reality from the reality outside. The fact that, in fiction, the reality outside the self is itself fictional only serves to complicate even further the characters'—and readers'—project of distinguishing the fictional or represented from the real.

James creates such doubt in the readers' minds as to the possibility of reaching beyond representation to any underlying truth that

his characters' confusion, alienation, inability, or refusal to participate in life might be understood as a form of radical solipsism. The
self defines itself as so separate from the world that, ultimately,
it comes to doubt the very existence of a world outside its own
representations.[7] Representation being indistinguishable from the
very reality that might validate it, an interminable chain of yet
further representations is generated, exposing a dimension of solipsism inherent in the tradition of radical skepticism. In *The Claim
of Reason,* as in much of the rest of his work, Stanley Cavell addresses the issue of solipsism as the logical outcome of radical
skepticism, an unavoidable and dangerous upshot of a mode of
thought that has characterized Western metaphysical philosophy.[8]

James's fiction dramatizes the problem entailed by solipsism, but
also suggests ways of confronting it. In revealing, recognizing, and
accepting the impossibility of distinguishing representation from
reality, James underscores the difficulty of representation while
insisting on its inevitability. Insofar as James is a novelist engaged
in the traditional task of representing reality, we may wish to understand him as indeed welcoming, if not celebrating, the inexhaust-
ible nature of representation. The interminable and illimitable
process of representation provides both the characters in the novel
and its readers with their only possible access to reality, the "reality" that fiction represents.

In other words, although James's characters and James's readers
may doubt the capacity of representation to reflect reality adequately, they also need to confront the possibility that it may indeed do so. Precisely because we can never close the gap between
the representation and that which is represented—after all, we
only have access to "it" in representation—we do not give up attempting to authenticate our experience. Although James's fiction
appears skeptical about the possibility of telling its own truth, it
nevertheless tries to do just that: its truth is that the struggle
to distinguish between representation and reality is unending. A
paradox, then, is implicit in James's novels. He appears to suggest
the illimitability or impossibility of representation, yet as his novels
successfully represent the confusion that we feel as a result of our
entrapment in the endless chain of representation, he succeeds in
undermining his own project. Insofar as his fictions "work," his
very success is an indication of his failure. The precarious balance
of the openness of his texts and their success in expressing this
openness suggest a closure implicitly inimical to a conception holding representation to be radically illimitable.

Resonating within the surface of James's novels, concerned as they are with the manners and morals of the upper classes and the clashes and crises of characters struggling to find and fulfill their desires, and underlying the richly rendered and extremely specified individual history of James's characters is a sense of the broader canvas, of history itself. A deeper sense, involving rupture and loss in James's work, is reflected not only on the level of action or content in his work, but also in the highly self-conscious way James problematizes the formal elements of the novel. The density and opacity of his language and syntax, the circumlocution which out-raged many contemporary readers[9] and continues to exasperate many modern readers, the claustrophobic quality of his handling of point of view, all serve to highlight and compensate for the loss of those certainties which ordered an earlier tradition.

James's emphasis on the precious achievements of a stabilizing social tradition, however precarious, finds its fullest expression in his over-elaboration of the surface quality of language and in his highly self-conscious manipulation of the forms of narration. The intricate elaboration of *artistic* form in James's novels would seem to reflect, resonate with, and rehearse the attempt to create *social* forms which can more or less adequately express and counter the experience of dislocation consequent on the loss of confidence in the imperatives of truth and ethics. Whereas these issues can be found throughout James's work, it is in what Matthiessen calls the "major phase" that James engages these issues most directly.[10]

If, as Brooks puts it, James's work "is a response to the loss of the tragic vision,"[11] this loss is reflected in James's last three com-pleted novels in the problematization of the ground which the tradi-tional novel takes for granted. To engage the problem of projecting a world devoid of tragic vision, the late works represent the strug-gle to define a self whose "ordeal of consciousness" takes place in an unstable network of linguistic and social relations characterized by the absence of "truth." The importance of the network of lan-guage, art, manners, social forms, and norms is emphasized pre-cisely because it lacks the authority of transcendence and compensates for this lack. All we have is the network of representation.

James's formalization of his material tends—like much of the modernist art of his successors—to subvert the very possibility of authoritative representation even as it insists on its unavoidability. The formal articulation of the last novels usurps the substance of the "worlds" they project and undercuts the possibility of reading them as unitary, or even as stably ambiguous representations of the world.[12] To see this is not to neutralize the relevance of James's fiction as an account of the world or "mimetic" project, but to highlight and complicate the issues on which the more thematic readings are based. James's subversion of the forms of his own artifice has, necessarily, critical implications for the understanding of his fictional world. In all of the late works, the self-reflective quality of the language, the hypertrophy of dialogue, the over-whelming extent of the characters' convoluted self-conscious medi-tations, the impenetrability of the syntax itself, all serve to highlight the act of formalization. Hence the importance of focus-ing on the fluid and continual cycle in which the reader is caught. The extreme formalization of the novel subverts its content, which is then re-thematized and once again subverted in a continuing oscillation.

In the following readings of the three novels of the major phase, I arrive at a reading of James which relates the complexity of formal elaboration to thematic interests. This study elucidates the most obvious quality of the late work, namely the opacity produced by its linguistic density, a quality too often explained away on insuf-ficient thematic or psychological grounds. Those qualities that may at first seem obstacles to understanding are in fact the proper ob-jects of understanding; indeed they constitute the project of under-standing. In these works, James reflects the experience of having to deal with the problem implicit in representation, namely, the way representation generates further representation. In many of the prefaces to the New York Edition, but specifically in the preface to *Roderick Hudson* and to *The Ambassadors,* he explicitly ad-dresses the author's need to arbitrarily limit the proliferation of his material.[13]

I argue that, in the course of his last three major novels, James develops a dynamic, critical, and inherently unstable or self-reflective mode of accommodation to this problem. As a prologue to the works of the major phase, I discuss *The Tragic Muse,* written some ten years earlier, to suggest how James focuses schematically on the problem of representation at this middle stage of his career. I then go on to analyze the late novels to reveal the increasing complexity of his fictional world in terms of plot and style, and to point out the possible responses developed by the characters, as well as by the readers of these fictions, to their represented worlds.

In *The Tragic Muse* James experiments with different ap-proaches to the subject of representation that will occupy his later work. By the time we come to read the books of James's major phase we realize that the maze of representation is, in fact, existen-tial—underlying and informing all human activity. James begins, however, at the most obvious place, namely, with the theater and artists whose license it is to represent.

Since the characters in *The Tragic Muse* are artists, the focus on audience in this book is broader than in the later work. It is via the dramatization of the artist/audience relationship that James explores different conceptions of representation and its functions, viewing this relationship as prefiguring, in incipient form, the relationships between the characters in the later novels.[14] In the novels of the major phase, each of the characters becomes audience for another's performance. This is particularly true when James develops more fully his conception of representation as deriving authority from the success of its performance. I am thinking more specifically of such instances as that of Strether recognizing that he has been audience to the drama of the enabling lie, discussed below, or of Maggie enacting her lie. If in *The Tragic Muse* the protagonists are actual artists with real audiences, in the later texts the characters are seen to be implicated in a world that makes the distinction between artist and audience hard to sustain. In *The Tragic Muse* the relationship between representation and reality is figured as a conflict, and only occasionally does James suggest the terms he will fully endorse in the later books: "These things were the fictions and the shadows; the representation was the deep substance" (325). Thus, what emerges as an opposition in *The Tragic Muse* will be worked out in the novels of the late phase as categories that, intertwined, provide the fertile ground not just for art but for experience in general.

The strength of James's late work lies in the way in which he manages to create a sense of a world and at the same time to suggest the problematic of such a creation. It is not just that he deals with the powerful and traditional themes of the novel—the struggles and the fears the self undergoes in generating a sense of self, its attempts to know and satisfy its desires for self-expression, marriage, respect, status, recognition, love; its desire and anxiety to know itself and be known by others; its attempt to escape and establish the limitations of selfhood through establishing a relation with another. It is also that at the same time James creates characters and generates a sense of a familiar world, in which all such constructs of selfhood are recognized *as* constructs. The self in James, then, is seen as a function of desire manifesting and generating itself as it enters a network of relations where there are no firm rules, no fixed formulae for achieving selfhood, a world where the self is seen as structured by the culture or the order of representation it enters.

The structure of the cultural setting in James's fictional world, as configured for and through the dramatis personae, as well as for the reader, is itself experienced as arbitrary insofar as it is not grounded in anything other than the need for signification. There is no transcendental given in the world that will direct, mandate, or legislate the struggles of the subject. Despite the dramatized problematics of such a situation, James succeeds in projecting a recognizable world, as his characters engage with other characters in their attempt to fulfill their needs and desires.

For the post-Saussurean, post-Derridean reader, the Jamesian text frequently reflects upon the problematics of the interpretation of signs with uncanny resonance. Let me exemplify James's interweaving of the mimetic and the semiotic through an analysis of the following passage in *The Golden Bowl*, which describes Charlotte's rehearsal of the predicament of illicit intimacy. I provide the passage in full since I shall be returning to it frequently, to indicate how contemporary theory can elucidate specific aspects of the Jamesian text.

> It appeared thus that they might enjoy together extraordinary freedom, the two friends, from the moment they should understand their position aright. With the Prince himself, from an early stage, not unnaturally, Charlotte had made a great point of their so understanding it; she had found frequent occasion to describe to him this necessity, and, her resignation tempered, or her intelligence at least quickened, by irrepressible irony, she applied at different times different names to the propriety of their case. The wonderful thing was that her sense of propriety had been, from the first, especially alive about it. There were hours when she spoke of their taking refuge in what she called the commonest tact—as if this principle alone could suffice to light their way; there were others when it might have seemed, to listen to her, that their course would demand of them the most anxious study and the most independent, not to say original, interpretation of signs. She talked now as if it were indicated, at every turn, by finger-posts of almost ridiculous prominence; she talked again as if it lurked in devious ways and were to be tracked through bush and briar; and she even, on occasion, delivered herself in the sense that, as their situation was unprecedented, so their heaven was without stars (220).[15]

Ostensibly, Charlotte and the Prince's problem, as expressed in this passage, is that they do not quite know how they are expected to relate to one another in the novel situation created by their marriages to the Ververs, father and daughter respectively. Adam and Maggie's continued intimacy, after their marriages, throw the Prince and Charlotte on one another's company with the result that they feel required to generate a code of conduct that will take account of the changes in their relationship. They are unfamiliar with the situation within which they find themselves, and consequently become aware of their need to interpret and act in unfamiliar ways.

The fact that the Prince and Charlotte exploit their freedom by having an affair suggests a typical Jamesian motif. Since the publication of "Daisy Miller," through *Roderick Hudson, The American,* and *The Portrait of a Lady,* up to and including the novels of the major phase, to name only a few obvious examples, James is associated with what his friend and contemporary, Howells, called the "international theme."[16] This motif is taken to represent the exploration of the problems encountered by the American sensibility in its meeting with the European sensibility.

Accepting, for the moment, the necessary oversimplification implicit in formulations of this sort (like Osmond and Madame Merle, Charlotte is American by birth and European only by adoption— the lines of demarcation blur), it seems that there is some measure of agreement among critics that James is acutely aware that his native America lacks the history and, therefore, the sense of tradition associated with Europe, his continent by adoption.[17] Schematically, America is characterized by vigor and vitality, while Europe is characterized by decadence and moral decay. Most critics who have written on James discuss the relationship between Europe and America. It is beyond the compass of this study to engage in an account of this criticism; suffice it to note that the broad consensus concerning this relationship views it as involving a conflict between good and evil, innocence and experience, open democracy and established tradition, expansive thrust and slow atrophy. Critics have further condensed these characteristics of the American spirit, as represented in James, into a term like "innocence," which is then contrasted with a concept of European "experience."[18] The token and overdetermined term which I will use in this work to describe the American ethos is the phrase, "American romanticism." This phrase can be understood as describing and ascribing to the American sensibility an unself-conscious assumption that transcendental essences, like the "good" and the "bad," are immediately present and manifest in the operations of everyday concrete life. In this perspective, the essential immanence of recognizable moral categories and unshakable truths is what characterizes a quintessentially American world-view.[19]

Rather than expressing an opposition, no matter how complex, the "international theme" is one of the many means James employs

to suggest not only the interdependence of such cultural constructs, but also their lack of any inherent substantiality. We may
be seduced into believing that terms such as country, home, and
even language might provide the contours of an identity; however,
they are soon exposed as sharing the limitations from which they
should serve as refuge. Osmond, Madame Merle, Maria Gostrey,
and Charlotte are all Americans by birth, but their experience in
Europe exposes the paucity of such cultural definition. Indeed, all
the ideas that would purport to offer stability and a sense of definition or self-definition seem to be prey to the same kind of destabilization in James's fiction, and this destabilization is inherent in the
very project of representation. The international theme in James
is the marker of a difference, ostensibly between Europe and
America, that dramatizedly fails to provide the kind of anchor and
stability normally associated with different countries and discrete
cultures. The function of this marker is to expose the limitations
of traditional attempts to find stability by placing traditional categories of thought in opposition to each other. The self requires
representational structures to attain some kind of stability, but
these very structures are exposed as affected by the instability
that the self is attempting to overcome. The need for and the danger
implicit in the representational structures shaping the self are also
shaped by the mode of narration James develops to express his
fictional worlds.

In its context, the passage cited above from *The Golden Bowl*
appears to express the difficulty experienced by the Europeans,
Charlotte and the Prince, in understanding the unfamiliar world
of the American Ververs. This difficulty might seem to represent
Charlotte's rationalization of her desire for the Prince. Insofar as
this rationalization is effective, however, it derives its efficacy from
Charlotte's rhetorical ability to persuade the Prince, and the reader,
of the possible validity of her perception. Here the motif of "the
international theme" is expressed in terms of a relation to language,
to sign. The world Charlotte describes is structured by a system
of signs that includes the characters who must act within it. For
the characters to "understand their position aright" they must establish a relationship with the world or the system in which they
move. The passage reveals, and the difficulty of the syntax seems
to confirm, that the signs, "the finger-posts" that should provide
the characters with points of orientation, are not intrinsically stable; the signs that are "ridiculous[ly] prominent" have also "to be
tracked through bush and briar."

The sense is that a sign can only be recognized as a sign, and thus fulfill its signifying function, within the context of its relationship to an entire system of signs. James can be seen to be using Charlotte's sense of the world to signify issues that come to dominate consciousness in post-structuralist literary theory. Charlotte's bewildered effort to recognize the signs and make out a "way" may be taken as a text that implies much that has been thought and said in the structuralist and post-structuralist perception of language and of our place within it.

The anxiety and freedom of Charlotte's "unprecedented" situation is condensed in the culminating phrase of the passage quoted from *The Golden Bowl*. In Charlotte's consciousness, her "heaven was without stars." For her, the absence of stars indicates the absence of that which would orient her course of action, moral or other.[20] In terms of the traditional trope, the stars represent the categorical imperative; their absence suggests the unsanctioned nature of representation in these conditions. Representation must then compensate for this lack, and arbitrarily assume a missing sanction.

The world that James describes in the late novels is always informed by the anxiety of such absence—namely, by the anxiety that there is nothing which legislates any particular course of action. Action, then, as rendered in the novels, would seem to be the product of a character's desire. In this light, interpretation, rather than being arbitrary is shaped by the terms afforded through the character's entry into the concrete situation. In James's discourse, the authority and mastery sought by representation is always subverted by the dramatized possibility of a different but equally plausible representation.

The issues shadowed by the absence of stars in Charlotte's heaven can be illuminated by reference to the work of Jacques Derrida whose work, so central to post-structuralist rhetorical criticism, is relevant here. For Derrida, Western metaphysics is a metaphysics of presence, and logocentrism, the term which he uses to describe this metaphysics, has according to him hypostatized the theoretically untenable dichotomy of presence/absence.[21] The absence of stars in James's passage signifies Charlotte's sense of the absence of an originary term which would guide her actions. The reader is asked to see Charlotte as thinking herself, or pretending to think herself, in an unprecedented situation which "would demand . . . the most anxious study and the most independent, not to say original, interpretation of signs." I would argue that James's characteristic use of the negative, as in "not to say" followed by that which should not be said, is an example of what in Derrida becomes a technique of writing under erasure, a means of both saying and indicating a logical or ontological problem, namely, the impossibility of saying.[22] What Charlotte is describing/ not describing is both describable and indescribable; she is talking of the "unprecedented." She is conjuring origin out of absence.[23]

When Charlotte thinks of the situation of the Prince and herself as demanding "the most anxious study and the most independent, not to say original, interpretation of signs," the necessity of representation is foregrounded precisely in the conditions that suggest its difficulty. How could an original interpretation be recognized as an interpretation? How can representation proceed if the origin of the system that can sanction it, in this case the stars, is absent? It is as though, without stars, the entire system that would make representation possible is unavailable. The passage dramatizes the need for some transcendental sign, some term that is not contingent, some categorical imperative that would sanction and stabilize the system. Charlotte's sense of the "independence" of her situation expresses both the lack of such a principle and the consequent need for it.[24]

Derrida's description of the *text* as instantiated and inhabited by *differance* provides a means of understanding the contradiction implicit in Charlotte's problem.[25] If the star, the centering term, were present, navigation or representation would be a process of learning how to make use of the given term in order to move in the desired direction. But when the lodestar is absent, as is the case in Charlotte's world as she perceives it, then even the signs that would "light [the] way" do not exactly lose their capacity to signify, but rather signify too much; at one and the same moment they are "ridiculously prominent" but also have "to be tracked through bush and briar." Without the foundation provided by the star there can be no intelligible system of signification and therefore no authoritative representation. But in this "unprecedented" situation Charlotte must act and, therefore, must generate impossibly original interpretations of signs. Representation is thus dramatized as a response to its own impossibility. One only need to represent, James seems to be suggesting, when one cannot.

In *The Golden Bowl* Charlotte chooses and acts on the basis of her own interpretation, simultaneously reconciling two logically exclusive views of representation. Through Charlotte, James emphasizes the necessarily arbitrary, and thus tendentious, and thus anxiety-provoking aspect of representation. The empty heavens figure the lack of a guiding authority, and the sense is double: no matter what direction she moves in, Charlotte is in principle lost;

and her sense of "extraordinary freedom" lies in the consequent need to act on the basis of arbitrary and unstable representations that are not determined by a transcendental authority. For James, representation is starless, a concept without presence or origin. Charlotte's manipulation? hypocrisy? self-delusion? repression? may be more wide-ranging than we suspected.[26] It is as though James is suggesting that interpretation, the basis for human action, involves a necessary and necessarily ungrounded fabrication of some guiding principle that will acquire the proportions and status of a foundational given.

In James's late novels, the situations are always unprecedented and the heavens always starless, and it is this that provokes and confers the fabulous liberty and anxiety associated with an "original" interpretation. When discussing the formalization of James's late work, what I had in mind is precisely the necessity to generate a system of signs, a formal structure, that is at once obscure and obvious. In the passage quoted from *The Golden Bowl,* Charlotte's enmeshment in unfamiliar signs can be seen to shape her desire as it both expresses and conceals it. Tact is not natural, behavior is not given. In the absence of a transcendental logos, representation, which cannot be avoided, is never grounded in absolute principles, but is dependent on relation to a system of signs that structures not only the world but the very consciousnesses that would interpret that world.[27]

Given this absence of "stars" James's problem then becomes how to represent a world (or characters, or the characters' representations of themselves and others in that world) where the possibility of representation is undermined by the absence of an orienting point or system able to guarantee the stability, credibility or reliability of those representations.

His method, which is also his aesthetic, is to focus on the representation of the consciousness of his characters as they struggle to define themselves in a world that defies definition. By highlighting the process of consciousness James succeeds at once in creating a mimetic world where characters act and interact with each other, while also suggesting the factitious nature of such a world. I outline below some of the strategies that James uses in order to achieve this twofold aim, while at the same time I indicate how these themes support my overall thesis, namely, that James both creates and problematizes the possibility of representing a mimetic picture of the world.

One of James's chief strategies is his use of the dramatic scene. Major earlier critics of James, such as Lubbock, Dupee, and Mat-

thiessen, as well as many after them, single out James's interest in
the theater for special attention.[28] The late works come after what
is taken to be James's failure in the theater. This failure, however,
was instructive for James insofar as it enabled him to refine his
handling of the "dramatic scene," which in fiction, as opposed to
drama proper, is characterized by the near-silencing of the narrative voice that ordinarily carries the authority of telling.[29] This
treatment of the scene opens up the entire question of authority.
Traditionally in the novel an omniscient, or even a partially omniscient (limited) narrative voice (often associated with the voice of
the author), seems to shape or confirm the reader's response to
scene, situation, character, action. Onstage drama and James's fictional dramatic scene are characterized by the absence of such a
voice.[30] Lubbock claims that James does manage to achieve the
immediacy of drama, and that the reader/spectator has to interpret
the scene unaided by author or playwright.

What Lubbock, Booth, and many critics who follow them consider the "*method*" of the dramatic scene, which allows James to
present and explore the movement of consciousness, is in fact an
aesthetic that tends to problematize the very project of representation. His handling of the authorial voice raises a wider problem—
the absence of an authority able to validate any given representation, and with it any interpretation of that representation.[31] The
missing authority of such an authorial voice can thus be seen as
analogous to the absence of stars in Charlotte's heaven. The problem of authority is expressed at different levels of the text, and
James's late novels problematize representation and interpretation
and explore the issues of consciousness and moral action in a narration which subverts its own authority. Examples of the self-
subversion of the narrative voice are analyzed in the following
chapters.

The readers' confrontation with the limits of their own interpretations is reinforced in the late novels, as they become aware of
the lack of a validating authority and find themselves engaging
in the same activity as the characters they would interpret. The
characters themselves are often seen as involved in interpreting
their own and the other characters' situations, often through
James's reflective use of the motif of reading and of writing. What
I am suggesting has the structure described by contemporary criticism as *mis en abyme*.[32] As they read, readers struggle to understand their own experience on the basis of their interpretation of
the characters' experience. But the characters themselves are involved in a similar activity as they struggle to understand their

own situations by interpreting the actions of the characters with whom they engage. Through these characters' involvement in the interpretation of the activities of other characters, James succeeds in suggesting the interminable process of representation, and its limitations: readers must interpret the characters interpreting and being interpreted in turn. In doing so, they experience not only the limitation (in terms of "criteria of truth") but also the inescapability of representation, and ultimately its success in establishing itself—whether it stands for some "reality" or "truth"—as the basis for the characters' actions as they interpret each other. Moreover, these characters interact in what is an irreducibly ethical context, namely, they have to make decisions which affect, for good and ill, not only themselves but other characters, who also act and make decisions. Yet, the characters act on the basis of interpretations which, certainly for the reader, but often even for the characters themselves, are necessarily partial and interested.[33] The most obvious example of this structure of *mis en abyme* is the way the characters are dramatized as interpreting through acts of reading and writing. Self-reflection has become a commonplace of contemporary literary discourse, yet what distinguishes self-reflection in James's late works is his thematization of the difficulties of reading and writing. Time after time we see characters whose profession is to write, reflecting on the impossibility of writing.[34]

Although it might seem that I am describing the familiar ambiguity of James's fiction, something else is involved. In his late fiction, James writes narrative which dramatizes the problematics and deals with the implications of a radical conception of representation, which assumes that freedom is foisted on us precisely because of the absence of any grounding terms.[35] His narrative establishes not the ambiguity of language, but *difference* that cannot be recuperated through the invocation of an hypostatized origin, a conception most fully formulated in post-structuralist criticism.[36]

Freedom is a concept that properly belongs to an ethical discourse, and what is most interesting in the novels under discussion is the way the seemingly antithetical worlds of a semiotic and an ethical discourse can be seen to meet in late James, where the semiotic implies the ethical. Were it not for the *necessary impossibility* of being sure that any sign, any representation, means what it says, the characters in James's novels, and his readers, would not be free to understand their experience on the basis of their interpretations. Interpretation would be determined and fixed by the signs and representations that produce it. James's late work, however, points to his uncomfortable acceptance of the discontents of a freedom structured by the instability of the terms, or signs, within which the characters, the readers, and the author construct meaning.

The problematic theme of freedom has been singled out, from as early as 1926 when Ezra Pound wrote about it, as the dominant issue in James's work.[37] The "ordeal of consciousness" in this view is primarily the ordeal of the individual struggle to achieve and preserve autonomy of self in the face of conflict, whether seen in personal, or in social terms.

Although concern with the theme of freedom is evident from the beginning of James's career, as his work develops the figure of the freedom-denying, immoral manipulator becomes increasingly associated with the figure of the aesthete.[38] But by the end of his career, the familiar opposition that critics have found in James's work between the aesthetic and the ethical is undone, and James's last works suggest that the ethical moment is instituted in the aesthetic moment.[39]

The aesthete in James is the figure whose overriding concern is with form, with the way things and people look. The distinction between people and things is collapsed as a result of James's emphasis on the way people/things are assessed and used by the aesthete. The Jamesian aesthete is only concerned with his own specific, and generally self-interested, conception of the beautiful.

By the time he publishes *The Portrait of a Lady* (1881), James has fully worked out the motif of the aesthete as immoral manipulator. Whereas any condemnation of Madame Merle's exaggerated concern with external form might be mitigated by her dramatized concern for her daughter Pansy, Osmond is the paradigmatic Jamesian aesthete; his withering aestheticism—as dramatized through his effect on Isabel's development as well as on Pansy's life—and his denial of their freedom, characterize him as a human monster. Solely and self-consciously concerned with appearances and with the way things, and primarily he himself, will appear in the eyes of others, he uses people as instruments for his own self-aggrandizement, and is seen as opposed to any moral impulses such as the ones that Isabel wants to have.

In *The Portrait of a Lady* James also develops another, more interesting and more problematic aesthete, in the character of Ralph. Ralph is representative of a long line of figures who, in the prefaces to the New York Edition, James describes as "reflectors." James's reflectors are gifted with developed and highly sensitive consciousnesses, through which the people and events they observe are portrayed. They are characterized above all by their capacity to see. Primarily spectators, these characters watch and are not, in James's early work, participants in the central dramatized action.

Like many of James's reflectors, Ralph is characterized as a sympathetic and sensitive man whose own personal autonomy is maintained by his distance from ongoing life and sustained by the curiosity and interest with which he looks on. It is this overinvestment in the activity of looking that is dramatized as immoral, creating the link between the reflector and the aesthete.[40] Neither can engage the ethical life of choice and consequence; both are concerned, for different reasons, with appearances, with the way things look, and with the act of looking. In James's discourse, both are aesthetes.

The seemingly irreducible opposition in James between aestheticism and ethics takes me back to the problematic of authority, and more specifically the problematic of mimesis. A semiotic perspective on the activity of observing shows how James's aesthetes are responsible for producing the ethical.[41]

In the final chapter of his book *Narrative Crossings,* with James's dramatic scene in mind, Gelley suggests that awareness of the limitations affecting the mimetic approach reveals a connection between the activity of "seeing" in the non-mimetic or semiotic text and the significance of this experience for the spectator. Gelley thinks of the scene "as a scene of desire,"[42] which shapes and expresses the *spectator's* fantasy. The dramatic scene focuses as much on the spectator as on the scene he witnesses.

> A theory of the scene in fiction could be used to test certain assumptions of a mimetic and representational model of narrative, assumptions like that of the "proximity" of the reader to what is represented. It could help us to account for the interplay of the staged or the "spectacle" (cf. the theatrical sense of the root term in Greek, *skene*) with the seen, the specular investment appropriate to a given form of narrative. For the reader enters the narrative as an unsituated variable subject, not as an absolute instance of vision, superior to what it views. The scene brings into play a type of *specular investment* that reveals the reader as both an agent of disclosure and an object of fixation. (my emphasis)[43]

For Gelley the emphasis on *seeing* in James's text, which would seem to support its mimetic dimension, in fact problematizes the mimesis by drawing attention instead to the potential for fantasy production on the part of the reader, who is seen as "an unsituated variable subject, not as an absolute instance of vision, superior to what it views." If we understand the reader as investing the scene he views with his own fantasies, then, by the same token, this dynamic also applies to spectators *in* the text as they participate in the scene by looking. Gelley would seem to support such a position when he writes that the scene can be though of as disclosing the structure of *mis en abyme,* "since the agent of disclosure, the viewer of the scene, is himself part of another scene that includes the first."[44]

Through an exploration of representation in the late works, I attempt to show how in his handling of the spectator James closes the seemingly irreducible gap between aestheticism and ethics. In *The Ambassadors,* James succeeds in projecting a "world" which dramatizes the problems implicit in representing a "world" constructed through mediation. James's difficulty in this novel has to do with reconciling an awareness of the mediated nature of experience with traditional moral imperatives. Strether learns to accept the value of the lie in the "virtuous attachment," but the novel ends, nevertheless, with his moral renunciation of further involvement in the lives of those around him. In *The Wings of the Dove* the interminable chain of mediation is taken for granted and expressed in the characters' endless construction and interpretations of each other's and their own secrets. But the novel also dramatizes the necessity of judging the interpretations and actions it represents. Densher cannot live with his and Kate's lie, and his judgment leads him, like Strether, to renounce further engagement. By the time he comes to write *The Golden Bowl,* James finds a way to reconcile his sense of the constructed nature of the world with the possibility of moral action.[45] Maggie learns to lie, but unlike James's earlier protagonists she learns to construct a self through her fiction, to shape and affirm positive engagement in ongoing life.

2
Artist as Audience: *The Tragic Muse*

"To 'do something about art'—art, that is, as a human complication and a social stumbling-block—must have been for me early a good deal of a nursed intention, the conflict between art and 'the world' striking me as one of the half-dozen great primary motives."[1] Thus, in his preface to the New York Edition, James describes his intention in writing *The Tragic Muse* (1890).

In light of the preface, it is possible to understand *The Tragic Muse* as a traditional nineteenth-century novel whose distinction is that its protagonists are artists. Such a view would take James to be exploring the allure and value of art versus the concrete attractions of the great world. The primary vehicle for this exploration would be the characterization of Nick Dormer, the politician who turns his back on politics and chooses to become a portrait painter.

In this chapter I suggest that, in *The Tragic Muse,* rather than treating art in either purely aesthetic or social terms, art becomes the ground on which James reveals the problematics implicit in the project of representation: does representation in art reflect the world or aspects of the world, or does it shape our perception of the world, possibly to the point of distorting it? In staging the conflict between art and the world, James at once dramatizes the limitations inherent in the representations of art—art cannot adequately represent the world—and suggests the inescapability of such representation.[2] To borrow the language of the preface: there is no going behind the representation that is art (91).[3]

A natural question, of course, is why so much of James's work—stories, novellas, novels—deals with the explicit subject of art. Why is this so important to him? What is at stake beyond a possibly narcissistic involvement in his life as an artist, and how are we to understand it?[4]

My thesis is that for James the problem of art is inextricably linked to a consideration of the nature of reality and of the multifaceted problems of representation within it. By the nature of reality I mean something quite simple, namely, an examination of how the individual, as part of a community, can distinguish his or her fantasies about reality—or even fantasies about him or herself, from something that might really exist outside of individual consciousness, that might really *be* out there.[5]

One of the motivating reasons to distinguish the real from the imagined or fantasized has to do with a desire for the security of community, which can in part be fulfilled if individual experience is shared and confirmed by others. If individual experience is not shared, then individuals are potentially trapped in their own consciousness. In the extreme, such isolation within one's private representation is tantamount to a solipsistic cutoff. The danger of such isolation is a problem for James's readers, as it is for his characters. A sense of community that promotes some degree of intimacy may help to contain this threat of isolation, even as it provokes different fears.[6]

Art plays a role in constructing a sense of community. Art itself, as it is produced by an individual, becomes the basis for a shared experience of reality. Since the reader's response is integral to the creation of whatever significance we attribute to James's art, as he writes and as the reader reads, some common reality, however limited, is established, on the basis of which some sense of community is constituted.[7]

Our sharing of such a common human-made reality may serve as a basis for talking about other aspects of our experience. In other words, the made world of art, precisely because it is made, may become a testing ground for the reality in and from which this art is made. The grounds of art provide a relatively neutral formal field on which we can negotiate a relationship both with reality and with art.

James's preoccupation with art is in good part rooted in this concern with contact and communication, as mediated through his representations of the endless process of representation. He uses literature and the writing of literature in his work as a means of engaging the problem and as a means of affirming a need to continually negotiate the gap between appearance and reality through the engagement with art. For James, the function of art is to provide the grounds for the ongoing negotiation required to distinguish appearance from reality and to distinguish among more or less adequate representations of "reality" within the field of his characters' experience.

In confronting these issues, *The Tragic Muse* anticipates James's last completed novels.[8] It does so by directly engaging art as a paradigmatic instance of the process of representation and the role of this process in facilitating or blocking communication. In this book we have not only a range of artists and of conversations about art and the project of aesthetization as such, but also, by extension, an exploration of the meaning, status, and value of the representations attempted and achieved in art. Indeed, its central issue has to do with the status of art and, therefore, the status of reality. Within *The Tragic Muse* art becomes a means of testing what it is that we call reality. When Peter Sherringham accuses Miriam Rooth of never getting off the stage, what he is doing for himself, for James, and for the reader is attempting to define what is meant by "reality."

The Tragic Muse is especially useful in defining issues of art and reality, and the transaction between artist and audience. It schematically lays out the issues of mediation and representation as they figure in the experience of its main characters, most of whom are artists. Three artists, and each one's relation to their public, are juxtaposed in *The Tragic Muse*. Nick Dormer is an artist who eschews the idea of pleasing his public and thus becomes his own sole audience. Gabriel Nash is an aesthete who transforms his life into art and thereby casts everyone, including himself, in the role of both artist and audience. Miriam Rooth is a successful actress whose continuous representation of the range of human emotion unfolds in unremitting transaction with an audience. She epitomizes the issue of the artist/audience thematic as James conceives it.[9]

James's preoccupation with the role of the artist and the necessary corollary, the role of the public, allows him to explore not just "the happy and fruitful"(80) conflict between art and the world, but the "terror" and "horror"(95) of having to distinguish and negotiate the conflicting claims of "art" and "world" in a piece of fiction. Since that fiction itself claims to represent the world, it renders the very distinction it seeks to make almost impossible to conceptualize. Inscribed within *The Tragic Muse,* itself the product of an artist addressing himself to a reading public, is a dramatic exploration of the problematic of representation, as representation itself is felt to be the ground on which artist and audience meet. James himself is the arch-analogue for all the artist figures of the novel as he establishes contact with his own audience on the basis of his representation, which is *The Tragic Muse.*

The novel opens in an art gallery, where a discussion of the problematic status of art provides the organizing frame in which

James at once creates a world that allows him to communicate with his readers and explore the difficulty of that communication. When almost at the beginning of the novel Nick Dormer says that "All art is one"—he might well be speaking for James who, in *The Tragic Muse,* is about to show how this both is and is not the case (14).[10] My point here is twofold: First, James's novel, in a self-reflective mode, makes the subject of "art" central; and second, since the issue is raised *in* a novel, in the context of characters struggling to make choices and fulfill themselves in a particularized social world, the very issue of art is itself experienced as an existential problem.

James constructs a fictional world which conforms to and confirms certain novelistic traditions—for instance the requirement for exposition of the opening scene. I stress this point because James uses traditional novelistic strategies to tap, express, and contain strengths of feeling that he will invest in such subjects as art, which at this point in the tradition lie outside the range of the contemporary novel. The very possibility of representation will now bear the pressure associated with traditionally more emotive issues. The exposition will organize a novelistic examination of the subject of art as the fictional world is established.[11]

Broadly speaking, James lays out a crude opposition between "art" and "life," where "life" is associated with the world of politics, specifically English politics.[12] Lady Agnes, Nick Dormer's mother, is presented as a typical upper-middle-class English woman, the widow of (in her mind) a prominent member of the House of Commons. Her ambition is that her son Nick continue the family tradition. "[T]he general sharp contagion of Paris" (19) largely consists for her in the almost sinful attraction that art poses for her son, himself a frustrated artist. As Nick and his sister Biddy wander off to look at contemporary French art, Nick characterizes Lady Agnes's view of art:[13]

> Mother wouldn't like it. She has inherited the queer old superstition that art is pardonable only so long as it's bad—so long as it's done at odd hours, for a little distraction, like a game of tennis or of whist. The only thing that can justify it, the effort to carry it as far as one can (which you can't do without time and singleness of purpose), she regards as just the dangerous, the criminal element. It's the oddest hind-part-before view, the drollest immorality. (17)

The stated area of contention is "art." For Nick, Lady Agnes's "philistine" (125) view is a kind of "immorality," but the competing claims for the status and role of art are inscribed here within a broad generational conflict between Nick and his mother. The generational conflict is of prime importance in that we are not considering a theoretical text but a novel, no matter how schematic. The discussion of art only "lives" in terms of its impact on the lives of the various characters of this novel. As readers, we experience the claims the characters make for art in terms of our experience of them as dramatis personae in a more or less traditional piece of fiction. On the one hand, the fictional world becomes concrete as matters of marriage, money, tradition, family, profession, competition, generational conflict, etc., are seen as central to the characters' concerns. On the other, the problem of art and representation ranks as a central concern in James's own work of art—this *novel*. Nick is slated for the Commons but wants to be a painter; Biddy is represented as wanting to be a wife (Peter Sherringham's) but dabbles in sculpting; Peter Sherringham, a rising young diplomat, does not want his avocation as a theatergoer to interfere with his career. The question of Nick's occupation is linked to money—the plot creates a situation where there may only be enough money for the relatively impoverished family if Nick enters Parliament. The broad arena in which the protagonists will assert their individual wills and make their individual choices is framed, however, by the question of representation. Hence representation comes to be experienced by the characters, as well as by the readers, as the most personal, and dramatic, of life issues.

The relation between reader and text, or artist and audience, acquires particular resonance in *The Tragic Muse,* where problems of intimacy are cast in the context of couples, with specific emphasis on the question of the artist/audience relation. Problems of intimacy arise in the context of presenting two couples, when in each couple one partner is an artist. Time and again, the question of the relationship between artist and audience arises, the primary audience being the other partner in the couple.

The exposition of the first scene provides a frame, as it immediately brings together the four main characters of the novel: the about-to-be painter, Nick Dormer; the aesthete figure, Gabriel Nash; the tragedienne, Miriam Rooth; and the avid theatergoer, Peter Sherringham. It is useful to begin the analysis with Gabriel Nash, since his status as "artist" is the most equivocal: Is he artist or is he audience?

The figure of Gabriel Nash and the contrast to him that is provided by Nick Dormer are used to suggest the appeal and the dangers of overaesthetization.[14] We learn that Nash has written an interesting book, which received some critical success, but that he has since eschewed writing in favor of transforming his entire life into "art." His equivocal status extends to his cultural position. While we are asked to see the Dormer contingent as typically English and their behavior as typical of the English abroad, Biddy, on first noticing Nash "would have taken him for a foreigner" (20). From the beginning he resists easy categorization. The ambiguities surrounding Nash bear as much on the question of how he lives as on the significance of his iconoclasticism, as his search for the beautiful erases the boundaries that distinguish life from art.

> "I drift, I float. . . . If such a life as mine may be said to have a direction. Where there's anything to feel I try to be there!"
> "I should like to get hold of you," Nick remarked.
> "Well, in that case there would be something to feel. Those are the currents—any sort of personal relation—that govern my career." (23)

Jonathan Freedman has noted that Oscar Wilde almost directly lifts lines from Nash's speech and includes them in *The Picture of Dorian Gray.*[15] Gabriel Nash's identification as an aesthete is even further strengthened when he answers Nick's question as to what he has been doing: "'Oh, living you know'; and the tone of the words seemed to offer them as a record of magnificent success" (263).

Questions of "tone" or what it means to be an artist and, more specifically, what it means to be a writer, are the focus of an exchange between Gabriel Nash and Nick Dormer. Nash, the once successful writer, reveals that he has abrogated the attempt to reach an audience.[16] Insofar as he allows no distinction between life and art he also collapses the distinction between artist and audience and occupies both positions. In so doing, he appears to forfeit the possibility of communication and remains sealed in a private universe. Nash says:

> "And why should one call one's self anything? One only deprives other people of their dearest occupation. Let me add that you don't *begin* to have an insight into the art of life till it ceases to be of the smallest consequence to you what you may be called. That's rudimentary."
> "But if you go in for shades, you must also go in for names. You must distinguish," Dormer objected. "The observer is nothing without his categories, his types and varieties."
> "Ah, trust him to distinguish!" said Gabriel Nash, sweetly. "That's for his own convenience; he has, privately, a terminology to meet it. That's one's style. But from the moment it's the convenience of others,

the signs have to be grosser, the shades begin to go. That's a deplorable hour! Literature, you see, is for the convenience of others. It requires the most abject concessions. It plays such mischief with one's style that really I have had to give it up." (28)

Via Nash, James outlines the aesthete's position and its built-in contradictions. Nash may think he has transcended a need for the audience in his search for artistic perfection. James, however, exposes a basic inconsistency in this position, as we recognize the self-defeating aspects of a stance denying the community afforded by an audience and, at the same time, requiring communal approbation. While Nash speaks, he is described as looking "cheerfully, hospitably, at Biddy; not because it was she, she easily guessed, but because it was in his nature to desire a second auditor—a kind of sympathetic gallery" (22).

However, although Nash's aesthetic position is exposed as ridden with potential contradictions—after all, what is the meaning of art without an audience?—Nash's character performs what James calls "ficelle"-like functions whether he will or no. The novel seems to be making the point that, irrespective of the individual's will to engage, life necessarily situates the subject in a position of affecting others and others' lives. It is directly through Nash's intervention that Nick Dormer meets Miriam Rooth and that Miriam meets Peter Sherringham; he is also instrumental in Nick's decision to become a painter. The kind of autonomy Nash seems to wish for is proven existentially untenable in the way the novel works out its plot.

Autonomy has long been recognized, in one guise or another, as a major Jamesian theme. I suggest that here it appears in the guise of the observer attempting to remain outside human feeling and human activity. Gabriel Nash drifts in and out of the major characters' lives, and by the end of the novel he just quietly disappears. The sense is that having his portrait painted by Nick is really the end of him: "he has melted back into the elements—he is part of the ambient air" (516). Examined through the prism offered by the aesthete Nash, the issue of the autonomous observer can be seen to touch—in more ways than one—on the status and function of art and, specifically, on the problematic of the immediacy of art and representation.

Two views of art that James will explore further in the later novels appear here. The first, represented by Nash, is a view that wants art to totally dissolve the border which constitutes art as art. Nash wants life to be indistinguishable from art, and he attempts to shape his own life in such a mold. He goes wherever there is anything to be felt or any beauty to be experienced. He wants art/life to be totally one—immediate—with no boundary and no mediation separating the self from experience. His goal is to import the beauty that is art into the experience that is life. In contrast, Nick has "formulas," and talks about the artist's need for shades and for a language that will allow him to make discriminations.

The novelistic point that James makes has to do with the attraction between these two figures. It is Gabriel Nash who attempts to persuade Nick Dormer to be serious about his own capacity to make art, to paint. For Nash, nothing is quite as serious as art, and all other "representations" are secondary. Nash in fact cracks a joke, comparing Nick's representation of his constituents to representation in art. As I hope to show that comparison was later to become the basis for a more extensive examination of the problem of mediation in *The Ambassadors*. Through the relationship between these two "artists" in *The Tragic Muse*, James explores the limits of different views of art. When Gabriel tells Nick he does not have to know how to paint, he is formulating a new aesthetic calling for the dissolution of the *frame* of art. This frame, however, is what separates art from the observer and this is the gap that art continually attempts to overcome. Through the figure of the observer, James conveys the pain of removal and of distance— aesthetic and other—and to some extent, his art strives to bridge this distance. The categories of observation keep the artist out of life, but they also afford the possibility of distinguishing art from life—a distinction that Gabriel Nash is set on dissolving. He talks of himself and his life as if he were an artistic text, and the problem with this credo is precisely the failure to distinguish between art, an artificial form, and life. Living is, for Nash, an experiment in style. The exchange with Nick exposes both the attraction and the paradox implicit in Nash's credo: Nash's "I make it my business to take for granted an interest in the beautiful" (120) points to the paradox implicit in the *framing* of art, which makes aesthetic distance possible and, in turn allows a chance for observation.[17] In keeping "life" framed, the frame of art separates the two categories and reinforces distance.

Nash is dramatized as a figure marginal to the ongoing life represented in the novel. Nevertheless, James gives a sense of the problem that his art both expresses and is designed to overcome: our separation from the thing itself. James's representation reflects both the difficulty of representation, which is always removed from its referent, and the difficulty of alternative conceptions.

The oversimplification inherent in Nash's position—he has characterized his system as the attempt to be "simple"(116)—is brought out in his exchange with Nick as they walk along the Seine. In the context of the palpable human history of Paris, the crudity of Nash's "aesthetic" conception of art is exposed. Critics have long been divided over whether James's own art is over-aesthetized, but in the context of *The Tragic Muse* the figure of Gabriel Nash is used, negatively as it were, to suggest the cogency of maintaining the boundary separating art from life. In the following conversation with Nick Dormer we begin to see how Gabriel Nash's program to concentrate on the beautiful and thus dispel "dreariness" (119) can be understood as an attempt to escape the pain and violence of human history. Gabriel and Nick discuss the relative claims of Nash's "life as art"—my expression—versus traditional art:

Our young men, gossiping as profitably as I leave the reader to estimate, crossed the wide, short bridge which made them face towards the monuments of old Paris—the Palais de Justice, the Conciergerie, the holy chapel of Saint Louis. They came out before the church, which looks down on a square where the past, once so thick in the very heart of Paris, has been made rather a blank, pervaded, however, by the everlasting freshness of the great cathedral-face. It greeted Nick Dormer and Gabriel Nash with a kindness which the centuries had done nothing to dim. The lamplight of the great city washed its foundations, but the towers and buttresses, the arches, the galleries, the statues, the vast rose-window, the large, full composition, seemed to grow clearer as they climbed higher, as if they had a conscious benevolent answer for the upward gaze of men. (120)

Their walk continues, but whereas Nick thinks of "the old Paris, of the great Revolution, of Madame Roland . . ." and feels the need to create his own composition, Nash says:

"I go about my business,like any good citizen—that's all."
"And what *is* your business?" [queries Nick.]
"The spectacle of the world."
Nick laughed out. "And what do you do with that?"
"What does any one do with a spectacle? I look at it." . . .
"I wish very much you had more to show for it."
"To show for what?"
"Your little system—the aesthetic life." . . .
"Oh, having something to show is such a poor business. It's a kind of confession of failure." (122–123)

I quote at length in order to bring out several points. First, it is precisely at this stage, as Nash elaborates his aesthetic system, that the novel refers to a real historical Paris—to real buildings which conjure up a concrete and bloody history.[18] Second, while Nash remains the outsider, contemplating the "spectacle," Nick feels "a certain soothing content; as if [the church] had been the temple of a faith so dear to him that here was peace and security in its precinct" (121).

It is almost as if art's concrete achievements, as well as the real and violent historical backdrop for those achievements provoke Nash to an aesthetic retreat. The world becomes "spectacle for Nash," and thus allows him to maintain a safe distance, as audience.[19] If the function of art, at least in part, is to lay the grounds for an experience that will foster a sense of inclusion and community, this is clearly not true for Gabriel Nash; his explicit search is for a beauty that will counter the ugly, the violent and the passionate, leaving him in a state of splendid isolation. The oversimplified aestheticism that would select only the beautiful from ongoing human experience and exclude the ugly, the bloody and the violent which, it seems, is the position ascribed to Gabriel Nash, is highlighted through Nick Dormer's contrasting response.

By inviting comparison between Gabriel Nash's "art" and the "objects" that James urges us to think about, the text leads readers to favor Nick Dormer's—and I argue, James's own—aesthetic position. The juxtaposition of Nick and Nash works to Nash's disadvantage, and we learn that, in the objective or the real world, real history has a role. Gabriel Nash's attempt at "the aesthetic life" puts the blood of life, revolution, and history behind him; he simplifies life to the point of not having to contend with those aspects of human experience that involve ugliness, dreariness, and struggle.[20] As a removed and even remote spectator, Gabriel Nash does not participate in the struggle to find a partner, make a living, or compete for an identity in a community of peers. Gabriel Nash's role as a character in this novel thus dramatizes the paradox inherent in his retreat from the passional. As readers, we experience his search for beauty as cutting him off from the ongoing life of the novel: at the end he simply disappears—as though the spectator or audience who does not participate, engaging only one side of the artist/audience dyad, is bound to disappear. Gabriel Nash is one of a long line of aesthete figures in James's ouevre who find themselves marginalized, as events in which they themselves are implicated have unforeseen repercussions. As he eschews the role of artist, Nash also loses his role as audience or spectator.

*****

If Gabriel Nash's trajectory is from artist to audience to disappearance, Nick Dormer's career follows the opposite course. He chooses to give up his seat in Parliament, where he "represents" his constituents, to retreat to his studio where, as a portrait painter, he represents the subjects of his work in painting. In terms of the novel's schematic treatment of the problems attendant on representation in the context of the artist's relationship with his audience, Nick exemplifies dynamic possibilities as he moves from one position to another, and he articulates many aspects of the central problem that the novel explores. But an examination of Nick's crisis provides above all a sense of how Nick's specific attitude to art, to politics, and, most important, to the notion of an audience, is part of an articulated life; it is intricately connected to his biography.

As a young man in public life, Nick has been subject to the prying eye of his constituents. In the following passage we begin to have a sense of the two related poles that shape Nick's experience.

> He was suspected of having a studio in an out-of-the-way quarter of the town . . . incongruous as such a retreat might seem in the case of a member of Parliament. It was an absurd place to see his constituents, unless he wanted to paint their portraits, a kind of representation with which they scarcely would have been satisfied.[21] (61)

Which activity constitutes satisfactory representation? And for whom? From the beginning Nick is presented as the embodiment of a conflict between politics and art. He is reluctant to run for Parliament but succumbs to family pressure. He wins his seat with the help of his cousin Julia Darrow, Peter Sherringham's sister—the woman to whom he will become betrothed and who will later break off their engagement. If as a politician Nick had to represent his constituents to *their* satisfaction, as an artist he insists on the freedom not to please a public he sees as too facile. Nick's choice to run and then to relinquish his seat in Parliament must be understood in a double context: his conception of art and his relationship to his family—including his deceased father and, of course, his betrothed, Julia Darrow. In the context of the ongoing life of the novel, in which Nick is seen as making choices, James is able to suggest the levels of complexity underlying the process of becoming an artist, and the bearing of this process on the artist's relation to his or her audience.

We have already seen how Nick's response to the art of Paris inspires him to become artistically creative: "The great point is to do something, instead of standing and muddling and questioning; and, by Jove, it makes me want to!"(121). But from the beginning, even before he has chosen to become a painter, Nick has doubts about the role an audience should play in the life of an artist. In the course of the conversation already cited, Nash says:

> "I take my stand on my nature, on my disposition. I'm not ashamed of it. I don't think it's so horrible, my disposition. But we've befogged and befouled so the whole question of liberty, of spontaneity, of good-humour and inclination and enjoyment, that there's nothing that makes people stare so as to see one natural."
> "You are always thinking too much of 'people.'" (123)

After Nick has thus noted the paradox implicit in Nash's system of "simplicity" and "spontaneity," as the conversation proceeds, and especially through the foil that Nash provides, it emerges that Nick himself abides by a fairly traditional notion of the painter's task—to produce beautiful work. I emphasize this point since, even at this stage of his career, Nick has a conception of beauty that stands independent of people's appreciation. As we will see later, this desired freedom also contrasts with Miriam's dependence on her audience.

Nick's attitude to art and to a potential audience emerges clearly in the context of the exchange during which Nash is trying to persuade Nick to become a painter and give up the idea of re-entering parliament. For his part, Nick confesses his considerable attraction to the idea of becoming a painter but describes the lure of the aesthetic life as a "violence . . . that tears [him] to pieces. . . ." (126), for which the politics and public life to which he has been bred stand as an "antidote."

The pull exerted by politics is described in terms of duty to his family and to his family's traditions and expectations, which provoke Nick's counterbid for autonomy of action and expose him to guilt.

> He had the gift, so embarrassing when it is a question of consistent action, of seeing in an imaginative, interesting light anything that illustrated forcibly the life of another: such things effected a union with something in *his* life, and the recognition of them was ready to become a form of enthusiasm in which there was no consciousness of sacrifice—none scarcely of merit. . . . He found himself believing, because his mother communicated the belief, that it was in his option to transform the social outlook of the three women who clung to him and who

declared themselves dismal. This was the highest kind of inspiration, but it was moving, and it associated itself with dim confusions of figures in the past—figures of authority and expectancy. (171)

The terms in which he describes the violence of being torn are instructive, as he claims: "I'm a freak of nature and a sport of the mocking gods"(125).[22] If the echo of Oedipus seems somewhat forced here, remember that his recently deceased father had raised him for the House:

> "You don't know the atmosphere in which I live, the horror, the scandal that my apostasy would inspire, the injury and suffering that it would inflict. I believe it would kill my mother. She thinks my father is watching me from the skies."
> "Jolly to make him jump!" Nash exclaimed.
> "He would jump indeed; he would come straight down on top of me." (126)

Not only would his father "come down on top of him," but Nick imagines that Mr. Carteret and Mrs. Dallow would join him. Later, when he decides to leave the Commons, he breaks the news to Mr. Carteret, an old friend and colleague of his father's—clearly a surrogate father figure for Nick—with a sense that his news might speed his death (349) and that it might easily kill his mother as well (365).

To relinquish his seat is an apostasy that Nick experiences as exposing him to his father's and his family's revenge. In his family, as he goes to great lengths to explain, no one has ever had any aesthetic sense (125). His betrothed, Julia Darrow, indeed breaks off her engagement to him. As noted, his family and his entire class consider his commitment to paint as a species of immorality. The plot dramatizes Nick's understanding of his family's attitude, since he has an acute sense of their demands on him and of how his decision will frustrate their expectations of him, to the point of depriving them of their home and income. He has no less acute a sense of their anger toward him.

His decision to become a painter then, is for Nick, an act of great rebellion. We can well imagine that, for Nick, the very idea of an audience that he must please and satisfy might come to be associated with his resolutely displeased family. Nick so vividly experiences his family as limiting his freedom to choose and as a threat to his autonomy that he entertains a fantasy that they will retaliate—"jump down . . . straight on top of [him]"—for his ostensible aggression; after all, his apostasy might "kill" both his mother and Carteret. Insofar as so much violence colors his idea of family, it is not surprising that the choice of becoming a painter entails turning his back on all such commitments, on everything he imagines his family—or any audience—might demand of him.

Even Nick's most intimate commitment, his relationship with Julia Darrow, which he characterizes as the "abyss of intimacy" (179), is presented as inextricably linked with responsibility to an audience, as it requires him to undertake the task, impossible for him, of representing Julia's constituency in Parliament. Julia will not have Nick unless he undertakes to be her member for the borough. With a pun, Nick asks: "*Her* member—am I hers? . . . What a droll thing to 'represent', when one thinks of it! And what does *it* represent . . . ?" (165). The relationship between the couple is seen to hinge on his preparedness to be her member and represent her in public, the difficulty of which he experiences as an intolerable limitation of his autonomy. He has already rebelled against fulfilling his family's expectations and he ultimately finds himself unable to fulfill Julia's. He refuses to be trapped in the role of representing anyone else, even his lover. Julia, it seems, experiences a similar problem, albeit to a lesser degree; although she declares her love for him, she confesses that it is difficult for a proud woman to "adore" a man (187). The fact that the emotions associated with intimacy can be experienced as a limit to autonomy is further dramatized when Nick, wanting to communicate his love for her, says to Julia: "I hate you!"(185). With this couple, as with Miriam and Peter, James explores the continuity between the most personal kind of relationship, that of lovers, and what might appear the most impersonal—politician and constituents, artist and audience—in terms of the issues of autonomy and representation. In each case, the responsibility of representation will involve some unbearable limitation of autonomy.

The circumstances of Nick's decision to paint, and the particular attitude he develops towards his work and his audience, enable James to pursue the problem of separating reality and representation. Nick chooses the autonomy of the solitary painter who is not concerned with pleasing an audience. Unlike Miriam and Gabriel Nash, the two other artist figures who are full of a kind of "eagerness" for their respective artistic careers, Nick experiences severe doubts about the ultimate value of his painting and of painting in general.

Nick adopts an ostensibly idealist conception of representation that will later be moderated by a commitment to the activity of painting as such. Alone—and I stress alone—in his studio, Nick asks himself, with the "thrill abated," whether he has not committed a great mistake (417). After paying a visit to the National Gallery and looking at "Titian to Rubens and from Gainsborough to Rembrandt," he has been discouraged "not by the sight of the grand things that had been done" but because "he found himself calling the whole art literally into question" (418).

> Its weakness, narrowness appeared to him; . . . [the paintings'] place was inferior and their connection with the life of man casual and slight. They represented so inadequately the idea, and it was the idea that won the race, that in the long run came in first. He had incontestably been in much closer relation to the idea a few months before than he was today: it made up a great deal for the bad side of politics that they were after all a clumsy system for applying and propagating the idea. (418)

Through Nick, James dramatizes a possible strategy in coping with the difficulty inherent in the very project of representation. In debating the relative merits of one kind of representation over another, Nick had "no pretension of trying this question over again; he reminded himself that his ambiguity was subjective, as the philosophers said; the result of a mood which in due course would be at the mercy of another mood. It made him curse, and cursing, as a finality, was shaky; so he would throw out a platform beyond it" (419). The "platform" Nick finds is in doing, in "learning the beauty of obstinacy"(426) even though his painting might be "very bad" (419). I suspect that Nick here is really enunciating James's own personal commitment and relation to his own activity.[23] Unlike James, however, Nick keeps his audience at a great distance. He cultivates an "acute mistrust of the superficiality of performance" and feels himself cursed with an "odious facility" (482–483). On this basis he decides not to cater to the tastes of any contemporary audience but to work "quietly" and represent something he calls an "idea." His attempt is to create something that will be judged by posterity to belong in the category of the beautiful. When forgoing the attempt to please an immediate public, Nick aspires to something called "art."[24]

*****

The question of what Miriam Rooth represents, and how this issue is shaped by her relation to her audience, is by far the most complicated and most interesting in *The Tragic Muse*.[25] In the characterization of Miriam Rooth, James lays the ground he will explore in the three novels of his "major phase," namely, the radical difficulty, perhaps the impossibility, of distinguishing the *representation* of the "thing" from the "thing" itself, or appearance from reality.[26] In the "major phase" James will explore this not only in thematic terms but also in terms of the techniques he develops in his novelistic craft. In *The Tragic Muse* he begins to develop some of these techniques.

The most noteworthy aspect of the structure of *The Tragic Muse* is that we never get close to Miriam Rooth, the actress who *is* the tragic muse. We hear dialogue in which Miriam speaks, but we do not have access to her consciousness, and we only see her through the other characters in the novel, primarily through Peter Sherringham's eyes. In a passage that echoes the preface to *The Wings of the Dove*,[27] the narrative voice hammers home this problem.

> As to whether Miriam had the same bright, still sense of co-operation to a definite end, the sense of the distinctively technical nature of the answer to every question to which the occasion might give birth, that mystery would be cleared up only if it were open to us to regard this young lady through some other medium than the mind of her friends. We have chosen, as it happens, for some of the advantages it carries with it, the indirect vision; and it fails as yet to tell us (what Nick of course wondered about before he ceased to care, as indeed he intimated to his visitor) why a young person crowned with success should have taken it into her head that there was something for her in so blighted a spot. (276)[28]

From the beginning then, readers must believe the reports of the others, while simultaneously being aware that the representation of the novel's protagonist is mediated.[29] Even the syntax in the above passage seems of a piece with the later novels, so complicated and labyrinthine as to postpone and forestall direct engagement with the material it represents. With no direct access to the central figure in the novel we are thrown back to an awareness of the process of representation and the necessity for interpretation.[30] If there is "tragedy" in *The Tragic Muse,* surely a debatable point, it is in the fact that we have no purchase on the character that, ostensibly, is the subject of the novel.[31] Miriam is only available through others' representation of her.

The process of representation is so complex that there might even be a question of how immediately available the self is to the self. James brings out this problem through his focus on Peter Sherringham and his response both as audience and as lover—a crucial confusion—to the actress Miriam Rooth. James will use the relationship between Sherringham and Miriam, and their many discussions on the theater, to explore the interdependence between the dramatist/actor and the audience as a way of examining the centrality of representation in establishing even the most intimate sort of relations. As we will see in the case of Sherringham, James will even suggest that representation plays a role in how the self, as it represents itself to itself, establishes and consolidates individuality, even as it struggles to distinguish appearance or representation from the reality supposedly being represented.

Sherringham is presented from the outset as a man in love with the theater. The problem the novel dramatizes, both in its own mode of representation and in the relationship between Sherringham and Miriam, is the problem of whether Peter is merely falling in love with his own fantasy of the actress.

> It came over him suddenly that so far from there being any question of her having the histrionic nature, she simply had it in such perfection that she was always acting; that her existence was a series of parts assumed for the moment, each changed for the next, before the perpetual mirror of some curiosity or admiration or wonder—some spectatorship that she perceived or imagined in the people about her. . . . It struck him abruptly that a woman whose only being was to "make believe," to make believe that she had any and every being that you liked, that would serve a purpose, produce a certain effect, and whose identity resided in the continuity of her personations, so that she had no moral privacy, as he phrased it to himself, but lived in a high wind of exhibition, of figuration—such a woman was a kind of monster, in whom of necessity there would be nothing to like, because there would be nothing to take hold of. . . . The girl's very face made it vivid to him now—the discovery that she had positively had no countenance of her own, but only the countenance of the occasion, a sequence, a variety (capable possibly of becoming immense), of representative movements. (130)

Peter thinks of Miriam as having "the countenance of the occasion," and the novel dramatizes this problem, both in its own mode of representation—we do not have Miriam himself but only Peter's and Nick's and Gabriel's Miriams—and in the relationship between Peter and Miriam. This is the problem of "figuration." Figuration is "concretized" in this novel, resolves itself, and acquires a particular shape, in the problem of whether Peter is falling in love with anything beyond his own desire. As a corollary, the novel poses the problem of whether there is any way for authenticating, or for anyone else to know, whether this is the case. The issue is how to grasp one's own experience, how to distinguish one's fan-

tasy from reality or, to point yet again to the hackneyed but ultimately central issue of the novel, how to distinguish appearance
from reality, even when it comes to the awareness of one's own
most intimate feelings (130).

As the cited passage illustrates, Peter's uncertainty about who
Miriam really is results in all kinds of fantasies about *her* fantasies.
Peter thinks of Miriam as habitually playing to a fantasied audience: "her existence was a series of parts assumed for the moment,
each changed for the next, before the perpetual mirror of some
curiosity or admiration or wonder—some spectatorship that she
perceived or imagined in the people about her." Whether Peter is
correct regarding Miriam is impossible to tell, but in thinking of
her in this way, he is clearly establishing himself as audience and
possibly also as actor before the mirror of his own curiosity, admiration or wonder.

The pressure of the problem of his feelings for Miriam intensifies
with her growing success as an actress. Peter finds himself increasingly in love with her and increasingly unsure of who she "really"
is.[32] Sherringham asks her whether she was frightened the first day
she went to Madame Carre's and she replies:

"Do you think I was pretending?"

"I think you always are. . . . But excuse the audacity and the crudity
of my speculations—it only proves my interest. What is it that you
know you are?"

"Why, an artist. Isn't that a canvas?"

"Yes, an intellectual one, but not a moral."

"Oh yes, it is, too. And I'm a good girl: won't that do?"

"It remains to be seen . . . A creature who is *all* an artist—I am
curious to see that."

"Surely it has been seen, in lots of painters, lots of musicians."

"Yes, but those arts are not personal, like yours. I mean not so much
so. There's something left for—what shall I call it?—for character."

Miriam stared again, with her tragic light.

"And do you think I've got no character?"

He looked up at her an instant—she seemed so "plastic"; and then,
he answered: "Delightful being, you've got a hundred!" (146)

The question of Miriam's "real" character, whether she has it
and whether such a thing exists at all, frames the issue of the status
and function of art in the sections of the novel dealing with the
relationship between Miriam and Sherringham.[33] For Peter, Miriam's "plasticity" is both the source of her appeal and the cause
of his distress.

He had the apprehension that she might do what she liked with her face. It was an elastic substance, an element of gutta-percha, like the flexibility of the gymnast, the lady who, at a music-hall, is shot from the mouth of a cannon. He coloured a little at this quickened view of the actress; he had always looked more poetically, somehow, at that priestess of art. But what was she, the priestess, when one came to think of it, but a female gymnast, a mountebank at higher wages? She didn't literally hang by her heels from a trapeze, holding a fat man in her teeth, but she made the same use of her tongue, of her eyes, of the imitative trick, that her muscular sister made of leg and jaw. (131)

Priestess or mountebank? Priestess *and* mountebank? The "imitative trick"—the ability to hold an audience—is precisely what works on Peter and makes Miriam's art successful. The conception of the audience as vulgar voyeurs and, concomitantly, the conception of the actor as exhibitionist is not only Peter's. As we will see, Miriam shares it. Nick too uses the term "mountebank" to describe what he feels when, as a politician, he addresses his constituents. Later Miriam will address Peter himself as a "mountebank." Gabriel Nash denounces the art of drama when he characterizes the audience at the theater as the "sweltering mass," whose only interest is getting their money's worth and being entertained before the suburban trains will take them home (50). Miriam herself confirms a sense that part of the connection with an audience has its roots in unsavory intimacy. When Peter finds Miriam's ambition to become an actress difficult to understand he calls her a "strange girl" and she replies:

"Je crois bien! Doesn't one have to be, to want to go and exhibit one's self to a loathsome crowd, on a platform, with trumpets and a big drum, for money—to parade one's body and one's soul?" (113)

In the dramatization of Peter's and Miriam's relationship, James suggests it is precisely in this relationship, itself a product of doubt about the reliability of representation, that the issues of representation are most usefully confronted.[34] If we are to understand Peter's interest in the theater as an attempt to test the limits of the real, an attempt to distinguish fantasy from reality, fact from fiction, to lose and find himself in "the vale of friction"(59) that is art, it is in the novel's representation of the relationship between artist and audience, maybe even author and reader, that such a position is best negotiated.

In relation to Peter and Miriam, James suggests that the dichotomy artist/audience is too facile. James's subject is precisely what disqualifies drama for Nash: the interdependence, the community with all its mixedness, the dependence of actor and dramatist on an audience. The novel contains innumerable discussions about the actor-audience relation, many extending not just to the theater but, as the passages about Nick and Gabriel Nash showed, to other arts as well. Miriam thinks of the audience as vulgar voyeurs who experience their own lives vicariously as they ogle her. In his treatment of her relationship with Peter, James seems to suggest that, on the contrary, "art" is the product of the relationship between artist and audience. From the beginning of Peter's and Miriam's relationship, James suggests that the art Miriam represents is attractive because of the relationship between the audience and the artist. Sherringham wonders whether Miriam possesses "the celebrated artistic temperament"; in an awkward interjection that calls attention to him and emphasizes the full weight of his authority, the narrator says: "That Sherringham himself was of that shifting complexion is perhaps proved by his odd capacity for being of two different minds at very nearly the same time"(112).[35]

James dramatizes some sense of the complexity and the competition implicit in the relation of artist and audience in the scenes in which Sherringham proposes to Miriam. Sherringham has become convinced that he is in love with Miriam only *after* Madame Carre confirms that she will be a great actress (159). It is of a piece with the way even the most private of feelings need externalization or representation that Sherringham requires the confirmation of the celebrated actress (159).[36] As a mark of his recognition of Miriam's success he takes her to the Théâtre Française. In the intermission, thinking of Basil Dashwood, an actor and potential rival, he tells her he is better than a "young mountebank." "She turned upon him with a flush in her cheek and a splendid dramatic face. 'How you hate us! Yes, at bottom, below your little taste, you *hate* us!'"(241).

In the intermission, as part of a rite of initiation, he introduces her to the principal French actress and in the actress's dressing room, the theater's holy of holies, he proposes to her. He says:

"Give it up and live with *me*."
  "Give it up?"
  "Give it up and I'll marry you tomorrow."
  "This is a happy time to ask it!" she mocked. "And this a good place."
  "Very good indeed, and that's why I speak: it's a place to make you choose—it puts all before one."

"To make *you* choose, you mean. I'm much obliged, but that's not my choice," laughed Miriam. (247)

The question of her feelings for him remains unclear as his proposal is conditional on her giving up the stage, but the struggle for power and status between them emerges as she counters by requesting that he give up his career as a statesman and share her glory.

> "The husband of an actress? Yes, I see that!" Sherringham cried, with a frank ring of disgust.
> "It's a silly position, no doubt. But if you're too good for it why talk about it? Don't you think I'm important?" . . . Her voice sank to the sweetest cadence and her eyes were grateful and good as they rested on him. She sometimes said things with such perfection that they seemed dishonest, but in this case Sherringham was stirred to an expressive response. (250)

Once again, even as she rejects him in this most intimate of moments and insists that he remain *her* audience, even as he loses in this struggle for primacy, Sherringham responds to the perfection of her representation. His skepticism about her honesty, or about what lies behind her representation, elicits his emotional response. He is presented by James as seduced by her power of representation.

His second proposal to her is pretty much a variation, with some reversal, on the same theme; once again, this time more explicitly, her power to represent *creates* his response. After a lengthy absence, he sees Miriam perform in London, and after the play,

> he floated in a sense of the felicity of it, in the general encouragement of a thing perfectly done, in the almost aggressive bravery of still larger claims for an art which could triumphantly, so exquisitely render life. "Render it?" Peter said to himself. "Create it and reveal it, rather; give us something new and large and of the first order!" He had *seen* Miriam now; he had never seen her before; he had never seen her till he saw her in her conditions. . . . That idea of her having no character of her own came back to him with a force that made him laugh in the empty street: this was a disadvantage she was so exempt from that he appeared to himself not to have known her till tonight. Her character was simply to hold you by the particular spell; any other—the good-nature of home, the relation of mother, her friends, her lovers, her debts, the practice of virtues or industries or vices—was not worth speaking of. These things were the fictions and the shadows; the representation was the deep substance. (325)

This passage emphasizes the generative power of representation while underscoring the difficulty of distinguishing art from life, and hence appearance from reality.

The reunion of Peter and Miriam reverses the terms of their previous encounter. On their first meeting after the play, it is Miriam who addresses Peter as "Dear old master!" and he responds, "Oh, you honest creature!" (333).

It is Peter's honesty that is the issue when, in a conversation with Nick, we get a rare look at the possibility of Miriam marrying Peter, but this time from her point of view. What we find is that Miriam—no less than Peter—is locked in the maze of representation (450). Significantly, James gives us a glimpse of the way Miriam thinks of her relationship with Peter in the context of her sitting as a model for the other artist known to her—Nick Dormer. In his studio she is no longer an actor or an artist but the subject for Nick's art. She speaks to Nick of how she sees Sherringham as she relaxes from her own labor of representation. This is the only instance in the novel where the reader is privy to Miriam's thoughts, and even here we are not given her thoughts exactly, as we do not have access to her consciousness. Rather, we hear her conversation with Nick about Peter, in Peter's absence, with the result that, in this instance, we at least do not suspect her, if we did until now, of trying to manipulate Peter. She appears to be talking to Nick, but her comments are addressed to her mother. Miriam reveals that she does not believe Peter has ever been serious about marrying her:

> "He has never spoken to me as if he really expected me to listen to him, and he's the more of a gentleman from that fact. He knows we haven't a common-ground—that a grasshopper can't mate with a fish. So he has taken care to say to me only more than he can possibly mean. That makes it just nothing." (450)

Talking of herself and actors in general in the third person Miriam says: "People marry them to make them leave the stage; which proves exactly what I say" (453). Whether Miriam thinks that Peter would marry her if she agreed to leave the stage, or whether she does not believe that a man of his class would commit the social sin of marrying an actress remains unclear.[37] Since these alternatives are complicated by the possibility that Miriam is really in love with Nick Dormer, James appears to be suggesting the complex impenetrability of ever quite knowing what lies behind anyone's representations, even of themselves to themselves. If Miriam can be in love with Nick, she could also be in love with Peter.[38] As readers, we have been exposed to Peter's inner processes; although we tend to grant Miriam's acuity as she talks about Peter not knowing what he wants, it is hard for us not to take him seriously. James makes it difficult, if not impossible, to decide whether Miriam's interpretation of Peter's intentions is any more valid than the interpretation of her mother, who is convinced that Peter wants to marry Miriam. Miriam might be the victim of the way she represents her relationships to herself, even as she reaffirms her commitment to her profession: "It's rather cruel, isn't it, . . . to deprive people of the luxury of calling one an actress as they'd call one a liar? I represent, but I represent truly" (452).

Directly following this conversation between Miriam and Nick, James once again confronts us with the power and impenetrability of representation as we read Peter Sherringham's third proposal to Miriam when she comes off the stage on the opening night of her new play. When he asks her to marry him, Miriam responds, "Oh, I knew—I knew! That's why I entreated you not to come!" (462). Sherringham insists on the sincerity of his desire to marry her if she'll "renounce" the stage and she quotes him back to himself:

> "I've just shown that I'm a perfection of perfections: therefore it's just the moment to renounce . . . ? I was sure, I mean that if you did come your poor dear doating brain would be quite addled. . . . I can't be a muff in public just for you, *pourtant*. Dear me, why do you like us so much?"
> "Like you? I loathe you!"
> "*Je le vois parbleu bien!* I mean, why do you feel us, judge us, understand us so well! I please you because you see, because you know; and because I please you, you must adapt me to your convenience, you must take me over, as they say. You admire me as an artist and therefore you wish to put me into a box in which the artist will breathe her last. Ah, be reasonable; you must let her live!" (464)

In a moment that unites him with Gabriel Nash as he seeks to erase the distinction between life and art, Sherringham pleads with her: "The stage is great, no doubt, but the world is greater. It's a bigger theatre than any of those places in the Strand. We'll go in for realities instead of fables, and you'll do them far better than you do the fables" (466). Initially, Miriam seeks to maintain the life/art distinction: "My talent is the thing that takes you; could there be a better proof than that it's tonight's exhibition of it that has settled you? It's indeed a misfortune that you're so sensitive to this particular kind of talent, since it plays such tricks with your power to see things as they are" (466).

But lest we be too ready to accept the comfort of the distinction Miriam seems to offer between appearance and reality, the stage and the world, she insidiously turns the terms around as she suggests to Sherringham: "Stay on *my* stage; come off your own" (467). Sherringham seems to be adopting Nash's position on the continuity of art and life in this battle of the sexes, while Miriam moves towards Nick's view as she says she will cling, come what may, to her "idea," by which she means her idea of art and its capacity to represent. She accuses Peter of snobbery when he refuses to contemplate the idea of living off her wages and talks of the pain of the artist's exposure to an audience as being "like a contortionist at a country fair" (474).

As she rejects Peter, Miriam makes a moving plea for the position of the artist and her relation to an audience in which the pain of exposure to strangers is justified by a commitment to a high ideal of art as the means of stirring people's "souls":

> "Ah, there's where life can help us, . . . there's where human relations and experience . . . suggest things, they light them up and sanctify them, . . . they make them appear worth doing. . . . I go in for closeness of union, for identity of interest. A true marriage, as they call it, must do one a lot of good!" (475)

James depicts Miriam during this speech as "sustain[ing] the rummage of [Peter's] gaze without a relenting gleam of the sense of cruelty or of paradox." If this bursts the bubble of Miriam's eloquence—what, after all, do "human relations" and "true marriage" signify in the context of Miriam's rejection of her suitor—James does not allow us to dwell on Peter's hurt. He describes him, albeit sympathetically, as stereotypically "British" in his refusal to allow art to "better" or to "bother" him. Peter may *not* be a British boor when he is described as thinking "Art be damned" (476), but in exposing Peter to this accusation James suggests something of the painful power of art as it becomes part of human experience.

Something like the pain of art and its inextricable entanglement with human experience seems to be indicated in the concluding image. Peter Sherringham does not propose again, although it seems he would have, had he not returned to the theater after a long absence to find Miriam already married. He is described as needing but a "fragment" of Miriam's new role as Juliet to

. . . read clear at the last, in the intense light of her genius that this fragment shed, that even so, after all, he had been rewarded for his formidable journey. The great trouble of his infatuation subsided, leaving behind it something tolerably deep and pure. (528)

These almost final words on Peter suggest that a balance has been achieved, leading us to understand that, for Peter at least, reality and representation have finally been sorted into an appropriate relationship. We are not told whether Peter remains a frequenter of the theater but his rush to marry Biddy casts some doubt on the balance he has putatively attained.

He felt somehow recalled to reality by the very perfection of the representation. (528)

3

The Story of the Story: *The Ambassadors*

THE ambassadors of this novel unequivocally represent the people who dispatch them.[1] Strether goes to Europe as Mrs. Newsome's representative,[2] but in the performance of this function he becomes an instrument for exploring the problems of representation in another sense: how to render or represent experience. In representing Mrs. Newsome, Strether's performance exposes the problems inherent in the act of representation itself.

Although *The Ambassadors* bears a real affinity to traditional novels—that is, it is about people, marriages and money, namely, the most concrete things that center the world of fiction—it notoriously makes it difficult for us to perceive with any precision the "things" that it is manifestly about. Though James works in the tradition of the nineteenth-century novel and manipulates its elements in a familiar way, finally what this novel engages is not only the elements themselves, but the problematics of presenting them or of re-presenting them.[3]

The novel suggests that the reason for this difficulty, which it itself enacts, is that reality is not only not immediately accessible, but that it must be mediated through the interlocking network of consciousness, language, and the forms of art. It is because of the way it deals with this process of mediation that the novel comes to reveal aberrations in the representation or mediation of things, which themselves become indeterminate and, perhaps, ultimately inaccessible.[4] *The Ambassadors* then, engages the radical impossibility of apprehending experience directly.

I find support for this view of the novel in my reading of James's preface to *The Ambassadors,* written some six years after the novel's publication. In his self-reflexive preface, James comments on the "process" of writing or artistic production. He recalls hearing of a friend's outburst in a Paris garden:

"Live all you can; it's a mistake not to. It doesn't so much matter what you do in particular so long as you *have* your life. If you haven't had

56

that what *have* you had? I'm too old—too old at any rate for what I see . . . Live, live!"(1)[5]

This outburst becomes for James a "dropped grain of suggestion," the "germ" of his novel. Having "plucked" the germ from the realm of life, the artist, according to James, finds himself faced with the problem of matching his germ, his "snippet," to the whole cloth of fiction. Within the multiple possibilities afforded by fiction, his task will be to delimit, to choose, always with the knowledge that his business will be as much or more to keep possibilities out rather than to keep possibilities in. What is kept out will shape what is kept in. The implication is that, like language, story-making functions in a system of relationships, and consequently, what is included in James's story will be defined in relation to what is excluded. Saussure's central insight that the linguistic unit is defined by the relations which set it off from other units has taught us that the most precise characteristic of every sign is its difference from other signs. This in turn has been used by others to support the idea that "every sign in some sense bears the traces of all other signs; they are co-present with it as the entities which define it."[6] A sense of this economy is surely what prompts James to write that "the equilibrium of the artist's state dwells less . . . in the . . . delightful complications he can smuggle in than in those he succeeds in keeping out" (5). And if what follows from Saussure's formulation is the co-presence of traces in every sign, for James the consequence of his insight is the recognition that the artist *"sows his seed at the risk of too thick a crop"* (5; my emphasis).

It is just this sense of the factitious inherent in the fictitious project which prompts the curious admission James makes in his preface.

> It comes to me again and again, over this licentious record, that one's bag of adventures, conceived or conceivable, has been only half-emptied by the mere telling of one's story. It depends so on what one means by that equivocal quantity. There is the story of one's hero, and then, thanks to the intimate connexion of things, *the story of one's story itself.* I blush to confess it, but if one's a dramatist one's a dramatist, and the latter imbroglio is liable on occasion to strike me as really the more objective of the two. (5; my emphasis)

James's conception of his own art is necessarily "licentious" in that it goes beyond the normal license of the "realistic" novelist. It plucks things out of life, out of context, and in doing so, simultaneously discovers both the need for limits and the illimitability of any chosen context.[7] The mimetic element, the story of the hero, has to be seen in the context of dissemination, which is precisely the risk of too thick a crop. The story of the hero is conditioned by that which conditions all art or writing, namely, the need to contend with illimitability, which can be seen as the story of the story. I take "the story of the story" to refer to the problem of representation, on which is predicated the very possibility of narrative. In his preface then, James steers the reader towards an awareness of the split between the mimetic story and the meta-story, but it is the intimate connection between these two that is the focus of this chapter.[8]

* * * * *

The story of James's hero hinges on Strether's embassy to Chad on behalf of his mother Mrs. Newsome. Strether is to represent the mother to the son and persuade Chad to leave Paris and return to his proper place, his home and family business in Woollett, Massachusetts. In the course of performing this mission, Strether's rationale for being in Europe is reversed, and Strether undertakes to represent the son to the mother. E. M. Forster described this as the "hour-glass structure of the novel.[9] Strether is thus an unreliable representative, and in the course of his reversal the center of interest shifts from his particular mission, his function as representative, to the workings of his consciousness and to the general problems involved in the project of representation itself.

It is in this displacement, I argue, that the story of James's hero and the story of the story converge. Strether's function as Mrs. Newsome's ambassador is to bear her specific message to Chad. His task is to convince Chad of the merit of his mother's wishes. As James's representative, Strether has an analogous function; he must persuade the reader of the palpability of the fictional world James projects in his novel. But the story of the hero dramatically illustrates the way in which the representative himself continually gets in the way of what he is supposed to represent. The displacing of what is supposed to be represented by that which represents it.[10] Like Strether, the representatives or signs used by James in *The Ambassadors* are themselves subject to the problems intrinsic to representation. Thus the story of the hero and the story of the story converge, and the inevitable result is that, like Mrs. Newsome, the artist James, "sows his seed at the risk of too thick a crop."

The plot of *The Ambassadors* derives its structure from two distinct but connected elements. On the one hand we have Strether's presence at the center of the novel, while on the other we have Mrs. Newsome's absence in distant America. The first has to do with James's undertaking, as his preface says, to employ "but one center and keep it all within [his] hero's compass."

> The thing was to be so much this worthy's intimate adventure that even the projection of his consciousness upon it from beginning to end without intermission or deviation would probably still leave a part of its value for him, and *a fortiori* for ourselves, unexpressed. (9)

This technique of making Strether's consciousness the single and incomplete medium through which all the events of the novel are refracted has been admirably dealt with by many critics, whose work has involved an examination of the pressures and profits of the free indirect style.[11] Clearly, James does not entirely accomplish what he claims in the preface; there is evidence of authorial intrusion obliquely exercised. However, the impression remains that events are mediated through Strether's consciousness. Indeed, for my purpose, the chief benefit derived and the main loss incurred as a result of this technique is to emphasize the unmooring of James's chief representative. If Strether's is the sole consciousness, there is no possibility of testing the adequacy of his representations. Encompassed in the text of his mind, what the reader experiences is the impossibility of verifying Strether's impressions, of measuring them against the impressions of other characters or against those of an omniscient narrator. Since everything is filtered through his "mind," the distinction between what Strether represents and how well or faithfully he represents it, falls away. He becomes a medium, and there is no possibility of checking how well he mediates, since the only evidence we have for this hypothetical quantity is the evidence provided by his own mediation. This absence of checks and controls could make for an unstable or unreliable narrative; what is more interesting, however, is the way in which it liberates the appointed ambassador for the performance of his mediating function.

The subjectivity that James foists on Strether through this particular narrative technique is paralleled by what I take to be the second closely related major structuring device, namely, the distance which separates Europe and America, the space which further underlines the unmooring of the representative. The centrality of this device, while it has received much critical attention, has not been fully explored.

Distance and absence are clearly of the essence in Strether's situation; Mrs. Newsome wouldn't need an ambassador is she were herself present. In other words, for Strether to have any function whatsoever in this novel, Mrs. Newsome *has* to be somewhere else, has to be absent.[12] But part of the functioning of any representative depends on the impression that it is in contact with that which it represents. There has to be a sense of possible referentiality, and certainly in the first part of this novel we see Strether in constant and anxious communication with his place of origin and the source of his authority. It is through this communication that James examines the relationship between the representative and the distant—the absent—source of his credentials. In the preface, adumbrating elements of the story, James writes that part of his success in this novel is his creation of Mrs. Newsome, who, "away off with her finger on the pulse of Massachusetts, should yet be no less intensely than circuitously present through the whole thing, should be no less felt as to be reckoned with than the most direct exhibition . . ." (10). From its inception then, it is the distance between Woollet and Paris which makes for the focus on the central issues of representation.

It is precisely this condition of absence that calls into being the story of James's hero. The story of the story is thus also conditioned by this enabling absence, without which we would have no need for Strether. Strether's situation, the paradigmatic situation of the representative, exposes the difficulties attendant on and innate to the enterprise of representation. If the process of embassy itself emphasizes the distance between Woollett and Paris and opens up the gap between the source of authority and its representative, in doing so it creates the need to bridge this gap with the minimum loss of intensity. There can be no identity between the source and its representative, the signified and the signifier, since this would remove the very possibility and indeed the need for representation. Therefore, the distance or differentiation between Mrs. Newsome and Strether must always be both maintained and bridged.

The clearest expression of the distance between the two continents and the need to bridge it is found in Strether's constant communication with Mrs. Newsome. His stay in Europe is characterized both by his sense of dependence on Mrs. Newsome's directives and by his sense of the freedom which his distance from her affords him. Their correspondence spanning the gulf between Europe and America has "to reckon with the Atlantic Ocean, the General Post-Office and the extravagant curve of the globe" (113).

In Paris with Waymarsh, the first thing we see Strether doing is "hastening" to the bankers where he expects to find letters from Mrs. Newsome. The bank is, uncannily, situated in the Rue Scribe. It is appropriate at this point to recall the number of ways in which Strether is associated with the world of letters. By profession he is an editor of the *Review* owned and overseen by Mrs. Newsome. His very name, as Maria Gostrey notes, is the title of a novel by Balzac, and he himself feels that he owes his identity to the fact that his name is inscribed on the cover of the review he edits. The letters, when he eventually finds them, "had reached London . . . and had taken their time to follow him" (59). James's emphasis on the temporal displacement implicit in correspondence is important. It seems that to correspond is to emulate Achilles in his fore-doomed attempt to overtake the tortoise. The time which separates Mrs. Newsome from Strether is unabridgeable, letters are always belated. The frustration caused by this displacement is demonstrated by Strether's thwarted impulse to read the letters in the bank, there and then, on the spot "which, reminding him of the post office at Woollett, affected him as the abutment of some transatlantic bridge" (59).

That these letters serve both to connect and liberate is brought out in Strether's attitude as he reads them with "such an extraordinary sense of escape" (60):

Four of the letters were from Mrs. Newsome and none of them short; she had lost no time, and followed on his heels while he moved, so expressing herself that he now could measure the probable frequency with which he should *hear.* They would arrive, it would seem, her communications, at the rate of several a week; he should be able to count, it might even prove, on more than one by each mail. If he had begun yesterday with a small grievance he had therefore an opportunity to begin to-day, with its opposite. He read the letters successively and slowly, putting others back into his pocket but keeping these for a long time afterwards gathered in his lap. He held them there, lost in thought, as if to prolong the *presence* of what they gave him; or as if at the least to assure them their part in the constitution of some lucidity. His friend wrote admirably, and her tone was even more in her style than in her voice—he might almost, for the hour, have had to come this distance to get its full carrying quality; yet the *plentitude* of his consciousness of *difference* consorted perfectly with the deepened intensity of the connexion. It was the difference, the difference of being just where he was and *as* he was, that formed the escape—this difference was so much greater than he had dreamed it would be; and what finally he sat there turning over was the strange logic of his finding himself so *free*.[13] (60–61; my emphasis).

In the preface, James wrote of his success in creating the character of Mrs. Newsome. This passage is a sample of that success, while also anticipating James's skepticism about the possibility of language evoking some kind of immediate presence, a notion for which Derrida later coined the term logocentrism. The quality and quantity of her communication is stunning. The illusion that her letters create for Strether is such that he relates to them as being even more expressive of her "tone" than is her voice. It is as though the writing is a stronger, more continuous, more accurate representation for Strether of the "real" Mrs. Newsome than her presence. Rather than highlighting the distance between them, Strether's consciousness of the difference between the effect of Mrs. Newsome "in person" and Mrs. Newsome as represented through her copious correspondence makes him feel the intimacy of their connection. For an as yet relatively naive Strether, it is the written word that carries the plenitude of meaning normally ascribed to speech.[14] When he receives Mrs. Newsome's letters, Strether "hears" from her.

Curiously, Strether responds to the letters with a feeling of freedom and youth. In Europe he feels himself "launched in something of which the sense would be quite disconnected from the sense of his past . . ." (20). The novel is seeded with references to time: Strether's guilty habit of looking at his watch; the clock he contemplates in the Tuileries; the Spanish clock whose inscription he remembers; at one point Strether even thinks of Chad as a clock he has temporarily succeeded in stopping. Altogether, Europe is characterized by its surprising capacity to make Strether feel young. It is as though the space which separates America and Europe separates Strether from his age, disconnects him from his past, from the encroachment of time, and allows him to reexperience youth. The difference that Strether finds in his present connection with Mrs. Newsome, when he hears from her, is just this sense of spatial and temporal separation from her, a separation which, through the written word, paradoxically conjures into being both an intensity of connection and a feeling of freedom. The space that is spanned by the transatlantic bridge focuses attention on the way the bridge separates as much as it joins, stressing difference and differentiation as much as continuity and conjunction:

> Again and again as the days passed he had had a sense of the pertinence of communicating quickly with Woollett—communicating with

a quickness with which telegraphy alone would rhyme; the fruit of a
fine fancy in him for keeping things straight, for the happy forestalment
of error. No one could explain better when needful, nor put more
conscience into an account or a report; which burden of conscience is
perhaps exactly the reason why his heart always sank when the clouds
of explanation gathered. His highest ingenuity was in keeping the sky
of life clear of them. Whether or no he had a grand idea of the lucid,
he held that nothing ever was in fact—for any one else—explained.
One went through the vain motions, but it was mostly a waste of life. A
personal relation was a relation only so long as people either perfectly
understood, or, better still, didn't care if they didn't. From the moment
they cared if they didn't it was living by the sweat of one's brow; and
the sweat of one's brow was just what one might buy one's self off
from by keeping the ground free of the wild weed of delusion. It easily
grew too fast, and the Atlantic cable now alone could race with it. That
agency could each day have testified for him to something that was not
what Woollett had argued. He was not at this moment absolutely sure
that the effect of the morrow's—or rather of the night's—appreciation
of the crisis wouldn't be to determine some brief missive. "Have at last
seen him, but oh dear!"—some temporary relief of that sort seemed
to hover before him. It hovered somehow as preparing them all—yet
preparing them for what? If he might do so more luminously and
cheaply he would tick out in four words: "Awfully old—grey hair." To
this particular item in Chad's appearance he constantly, during their
mute half-hour reverted; as if so very much more than he could have
said had been involved in it. The most he could have said would have
been: "If he's going to make me feel young—!" which indeed, however,
carried with it quite enough. (95)

On the face of it Strether is worried that he might be acting in
bad faith. As Mrs. Newsome's ambassador he ought not to respond
to Chad and to Paris. Strether views communication with Woollett
as a means for "keeping things straight." It seems that the rate and
rapidity with which things tend to go crooked can only be matched
by the speed of the cable; this medium alone—despite, and possibly because of its abbreviated form—might be luminous enough
and quick enough to adequately represent events in Europe. The
trick of brevity and speed might transcend the incalculable distance, might render im-mediate the mediating space. But Strether
elects not to send a cable, precisely because he knows that he
cannot bridge the space, because "very much more than he could
have said" had been involved in the impression of Chad that he
wanted to communicate.[15]

The second and more interesting element that emerges from this passage has to do with Strether's understanding of the general efficacy of communication and explanation. A gifted explainer, Strether seems to conceive his own role at least in part, as the duty to report to Mrs. Newsome. But Strether's ideal conception of personal relations assumes a rapport which obviates report, an immediacy of understanding or an acceptance of its unimportance that would appear to undermine Strether's integrity in his accepted role of ambassador. The passage above is illuminating in that it articulates Strether's belief in the need for some kind of presence precisely in the situation prompted by absence, namely, the situation in which he is called on to explain or represent a distant event. I suspect that Strether reflects the author's vain hope for immediacy, but even if this is not the case, the novel clearly exposes the irony of a wish that can only have status or only arises in the instance which conditions its impossibility. The need for explanation only occurs, in Strether's conception, in the absence of a personal presence, so that to deny or eschew the possibility of explanation is to rob himself of his own function as representative. It is no wonder that he chooses not to send his cable.

The ebb and flow of his correspondence with Mrs. Newsome marks the fluctuations of Strether's success as representative. The nadir comes at the juncture where he persuades Chad to cable his mother that he, Chad, intends to remain in Paris. It is as a result of this cable that the indomitable Mrs. Newsome sends out her next relay of ambassadors, headed by her daughter Mrs. Sarah Pocock. (As an aside, I should like to note that at this stage the comedy is something like that of the child's song "There was an old woman who swallowed a fly" or "The House that Jack Built." Mrs. Newsome first lets her son go, then sends Strether to fetch him, then sends Sarah to fetch them both—the effect piles up.)

The cable that Strether does eventually send, to express his appreciation of reenforcements, after Chad announces that the Pocock contingent has *already* departed, does not contain an explanation. It is a gesture in which he attempts gracefully to bow before what he already knows to be inevitable and which we know is far from being to his taste. Strether's message is his manner of reporting that he recognizes the failure of all previous explanation. He reflects on his own cable:

> He had added that he was writing, but he was of course always writing: it was a practice that continued, oddly enough, to relieve him, to make him come nearer than anything else to the consciousness of doing something; so that he often wondered if he hadn't really, under his

recent stress, *acquired some hollow trick,* one of the specious arts of make-believe. Wouldn't the pages he still so frequently dispatched by the American post have been worthy of a showy journalist, some master of the great new science of *beating the sense out of words?* Wasn't he writing against time, and mainly to show he was kind?—since it had become quite his habit not to like to read himself over. . . . He might have written before more freely, but he had never written more copiously; and he frankly gave for a reason at Woollett that he wished to fill the void created by Sarah's departure. (203–4; my emphasis)

In the light of all that has already been said—the basic, given situation of his distance from Mrs. Newsome; the dependency and the freedom afforded him by this distance; his sense of the innate impossibility of ever explaining—it is clear that of course he beats the sense out of words. His own story, the text of his own thoughts, the relentless logic of embassy, all suggest that the distinction implicit in "beating the sense out of words" is a distinction between two sorts of writing, one specious and the other what?—true? This distinction is the "hollow trick" that cannot hold, especially in the context of this novel. James's use of the word "trick" reflects his awareness of the trickiness and treacherousness of language itself.[16]

Like his author, Strether is dependent on the vagaries of writing to fulfill his function. Despite his doubts, in writing copiously Strether still feels that he is doing something even if he is only filling a void.[17] It is through the story of Strether-the-character that the story of the story of *The Ambassadors* emerges. In the absence of a presence that obviates the need for representation altogether, represented experience is necessarily refracted through the mirror of writing or of language. In this sense, the possibility is mooted that all writing is a "writing against time," an impossible attempt to recapture some lost dimension that may have existed in the vanishing past of lived experience. Writing in this sense is always the already foredoomed attempt to fill the space that opens between experience and its representation. Analogous to the distance between the novelist and his germ, between germ and story and, for that matter, between story and reader—the distance between Mrs. Newsome and Strether subverts the bridging of the gap that structures not only writing but human relations themselves. Such relations, Strether will come to realize, are always devoid of immediacy, always contaminated insofar as they are determined by an impersonal symbolic order.[18]

His most personal of personal relations, his relation with Maria Gostrey, is from its beginning implicated in this impersonal order.

Describing his initial contact with her, Strether has the following thoughts: Maria's eyes

> . . . had taken hold of him straightaway, measuring him up and down as if they knew how; as if he were human material they had already in some sort handled. Their possessor was in truth, it may be communicated, the mistress of a hundred cases or categories, receptacles of the mind, subdivisions for convenience, in which, from a full experience, she pigeon-holed her fellow mortals with a hand as free as that of a compositor scattering type. (21)

To be perceived is to be classified, typecast within the order of representation.

In a little noticed scene, after Strether's discovery that Chad and Madame de Vionnet are lovers, he posts a letter in which he confirms his continued support of them. The scene dramatizes Strether's acceptance of his own implication in the inescapable thicket of mediation. As he is about to post his letter he hesitates, and the alternative opens up to him of *not* posting his letter, simply leaving things as they are;[19] "[h]e mightn't see her at all; . . . he mightn't see any one at all any more at all . . .". "This alternative was for a few minutes so sharp that if he at last did deposit his missive it was perhaps because the pressure of the place [the post office] had an effect" (332–333).

The post office is of course the institution which arranges, organizes, and facilitates communication. Faced with the option of dropping out, of ceasing to communicate with the couple, it is the pressure of the place, which "perhaps" decides him.

> There was none other, however, than the common and constant pressure, familiar to our friend under the rubric of *Postes et Telegraphes*—the something in the air of these establishments; the vibrations of the vast strange life of the town, the influence of the types, the performers concocting their messages; the little prompt Paris women, arranging, pretexting goodness knew what, driving the dreadful needle-pointed public pen at the dreadful sand-strewn public table: implements that symbolised for Strether's too interpretative innocence something more acute in manners, more sinister in morals, more fierce in the national life. After he had put in his paper he had ranged himself, he was really amused to think, on the side of the fierce, the sinister, the acute. He was carrying on a correspondence, across the great city, quite in the key of the *Postes et Telegraphes* in general; and it was fairly as if the acceptance of that fact had come from something in his state that sorted with the occupation of his neighbours. He was mixed up with the typical tale of Paris, and so were they, poor things—how could

they altogether help being? They were no worse than he, in short, and he no worse than they—if, queerly enough, no better; and at all events he had settled his hash . . . (333)

In this "scene of writing," the submotif of correspondence that has structured the novel from the outset reaches its apotheosis. The post office symbolizes for Strether the place where the common man is seen in communication, one with another. In writing to Madame de Vionnet, Strether makes his final turn and ranges himself with the common man engaged in common pursuits; assignations fierce or sinister negotiated by writing are what characterize this common life. To communicate, to represent, to explain, to write, is to belong to this dreadful community, wielding this needle-pointed public pen, in which distance is bridged and abridged by representation in words. In concocting his own message and thus ranging himself as one more performer in this tangle of communication, Strether chooses to become arranged within the typical: typical in that he too acquires an identity as a result of his commitment to the world of type and the network of communication that constitutes the world of this novel and the story of its story.

*****

The enabling absence implicit in the community of the "dreadful needle-pointed public pen" also marks the characters of this novel as they represent themselves to one another and to us through speech. I believe that almost any segment of dialogue would illustrate this, but the most interesting example of the vacancy of the spoken word is found in the transformations of the expression "a virtuous attachment." On one level, Strether's various perceptions of the significance of this phrase is simply part of the novel's comedy of appearances, but the contradictions in its usage reveal something about James's use of language in this novel.

"A virtuous attachment" is the phrase Bilham offers Strether to explain Chad's remaining in Europe. Lacking any other, Strether accepts this explanation, but he is not entirely satisfied with it. It is only when he finally discovers that this description is a lie that he comes to accept it as revealing a truth. Bilham has said that Chad is "good" although he "isn't used . . . to being so good" (116). Strether asks him: "Why isn't he free if he's good?" and Bilham replies: "Because it's a virtuous attachment."

This had settled the question so effectually for the time—that is for the next few days—that it had given Strether almost a new lease on life. It must be added however that, thanks to his constant habit of shaking the bottle in which life handed him the wine of experience, he presently found the taste of the lees rising as usual into his draught. (117)[20]

How Bilham's answer settles the question is something of a mystery, and if it takes the reader less time than Strether before his potion is infected by the rising lees or the sediment of language, it is because the reader is aware of the different constructions that the American from Woollett and the cosmopolitan Bilham might put on words.

When he learns of Chad's "two particular friends" Strether assumes that the virtuous attachment is to both Vionnets, mother and daughter. He has long assumed that Chad is in the clutches of some woman of "easy" virtue and has been hard put in this light to understand Chad's positive transformation. So that when Bilham describes the attachment as virtuous, Strether wants the clarity conferred by Bilham's category or pigeonhole and he fastens on this description. But he recognizes a possible equivocation and tests the description with Maria, who says: "You say there are two? An attachment to them both then would, I suppose, almost necessarily be innocent" (118). In trying to make sense of the phrase they discuss the possible permutations of Chad's relation. If the attachment is to the daughter and if it is virtuous then Maria asks:" . . . why isn't [Chad] 'free'?" (119). The paradox Maria notices is that if the attachment is virtuous, then it is not an attachment of the sort that can explain Chad's lack of freedom. If Jeanne is available, then Chad is not fixed in his situation in Paris but can presumably marry her and return to Woollett.

In trying to clear the phrase of paradox they continue the discussion and consider the possibility that Chad's attachment is to the mother, Madame de Vionnet.

> Miss Gostrey entertained the suggestion. "She *is* a widow then?"
> "I haven't the least idea!" They once more, in spite of this vagueness, exchanged a look—a look that was perhaps the longest yet. It seemed in fact, the next thing, to require to explain itself; which it did as it could. "I only feel that I've told you—that he has some reason."
> Miss Gostrey's imagination had taken its own flight. "Perhaps she's *not* a widow."
> Strether seemed to accept the possibility with reserve. Still he accepted it. "Then that's why the attachment—if it's to her—is virtuous."
> But she looked as if she scarce followed. "Why is it virtuous if— since she's free—there's nothing to impose on it any condition?"

He laughed at her question. "Oh I perhaps didn't mean as virtuous as *that!* Your idea is that it can be virtuous—in any sense worthy of the name—only if she's *not* free? But what does it become then," he asked, "for *her?*"

"Ah that's another matter." (121)

We saw previously that if the attachment is to the daughter and is virtuous, then it is hardly an attachment; what emerges from this piece of dialogue is that if the liaison is with the mother it might *not* be virtuous, in which case "there's nothing to impose on it any condition," which is to say that if the liaison is illicit then once again it can hardly be considered an attachment.

The dialogue itself charts the course in which Bilham's description is seen to contain both one possibility and its polar opposite with the result that it becomes so all-encompassing or so paradoxical that it can be understood in two contradictory ways.

"You don't believe in it!"

"In what?"

"In the character of the attachment. In its innocence."

But she defended herself. "I don't pretend to know anything about it. Everything's possible. We must see."

"See?" he echoed with a groan. "Haven't we seen enough?"

"*I* haven't," she smiled.

"But do you suppose then little Bilham has lied?"

"You must find out."

It made him almost turn pale. "Find out any *more?*" He had dropped on a sofa for dismay; but she seemed, as she stood over him, to have the last word: "Wasn't what you came out for to find out *all?*" (122)

But Strether, even though he is aware of the problems implicit in Bilham's phrase, insists on understanding Bilham's description; and the next time he uses the phrase it is to tell Bilham that although at first he had not understood what he had meant, having since spent some time in the Vionnets' company, he now does.

"Oh," said little Bilham. "I don't think that at that time you believed me."

"Yes—I did; and I believed Chad too. It would have been odious and unmannerly—as well as quite perverse—if I hadn't. What interest have you in deceiving me?"

The young man cast about. "What interest have *I?*"

"Yes. Chad *might* have. But you?"

"Ah, ah, ah!" little Bilham exclaimed.

It might, on repetition, as a mystification, have irritated our friend a little; but he knew, once more, as we have seen, where he was, and his being proof against everything was only another attestation that he meant to stay there. "I couldn't, without my own impression, realise. . . . I understand what a relation with such a woman—what such a high fine friendship—may be. It can't be vulgar or coarse, anyway—and that's the point." (173–74)

The broad narrative irony reinforces our sense of Strether's almost desperate need to cling to whatever signposts are offered him. Strether only realizes in book 9 of this twelve-book novel that Chad's attachment is to Madame de Vionnet, when he finds out that she and Chad have arranged a marriage for her daughter. Even though he knows that Madame de Vionnet has a husband it is only after Strether discovers her and Chad on the river that he becomes aware that Bilham has lied and that she and Chad are lovers. But he still persists in the belief that the attachment is virtuous. He says to Maria:

"Well . . . it was but a technical lie—[Bilham] classed the attachment as virtuous. That was a view for which there was much to be said—and the virtue came out for me hugely. There was of course a great deal of it. I got it full in the face, and I haven't, you see, done with it yet." (349)[21]

In his last conversation with Chad, referring to Madame de Vionnet, Strether says: "You'll be a brute you know—you'll be guilty of the last infamy—if you ever forsake her" (354). For Strether the virtuous attachment is and is not a "virtuous" attachment. The novel dramatizes the twists and turns whereby the phrase includes what it would seem to exclude, conflating virtue and vice, attachment, and freedom to the point where finally the truth that is a lie is recognized as truth.

When James writes in his preface of the dangers attendant on the artist's sowing of the fictional seed, it is clear that the crop is at risk not because of weeds but because of too large a crop. The same is true of language. It is not that "true" language gets infiltrated by untruth. The lees of language are integral with it. Like the wine that becomes suffused, language becomes so sedimented that the distinctions apparently made by words are blurred.

Bilham's attitude suggests that the very illimitability of language is its limitation, and in the segment of dialogue in Gloriani's garden, he explicitly recommends that Strether not restrict himself to experiencing the world through the categories of a language which is inherently unreliable. Strether has just met the Vionnets and asks Bilham:

> "They then are the virtuous attachment?"
> "I can only tell you that it's what they pass for. But isn't that enough? What more than a vain appearance does the wisest of us know? I commend you . . . the vain appearance." (129)

In the discussion that follows, Miss Barrace wonders at Strether's tendency to subordinate experience to preestablished categories that cannot encompass or express experience. "You're wonderful, you people, . . . for not feeling those things—by which I mean impossibilities. You never feel them. You face them with a fortitude that makes it a lesson to watch you" (130).

It would seem that for Miss Barrace the complexity of what she sees makes the efficacy of moral action doubtful. The world of appearances is so complex that if you are not blinded, if you take it in, purposive action is senseless. For Strether, whose very function as representative implies action—which means persuading Chad to go home—such a vision, such a breadth of vision, is anathema. He cannot see what she wants him to see and still maintain his sense of purpose. If vision involves such a complicated, complex set of responses, if it will undermine all the assumptions on which he has come out to act, then vision radically undermines his status as representative. He says:

> "You've all of you here so much visual sense that you've somehow all 'run' to it. There are moments when it strikes one that you haven't any other."
> "Any moral," little Bilham explained . . . "But Miss Barrace has a moral distinction . . ."
> "Oh not a distinction"—[Miss Barrace] was mightily amused . . . "But I think I may say a sufficiency . . . I dare say . . . that I do, that we all do here, run too much to mere eye. But how can it be helped? We're all looking at each other—and in the light of Paris one sees what things resemble. That's what the light of Paris seems always to show. It's the fault of the light of Paris—dear old light!"
> "Dear old Paris!" little Bilham echoed.
> "Everything, every one shows," Miss Barrace went on.
> "But for what they really are?" Strether asked.
> "Oh, I like your Boston 'reallys'! But sometimes—yes."
> "Dear old Paris then!" Strether resignedly sighed while for a moment they looked at each other. Then he broke out: "Does Madame de Vionnet do that? I mean really show for what she is?"
> Her answer was prompt. "She's charming. She's perfect."

> "Then why did you a minute ago say, 'Oh, oh, oh' at her name?"
> She easily remembered. "Why, just because—! She's wonderful."
> "Ah she too?"—Strether had almost a groan. (131–32)

Besides emphasizing the indeterminate equality of words like "charming," "wonderful," "perfect," and "really," the dialogue offers an interesting view of Miss Barrace's aestheticism.[22] Unlike Strether who has not really seen the virtuous attachment but has understood it through a moral framework that, as we have seen, loses its capacity to adequately orient experience, Miss Barrace suggests that her moral sufficiency is based on the acuity of her vision. She looks at things in the light of Paris, in their plenitude, and thus claims to see without the distorting categories of a prior moral conception. Whereas Strether has been deluded by his imposition of the moral, Miss Barrace sees what things resemble. For her, the probe beneath appearances is tendentious. Resemblance is what vision offers; more than this is abstraction. To probe beneath appearances is to import some distorting typology. What things resemble is what they really are. The thrust of this metaphysic undermines what is usually understood by "reality." If Strether's hope—if, indeed, his entire story—is the attempt to penetrate what lies behind appearances, to test them for their capacity to represent, the comedy of appearances reveals that resemblances are all that is available.[23] Behind resemblance is only resemblance, which is to say that resemblance and dissemblance are not opposite poles that can be fixed by reference to the thing itself. The thing is not in itself, but is only available in some mediated form; to resemble is always to be reassembled. When Bilham says "I commend you the vain appearance" he speaks out of both sides of his mouth because it is the emptiness of appearances that constitutes the fullness of reality.

*****

As we have seen, what James seems to mean by the story of the story is concerned with the mediated nature of experience, which is dramatized in the functioning of Strether's mind. Most, if not all of the major scenes in the novel are compared in Strether's mind—and there is no other place in this novel—to one or another art form, which is to say that all experience in this novel is conceived as, or likened to, some other form of representation.

Two important scenes, for instance, occur in the context of Strether's visits to the theater. In the first, early in the novel, we see that for Strether the play is as much off as on stage.[24]

It was an evening, it was a world of types, and this was a connexion above all in which the figures and faces in the stalls were interchangeable with those on the stage.

He felt as if the play itself penetrated him with the naked elbow of his neighbour. . . . He had distracted drops in which he couldn't have said if it were actors or auditors who were most true. (44)

What is beyond and what is this side of the footlights is interchangeable. On their next visit to the theater, he and Maria share a box, and as they wait for the curtain to rise, Chad makes his first and long-awaited appearance. The drama begins and the play onstage suspends the play offstage; the framing art form, the theater, obtrudes into the ongoing drama in the box and it becomes impossible to say where the play begins and where it ends.

But the mediating effects of art in this novel are nowhere as obvious as in James's use of the fine arts, particularly pictures. Pictures for Strether have the capacity to go beyond words. During his first walk in Chester the impact of the English country is described:

Too deep almost for words was the delight of these things to Strether; yet as deeply mixed with it were certain images of his inward picture. He had trod this walk in the far-off time, at twenty-five; but that, instead of spoiling it, only enriched it for present feeling and marked his renewal as a thing substantial enough to share. (24)

Experience that cannot adequately be represented in language but that derives from some quality of the interaction of previous experience and imagination, gets communicated through this "inward picture." If previously we have seen that representation re-presents either an absence or something that is radically inaccessible, we see now that representation through art makes it impossible to distinguish what is "out there" from what is "in here." An impression is always a conflation of the external and the internal.

Contemplating the clock in the Tuileries, Strether feels that "the air [of Paris] had a taste of something mixed with art, something that presented nature as a white-capped master chef" (60). Nature and art are never simple polarities in Strether's mind. The interaction of mind with nature always brings with it some element of art so that any perception of any external scene is already structured by the imagination or by art, and thus any separation of external reality from the mediating function of the mind is arbitrary. Experience is never raw but is always precooked in the symbolic order.[25]

Such is the case in Gloriani's garden where for Strether the outdoor scene is inseparable from his own placing of it in the cultural context from which it derives its power. Ian Watt has written that James's style can be seen "as a supremely civilised effort to relate every event and every moment . . . to the endless network of general moral, social and historical relations."[26] I would emphasize that the linguistic order also belongs to this network and that it can manifestly be seen to be working in Strether's perceptions in Gloriani's garden.

> It was in the garden, a spacious cherished remnant, out to which a dozen persons had already passed, that Chad's host presently met them; while the tall bird-haunted trees, all of a twitter with the spring and the weather, and the high party-walls, on the other side of which grave *hôtels* stood off for privacy, spoke of survival, transmission, association, a strong indifferent persistent order. The day was so soft that the little party had practically adjourned to the open air, but the open air was in such conditions all a chamber of state. Strether had presently the sense of a great convent, a convent of missions, famous for he scarce knew what, a nursery of young priests, of scattered shade, of straight alleys and chapel bells, that spread its mass in one quarter; he had the sense of names in the air, of ghosts at the windows, of signs and tokens, a whole range of expression, all about him, too thick for prompt discrimination.
>
> This assault of images became for a moment, in the address of the distinguished sculptor, almost formidable: Gloriani showed him, in such perfect confidence, on Chad's introduction of him, a fine worn handsome face, a face that was like an open letter in a foreign tongue. With his genius in his eyes, his manners on his lips, his long career behind him . . . [he] affected our friend as a dazzling prodigy of type. (124–25)

This scene is too "thick" for prompt discrimination. Art and nature are indistinguishable in this perception because experience is itself suffused with art so that to understand experience is always to become embroiled in the mediations of art. Art is a product of tradition, a heaping up of images under whose assault the open air becomes "a chamber of state," a person can become an "open letter in a foreign tongue," and the milieu a mass of "signs and tokens." Nature is nurture, and the natural objects of Strether's perception, the "bird-haunted trees all of a twitter," are seen to belong to the order of artistic tradition as much as the convent or the historical buildings. Strether himself is implicated in this historical, social, and linguistic network. But his identified response to the surrounding scene is accompanied by an "odious suspicion of any form of beauty" (123). His New England background, his function as representative, everything points to his need to distinguish art from life. How is he to represent when his representation is from the start contaminated by his own response? How can he report what is out there when it is so infernally mixed up with what is internal?

By the end of the novel this "ascetic suspicion" has all but disappeared, and spending a day in the French countryside, Strether discovers the conditions that were from the first implicit in his mission. He takes a train ride "on the chance of seeing something somewhere that would remind him of a certain small Lambinet that had charmed him, long years before, at a Boston dealer's and that he had quite absurdly never forgotten" (318–19).[27] He looks for a piece of nature that would remind him of this piece of art and thus reverses the usual mimetic order: he does not look for art that will represent nature, but for nature that will resemble art.[28] He finds what he is looking for without once overstepping "the oblong gilt frame" (319). The quality of his experience is such that the distinctions between art and nature, between memory and current experience, between the internal and the external, all become irrelevant. Experience itself is rendered as a mediated and culture-bound construct.

> For this had been all day at bottom the spell of the picture—that it was essentially more than anything else a scene and a stage, that the very air of the play was in the rustle of the willows and the tone of the sky. The play and the characters had, without his knowing it till now, peopled all his space for him, and it seemed somehow quite happy that they should offer themselves, in the conditions so supplied, with a kind of inevitability. It was as if the conditions made them not only inevitable, but so much more nearly natural and right as that they were at least easier, pleasanter, to put up with. The conditions had nowhere so asserted their difference from those of Woollett as they appeared to him to assert it in the little court of the Cheval Blanc while he arranged with his hostess for a comfortable climax. They were few and simple, scant and humble, but they were *the thing.* . . . "The" thing was the thing that implied the greatest number of other things of the sort he had had to tackle; and it was queer of course, but so it was—the implication here was complete. Not a single one of his observations but somehow fell into a place in it; not a breath of the cooler evening that wasn't somehow a syllable of the text. The text was simply, when condensed, that in *these* places such things were, and that if it was in them one elected to move about one had to make one's account with what one lighted on. (323–24)

Here all the terms and modes through which experience is mediated merge and meld. It is as though this interpenetration and the overwhelming evidence of the mediated aspect of experience is the very condition which from the outset was in the nature of Strether's embassy. Pictures, play, nature, art, texts, all combine to contribute to Strether's sense of well-being, his general confidence. The representative from Woollett has finally recognized that the distinctions he had come to Paris to make must disappear in the network of interpenetrations in which he has perforce to function. The context is irreducible to its separate parts since he himself is part of it, embroiled in too rich a tradition to allow for neat discriminations. The multiplicity of codes in the symbolic order is *the thing* he becomes aware of, and it is thus impossible to represent parts of it without implicating the whole.

*****

Strether's initial response to Paris is instructive: early on in the novel he feels that any acceptance of Paris might give one's authority away:

> It hung before him . . . the vast bright Babylon, like some huge iridescent object, a jewel brilliant and hard, in which parts were not to be discriminated nor differences comfortably marked. It twinkled and trembled and melted together, and what seemed all surface one moment seemed all depth the next. (66)

James's work itself has been described in terms that mirror some of his images:

> The ultimate limitation of his art is his need to treat the world as sheer spectacle, to cleave to surfaces, to eschew the passional and therefore the ultimate moral depths.[29]

As I hope this chapter has shown, however, *The Ambassadors* disqualifies the differentiation of "sheer spectacle" from "moral depths." In this novel the spectacle is indeed sheer, sheer to the point of a transparency that yields nothing but further spectacle.[30] Spectacle necessarily remains sheer, its transparency continually calls for and consistently confounds any and every attempt to cleave its surface.[31] The central problem of this novel lies in what does not lie beneath the surface, behind the sheer. It is this that creates the need to disinter the lie that lies behind.

By the end of his day in the country we see how Strether comes to recognize and accept the conditions that make up his situation. In the fictional world that the novel projects, nothing is immediate. Strether has represented Mrs. Newsome, represented Chad, represented Madame de Vionnet, and above all has represented to the reader the mediating role of representation itself. Nothing in this novel is conceived or experienced except through participation in the mediating order of culture, which itself structures or in-forms the participant. The novel dramatizes the way in which it is impossible to separate the knower from the known. All representation is thus self-presentation, and self or subject is itself a function of the mediating representations of culture.

The story of the story does not cancel the story of the hero but is its necessary and problematic precondition. Strether's story enacts the issues and problems involved in the enterprise of representation and thus thematizes the story of the story. The story of the hero is the story of the story.

4

The Story of the Fabulous Center:
The Wings of the Dove

THE Wings of the Dove takes as its raw material traditional melodramatic fare: a fortune hunter conspires against an unsuspecting innocent heiress and may ultimately be responsible for her death.[1] Penniless, beautiful Kate Croy is in love with penniless, charming Merton Densher. In an attempt to "feather her nest" Kate persuades Densher to make love to the "dove" of the title, the mortally sick heiress Milly Theale.[2] Her manipulations are motivated by the hope that Milly will marry Densher, die, and leave him an inestimable fortune, thus enabling Kate and Densher to marry and live in the style to which Kate would like to be accustomed.

I take the above to be a more or less adequate summary of the basic plot of this novel. Yet this leaves out almost everything of interest and leaves me with the burden of trying to say why it is impossible to judge and dismiss Kate as villain or to regard Milly as merely innocent victim.

Much of the excellent criticism of this novel can be read as the record of one or another critic taking this or that side in the conflict the novel projects, a tug of war, with each critic straining for his or her particular favorite.[3] What interests me is the tug of war itself, the way in which the novel promotes such taking of sides even as it exposes the arbitrary nature of any position taken. The representation of this tug of war is itself implicated in a field where competing representations are experienced as exposing the ungrounded project of representation itself.

In the chapter on *The Ambassadors* I argued that through the use of only one "center," Strether, the novel foregrounds the mediated nature of experience and the general function of representation. In *The Wings of the Dove* James takes this further. *Multiple* "centers of consciousness" compete in such a way as to render impossible the clear designation of a "center," whether of consciousness or of the novel as a whole. It is this proliferation of centers that

78

invites participation in a tug of war, making the identification of hero or villain both urgent and irrelevant. Each of the novel's multiple centers of consciousness has to find a way of acting and responding to a situation made out of interaction with other centers of consciousness.[4] Thus, James involves us in a story in which each center must construct an understanding of its own situation based on an interpretation of centers outside itself. The novel then becomes a record of the way one center attempts to represent both itself and other centers. Hence to side with one character is both to fulfill and ignore the dynamic of representation that prompts such identification.

The problems engendered by the traveling center are further foregrounded through migratory imagery and shifty plot. Insofar as the characters of the novel are text imaged as text, the difficulty of designating a stable center is further problematized. Moreover, insofar as the plot in which Densher would marry Milly for her money is a displacement or deferral of the plot of Kate's marriage to Lord Mark for Maud Lowder's money, the problem of achieving an organized perspective for judgment becomes dizzyingly difficult. The Croys' materialism, obscenely coupled with Mrs. Lowder's social ambition, would force Kate into a loveless marriage. If this is wicked, so is the greed which would force Densher into Milly's arms. If happiness is the end that justifies Kate's resistance and thus her plotting, then the happiness Densher would seem to bring to Milly would justify anything. But then, the represented nobility and magnanimity of Milly's response to Densher would seem to prompt in him a responsiveness to her that transforms his pretense.[5] Pretext becomes text, and what becomes of his good faith to Kate in this con-text? In the end we do not know where we stand: we cannot quite sort out an appropriate judgment, hence we are caught in competing representations. This is not to say that the vertigo engendered by all this repetition precludes the conceptualization of characters that achieve all the marks of fully fledged, discriminated consciousnesses. Rather, it is the tension between the highly articulated surface of the novel and the inherent instability of such consciousness that invites engagement in the tug of war, as the reader seeks to represent both character and center in an attempt to organize his experience of the novel.

The Ambassadors makes it impossible to distinguish between surface and depth, and the reader, like Strether, is thus mazed within a world of undiscriminated appearances. *The Wings of the Dove* invites us to plumb the depths of the experience it dramatizes, in order to assess the relative value, legitimacy, and meaning of a variety of represented responses to its central situation. That situation, however, is a kind of bottomless hole, which the reader, like the characters in the novel, cannot fathom, namely, the state of Milly Theale's health and the source of the debility that culminates in her death.[6] Because the "central" situation cannot be fathomed, both the judgment and the interpretation so urgently called for prove impossible.

By virtue of the enigmatic opacity of the "reality" at the center, and due to the dramatized problems of all those in the novel—Kate, Merton, Susan Stringham, Milly herself—who try to interpret it, the reader is more than usually implicated in the struggle to decode. Thus, the novel renders not only the problematic of representation but the accompanying anxiety. Because of the way the novel renders its "realities" through the agency of mediating consciousnesses, which are simultaneously made palpable and rendered problematical, it calls into question not only the object of perception, but also the perceiving subject. All the interpreting and judging consciousnesses of the novel, including that of the reader and of the "omniscient narrator," become equivocal due to the emphasis placed on consciousness itself and to the complexity of its mediation.[7] So problematicized is the field of meaning and judgment that all its elements, down to the title—unlike the title of *The Ambassadors*—remain undecipherable. *The Wings of the Dove* is an image as occult and finally uninterpretable as Milly's ailment.

As with *The Ambassadors,* the preface to the New York Edition reflects the concerns of the novel more than most readers have perceived. James emphasizes the matter of shifting centers and off-centered structure:

> . . . there could be no full presentation of Milly Theale as *engaged* with elements amid which she was to draw her breath in such pain, should not the elements have been, with all solicitude, duly prefigured. If one had seen that her stricken state was but half her case, the correlative half being the state of others as affected by her (they too should have a "case," bless them, quite as much as she!) then I was free to choose, as it were, the half with which I should begin. If, as I had fondly noted, the little world determined for her was to "bristle"—I delighted in the term!—with meanings, so, by the same token, could I but make my medal hang free, its obverse and its reverse, its face and its back, would beautifully become optional for the spectator. I somehow wanted them correspondingly embossed, wanted them inscribed and figured with an equal salience; yet it was none the less visibly my "key," as I have said, that though my regenerate young New Yorker, and what might depend on her, should form my centre, my circumfer-

ence was every whit as treatable. Therefore I must trust myself to
know when to proceed from the one and when from the other. Prepara-
tively and, as it were, yearningly—given the whole ground—one began,
in the event, with the outer ring, approaching the centre thus by narrowing circumvallations.[8]

The metaphors of James's discourse are revealing. What we have
in the medallion image is a figure/ground situation. The "spectator"
or reader will choose what to designate as "obverse" or "reverse"
and will decide what will constitute "face" or "back" in this "free
hanging medal." Moreover, since the "circumference" is "every
whit as treatable" as the "centre," the distinction between these
two elements becomes problematic; it becomes difficult, if not impossible, to *designate* a clear center.[9] Further, since the issue of
what will be "face" or "back" becomes something for the reader
to decide, the reader must become aware of the arbitrary and tentative status of his choice. All of which is to say that James's own
"trust" in the distinction between the "narrowing circumvallations"
and the "centre" becomes questionable. To mix the metaphors of
the two prefaces, just as *The Ambassadors* has a story that will
yield "too rich a crop," in *The Wings of the Dove* meaning itself
seems to "bristle"——in indeterminate fields, or alternating sides
of a medallion, at variable distances from an indeterminate center.

James's preface makes it clear that the problem of representing
the center derives from the nature of Milly Theale's situation. The
terms of his description of her and of her situation expose the
factitiousness of his assessment. Milly's struggle to live provides
James with the "idea" for the novel, which, ". . . reduced to its
essence, is that of a young person conscious of a great capacity
for life, but early stricken and doomed, condemned to die under
short respite, while also enamored of the world. . . ."[10] While it is
clearly in Milly Theale that James conceives of the center of the
novel, her struggle to live, ". . . to 'put in' before extinction as
many of the finer vibrations as possible . . . (288) . . . would inevitably determine, in respect to her, the attitude of other persons,
persons affected in such a manner as to make them part of the
action" (291). It is the participation of these "other persons" in
Milly's life that transforms the ostensible still center of the novel
into a raging whirlpool.

Their participation (appealed to, entangled and coerced as they find
themselves) becomes their drama too—that of their promoting her illusion, under her importunity, for reasons, for interests and advantages,
from motives and points of view, of their own. . . . Somehow, too, . . .

one would see the persons subject to [the promptings] drawn in as by
some pool of a Lorelei. . . . I have named the Rhine-maiden, but our
young friend's existence would create rather, all round her, very much
that whirlpool movement of the waters produced by the sinking of a
big vessel or the failure of a great business; when we figure to ourselves
the strong narrowing eddies, the immense force of suction, the general
engulfment that, for any neighbouring object, makes immersion inevitable. (291–93)

It seems that the dark fact of Milly's abbreviated future, the wreck
of what James calls his "vessel of sensibility," creates a center
which draws into itself all the other characters of the novel. It is
the vortex or "whirlpool" created by Milly's illness that, in drawing
into itself everything else in the novel, precludes the determination
of a clear center. In its own collapse this "whirlpool" exposes the
unknowable nature of "centre" and the consequent need for its
construction through representation.

Such absence of center, however, is not a repudiation of *structure*. Rather, it is an invitation to consider the contradictions implicit in both our own and James's normative conception of
structure. We tend to think of structure as defined by a coherent
center, whose function is, precisely, to center the surrounding
structure. Yet this novel exposes the limitations and contradictions
inherent in this view: on the one hand the whirlpool of centers
suggests that the novel decenters itself, while on the other hand,
despite the absence of a center, it successfully projects an elaborate surface that leads us to reflect on the problems of center and
of representation.[11]

Milly and her plight—her mortal illness—are the "germ" from
which, James tells us, the novel grew. Yet Milly and her illness are
both wrapped in obscurity, constituting, in fact, what I have called
the black hole, the tantalizing absence, the whirling eddy at the
ostensible but illegible center of the action. We not only never
learn what the illness is, but we never see Milly directly engaged
with any aspect of it. All we see is the process whereby Milly
may be seen to mystify herself, and others, through simultaneous
revelation of the "fact" of her illness and concealment of its nature
and substance. We also see the process whereby the morally ambiguous response of others to this elusive "fact" either destroys or
creates her; at the end of the novel we are not sure which.

*****

James's focus on the problem of representation determines the shifty structure of the novel. However, it is precisely the shifty structure of the novel that allows us to focus on the problem of representation. James's strategy of foregrounding the process of representation rather than stabilizing the object of representation is his use of what he calls in the preface the *"indirect"* presentation of his main image.[12]

The first and second book of the novel deal with Kate Croy and Merton Densher, and it is not until the third book, some seventy pages into the novel, that we are introduced to Milly Theale, the ostensible center of the entire story, and her companion Susan Stringham. Even then we do not directly learn of Milly's supposed illness. Rather, in the mode constitutive of the composition of this novel, we learn only indirectly, through Susan's reflections on her relationship with Milly, that there is something hidden beneath the surface that Milly presents: for Susan, to deal with Milly is to become involved in "duplicities and labyrinths," to acquire "an education in the occult" (70). We learn through Susan that Milly "was alone, she was stricken, she was rich, and in particular, *she was strange* . . ." (72, my emphasis).[13]

The question of how to interpret Susan's interpretation of Milly depends on how we interpret Susan. But as we are given Susan's perception of Milly we learn about Susan herself. Despite her pastoral role—Susan *Shepherd* Stringham is her full name—and even though she thinks of herself as unsuited for "duplicities and labyrinths," she is clearly capable of prevarication and subterfuge. She enters into the plot to "deceive" Milly—is indeed instrumental in its formation—when she encourages Milly to believe that Kate does not reciprocate Merton's love. Susan Shepherd is a novelist manqué, a New England widow; a writer who specializes in romantic literature for ladies, "a mere typical subscriber, after all, to the *Transcript,*" a magazine whose specialty is "love-interest" (73). From the onset she is deeply attracted to Milly, in whom she discovers "a New York legend of affecting, of romantic isolation" (72). "To *be* in truth literary had ever been [Susan's] dearest thought, the thought that kept her bright little nippers perpetually in position" (73). Susan is thus presented to us as an author, of sorts, an observer, whose speciality, we learn, is the domestication of the exotic. In Milly, Susan discovers an opportunity to exercise her literary imagination: ". . . but all categories failed her—they ceased at least to signify—as soon as she found herself in presence of the real thing, the romantic life itself. That was what she saw in Mildred . . . (73)."

Thus we see "Mildred" through Susan's shaping eye and we discover that this eye is shaped to see "Romance." We learn that Susan thinks of Milly as a modern-day princess, and of herself as a court attendant. Not only are we then given a picture of Milly, and an almost stereotypical picture of Susan, but we are also made aware of the process of representation by which these interdependent portraits emerge. Our inability to approach the characters except through the medium of a limited and partial consciousness makes us question the grounds of our own response. At this stage, Susan is our sole avenue of approach to Milly so that, even as we question, we are necessarily aware of the limited nature of our perspective. The question we confront, and which remains undecidable, is the extent to which Susan's investment in this view of Milly derives from her own romantic proclivities, her own predilection to represent her life as cast in the romantic mold.

Faced with Milly, Susan's perplexities are unrelenting and they reflect perplexities intrinsic in representation. To what extent, for instance, is Susan responding to something in Milly's character?[14] From the moment of Milly's first appearance Susan senses in her "some deeper depth than she had touched" (78). She wonders whether Milly does not represent "one of the finest, one of the rarest . . . cases of American intensity," and although she quickly dismisses the possibility that she is "merely going to [be] treat[ed] to some complicated drama of nerves" (78–79)—which explanation would have been "coarse"—Susan Stringham "found herself . . . in presence of an explanation that remained a muffled and intangible form, but that, assuredly, should it take on sharpness, would explain everything and more than everything, would become instantly the light in which Milly was to be read" (79).

The significance of Susan's vocation as reader is self-evident; the Susan who "writes" is also the Susan who, like everyone in this novel, "reads." Milly must be "read" and we must confront the problematics of such reading as they arise in the mystifying context of the presentation. We have here a deepening sense of Milly's inscrutable mystery, as well as of the way in which this mystery is "read" which is to say, represented, by Susan. But since Susan, herself a writer, is the object of James's, another writer's, irony, the self-consciously fictitious dimension of the world of this novel is foregrounded: reading and writing, both strategies of representation, merge. Susan, the reader/writer, is stimulated by Milly's "strangeness," her mystery. Susan becomes paradigmatic of all the other characters, as well as of the reader, perhaps even of the author, whose interest in Milly derives—like Susan's—from a sense of some "*void to be filled*" (74; my emphasis).

The difficulty inherent in our reliance on Susan's mediation for an image of Milly is brought out in James's need to emphasize that, although Susan is a particular kind of reader/writer, we cannot ignore her representation of Milly or simply dismiss it as unreliable. The image we create of Milly through the medium of Susan's consciousness is the image to which we respond. Even though we might be aware of the potential distortion involved in this second-hand sight, it acquires a persuasive rhetorical function.

> Such a matter as this may at all events speak of the style in which our young woman could affect those who were near her, may testify to the sort of interest she could inspire. She worked—and seemingly quite without design—upon the sympathy, the curiosity, the fancy of her associates, and *we shall really ourselves scarce otherwise come closer to her than by feeling their impression and sharing, if need be, their confusion.* She reduced them, Mrs. Stringham would have said, reduced them to a consenting bewilderment; which was precisely, for that good lady, on a last analysis, what was most in harmony with her greatness. (79; my emphasis)

James's uncharacteristically bold authorial intrusion, adjuring us to "share" the other characters' "impressions" as they are mediated through Susan, not only underscores the imperative—to participate in an equivocal point of view—but also dramatizes the problems of *any* perspective, including that of the narrative voice itself: writing involves interpretation and is not necessarily more authoritative than reading. We must see, for the time being, as Susan sees, but how can we know that even what she thinks she is sure of is as she thinks it to be?

In fact, though we must share Susan's impressions, we never get, either through her or through anyone else, a clear definition of Milly's condition, of the nature or "reality" of her ailment. From the beginning, that "reality" is both secret and mysterious, constituting an absence soliciting representation.[15] This becomes evident in the third book, in the course of the first direct presentation of Milly as a character, which occurs in the scene which I have been discussing. Susan Stringham follows Milly on her Alpine walk and, without revealing her presence, discovers her friend dangerously "perched" on the edge of a steep abyss. "A thousand thoughts" passed through Susan's mind, the first among them the possibility "of a latent intention . . . in such a posture; of some betrayed accordance of Milly's caprice with a horrible hidden obsession" (84). Up until this point there has been no hint of any morbid obsession; Susan's imaginative leap, her filling of the "void," of the abyss, is a measure of the kind of representation that Milly's mystery provokes.

Representation fills the void, and our sense of a "horrible hidden obsession" is confirmed when, without explicit reference to her experience on the precipice (and, in fact, about a hundred pages later), Milly asks Susan "abruptly, with a transition that was like a jump of four thousand miles, . . . 'What was it that, in New York, on the ninth, when you saw him alone, Dr. Finch said to you?'" (86). We are told that Milly is guessing, chancing her luck; there is no way she could have known that Susan had conferred with Milly's doctor in New York. "Yet why had her mind been busy with the question?" (87). As far as Susan knows, Milly had suffered from some slight illness prior to their departure for Europe, but under the impact of Milly's abrupt question Susan feels that it was "as if [the doctor] had said something that immensely mattered. He hadn't, however, in fact; it was only as if he might perhaps after all have been going to" (86–87).

This incident foreshadows Milly's labyrinthine concern with her health and dramatizes not just Milly's deviousness but the dynamic of the process of representation. That the doctor had after all revealed nothing of any importance is juxtaposed to the significance which Milly attributes to his possible pronouncements. What follows confirms both that Milly does conceal some secret and, further, that we have no way of assessing the significance of this secret; there might not really be a secret worth concealing. When Susan asks Milly, "But are you feeling unwell?" (87), Milly's response (in her first sustained dialogue) is enigmatic, if not disingenuous:

"I don't know—haven't really the least idea. But it might be well to find out."

Mrs Stringham, at this flared into sympathy. "Are you in trouble—in pain?"

"Not the least little bit. But I sometimes wonder—!"

"Yes"—she pressed: "wonder what?"

"Well, if I shall have much of it."

Mrs Stringham stared. "Much of what? Not of pain?"

"Of everything. Of everything I have."

Anxiously again, tenderly, our friend cast about. "You 'have' everything; so that when you say 'much' of it—"

"I only mean," the girl broke in, "shall I have it for long? That is if I *have* got it." (88)

The language of their exchange sets in relief the bafflement that pervades our sense of Milly's situation. The indeterminate "it" provokes all kinds of possibilities, and when Milly concludes with the asseveration that the matter with her is that she doesn't think she has the "power to resist the bliss of what [she *has*]!" (89), this bafflement is exacerbated.[16] Is Susan reading too hard? Are we? What is the status of all this "talk of early dying?" (90). Is Milly suffering from an incurable disease? What is the specific nature of the disease? What is the source of this mystery or secret? Why doesn't Milly simply say what is wrong with her? *Is* anything wrong with her? What is the point of all this mystification?

*****

The point of all this mystification, which is intensified when Milly gets to London, is to emphasize the problematics of representation. The mystification necessarily draws the reader into the process of constructing a representation whose adequacy can never be tested. It is not clear whether the purpose of Milly's journey is to see a doctor or to meet Merton Densher: is she concerned about her health, about dying, or is she concerned with meeting a potential lover, with living? Milly confesses to Susan, "possibly with a certain failure of presence of mind, that the last thing she desired was the air of running after [Merton Densher]" (93). Is Densher then the smoke screen that hides her true goal in going to London, namely to see a doctor, or are we to understand this the other way around—she goes to see Densher and her apparent ill health is the smoke screen? Or is it possible that she goes for both, and that the smoke screen functions to mask her great need of privacy, of secrecy? Does she simply need a smoke screen?

The novel gives us no clue as to which it is, or might be, and Milly herself, whatever her motives, contributes to the obscurity. Once again, readers find themselves in a position where—in the absence of unambiguous information, positively in the presence of mystification, of "consenting bewilderment" (79)—they are forced to construct a representation that will allow them to understand Milly's actions and motives. Readers are coerced into creating an orienting center which will give shape, structure, and form to their experience of the novel. Their activity, I would hold, is analogous, not only to all the characters' activity in constructing a view of Milly and of each other, but also to Milly's activity, opaque though it is, in constructing an identity for herself.

The unmoored status of Milly's representation of herself to herself is further exposed in the way James presents her visits to her doctor. It is characteristic of the darkness surrounding Milly's complaint that we never learn her doctor's specialty: her consultations with the famous Sir Luke Strett serve only to deepen the puzzle of her health. Milly's first visit to him exemplifies the way the novel defers its own central issues: the doctor does not have time to see her. When she does finally see him she imagines that "simply by his genius" he has "found out . . . literally everything" about her.

> Now she knew not only that she didn't dislike this—the state of being found out about; but that, on the contrary, it was truly what she had come for, and that, for the time at least, it would give her something firm to stand on. She struck herself as aware, aware as she had never been, of really not having had from the beginning anything firm. It would be strange for the firmness to come, after all, from her learning in these agreeable conditions that she was in some way doomed; but above all it would prove how little she had hitherto had to hold her up. If she was now to be held up by the mere process—since that was perhaps on the cards—of being let down, this would only testify in turn to her queer little history. (154)

The characteristic use of the double negative, discussed briefly in chapter 1, affirms at the same moment that it qualifies. We learn, first and foremost, of the absolute faith, and of the naivete of the faith, that Milly places in the great doctor. From the minute she makes contact with him she credits him with nothing less than omniscience. She assumes that he has found out "literally everything," but since neither we nor he ever know of what this "everything" consists, the literal becomes indistinguishable from the figurative, the representation from that which it would represent. Milly projects on to this doctor unlimited knowledge of her secret self. She feels that she has been exposed, understood, and in the process has come to understand herself. For Milly, we are led to feel, the secret of her health—the fact that she is going to die, and soon—constitutes this "self," constitutes her center. Milly's consultation provides her with the firm foundation she has long sought; it will be what "positively bears [her] up" (156).

Paradoxically, it is because Milly is the "heir of all the ages"[17]—the American girl who has everything—that she in fact has nothing and therefore desperately needs the identity provided by her secret. To have everything is to have nothing, in the sense that without limits there is nothing to provide Milly with the strictures and liberties of form. To have no boundaries is to be deprived of a self; implicitly, the self is a structure or shape that defines the individual against some theoretical notion of infinity or limitlessness. In her meeting with the doctor, both Milly and Sir Luke deal with the danger of her total freedom. The doctor attempts to discover for her some relation that will place her in a context; Milly resists this attempt. She is an orphan, with no father, mother, sister, or brother to care for her, with no one in the world to whom she owes an explanation, no one in the world to limit her freedom. This is an intolerable state. This total freedom is only the obverse of total annihilation. It is against this background that Milly's mysterious malady can provide her, in her crisis, with an identity not otherwise available to one so radically free. The origin of the word "secret" is "to set apart," and it is etymologically linked with "crisis." The secret by which Milly defines herself is her crisis, her sense that "she was in some way doomed" (156). She tells Sir Luke, "Nobody can really help. That's why I'm by myself today. I *want* to be . . . I like you to see me just as I am. Yes, I like it—and I don't exaggerate. . . .—it quite positively bears me up" (156).

In this perfectly circular logic Milly confirms her sense of self by locating in the doctor's response to her confirmation of her sense of doom. But Sir Luke does *not* quite confirm the gravity of Milly's case. He asks her to stay in touch with him and recommends that she leave London. But since the members of English society leave London at this time of year anyway, it is difficult to take from this prescription anything other than a general concern for Milly's well-being. On the basis of what we are given of the doctor's directions it is impossible to conclude that anything is seriously the matter with her. On the other hand, he does not dismiss her outright. Milly's "case," if she has one, remains obscure. But for the most part, this lack of clarity derives not from what Sir Luke says or does not say, but from the power of Milly's response to him.

As he ushers her out of his consulting rooms, Milly asks him:

> "So you don't think I'm out of my mind?"
> "Perhaps that *is*," he smiled, "all that's the matter."
> She looked at him longer. "No, that's too good. Shall I, at any rate, suffer?"
> "Not a bit."
> "And yet then live?"
> "My dear young lady," said her distinguished friend, "isn't to 'live' exactly what I'm trying to persuade you to take the trouble to do?" (160–61)

Despite the ambiguous nature of Sir Luke's response to her, Milly is more convinced than ever of the seriousness of her illness.[18]

Why would the doctor exhort her to live if there weren't a problem in living, "unless it came up, quite as much, that one might die?" (162). Why otherwise would the doctor have affirmed the obvious? There would have been no necessity for affirming the possibility that she will "live" if this affirmation were not made in the face of the fear that she will die. In Milly's labyrinthine, super-subtle mind, affirmation becomes indistinguishable from contradiction. Having read confirmation of her doom in the doctor's words, "she would affirm, without delay, her option, her volition" (162). The function of Milly's embrace of her disease—her imminent annihilation— enables her to discover and exercise "volition" and "affirmation," the attributes of self.

Milly's sense of her doom then substitutes for her lack of a center: the absence of center is thus replaced and concealed by the presence of "doom." But doom—in the form of death—is the ultimate enigma, the ultimate absence, so that absence is represented to the self *as* the self. The self is constituted by absence, by secrecy. The very word "enigma" has its roots in the Greek "ainos" which means fable, story, or tale. Milly constructs a story to curtail her intolerable freedom, to provide her with a sense of self, and this story or representation itself entails its own enigma, its own enigmatic, fabulous origin.[19]

* * * * *

However we choose to understand Milly's "case," it is what constitutes the missing center of the novel. The significance and meaning of Milly's illness is the blank to be filled in by Milly, the characters she interacts with, and the reader. James, in the authorial intrusion noted above, and in keeping with the program elaborated in the preface, has explicitly told us that we should come closer to Milly through her "associates' . . . impression[s]" (79). We have seen how Susan interprets, constructs, construes Milly's mystery, and we have seen how Milly herself relates to this. As the novel develops we see how all of the major characters sense this mystery and order their behavior accordingly: the very plot of the novel consists of their response to their representation of Milly's "case" and their conduct in relation to it.

Almost from their first meeting, Kate has an intuitive sense that Milly's appearance conceals some deep, dark secret. Kate's "perception" is "of the high happiness of her companion's liberty" (116). But despite Milly's obvious freedom, her wealth, her opportunities, despite her ignorance of any "flaw," in Milly, any "rift within the lute" (116), Kate has an unformed but "latent impression" that there is something in Milly's situation that prompts compassion and not envy; she would not want to exchange places with her. It seems that even on the basis of their slight acquaintance Kate feels that Milly's ostensibly brilliant future conceals some mystery, some source of future unhappiness (116).

Before discussing how Kate begins to plot on the basis of her representation to herself of Milly's secret ill health, it is useful to consider the context in which Kate is reunited with Densher and is discovered by Milly. Kate and Densher meet in the National Gallery where, by "coincidence," Milly bumps into them. The meeting is presented through the medium of Milly's consciousness: she has gone to the National Gallery to "lose [her]self" (187), to leave the "personal question" outside. Feeling herself "too weak for the Turners and Titians" (188), she gives herself up to watching the copyists and counting the American tourists. "That perhaps was the moral of a menaced state of health—that one would sit in public places and count the Americans" (188). She watches some women copying the masters and wishes she herself were a lady copyist—they "seemed to show her for the time the right way to live" (187).[20] But the copyists copy a copy of a copy, thus suggesting the interminable chain of representation as well as the power of representation to order experience.

> She should have been a lady-copyist—it met so the case. The case was the case of escape, of living under water, of being at once impersonal and firm. There it was before one—one had only to stick and stick. (187)

For Milly, the National Gallery was to have been a "refuge" (188), a place in which she could escape her personal life contemplating art. But art proves too strong, too lifelike: the attenuated, mediated, submerged art of the copyists is more in keeping with her situation. The ensuing scene dramatizes however, how art and "reality" are not so easily kept apart. Merton Densher appears, as if stepping out of the frame of a picture.

Milly had been watching three Americans—a mother and two daughters; she both takes pleasure in and feels guilty about seeing them as stereotypical: "she *knew* them" (189). Thinking that they refer to a picture, she overhears the mother say: "Handsome? Well, if you choose to say so. . . . In the English style" (189–90). But then Milly notices that the only pictures on the walls are Dutch, and that the ladies refer not to a picture but to a person, Merton Densher, accompanied by Kate Croy.

The reduplication of the Lambinet scene on the river between Strether and the lovers in *The Ambassadors* is striking: art comes to life, becomes life. Milly, a character in a piece of art, a novel, attempting to escape the life that novel creates for her—her illness—retreats to art only to find herself returned, with a bang, to a life in which she "knew herself handled" (191). As we learn elsewhere, "the margin flood[s] the text" (131), and the status of Milly's illness is all the more difficult to establish the more clearly one perceives how assiduously the novel problematizes the relationship between life and art. The interpenetration of the realm of life, Milly's life, and the realm of art, the world of the Dutch paintings in the museum, creates a sense of the instability of representation and serves to heighten the ungrounded nature of representation.Each character seems to be solipsistically locked in his or her own representation of reality.The scene in the museum dramatizes the absence of any authority capable of sanctioning a unified perspective, and insofar as it produces a sense of the dizzying possibilities of art, it in fact provides a mimesis of the confusion that is life. (We later learn that Densher's mother was also a copyist.)

Beginning to act on her representation to herself of Milly's illness, Kate tells Densher, "[Milly] particularly likes *you*. I say old boy, make something of that" (206). Kate tells him that Milly is in love with him (211), and convinces him to cultivate this relationship, even in the face of Densher's sense that he will be "a brute of a humbug to her" (211). The suggestion of humbugging emerges when she tells Densher that she thinks it possible that Milly is mortally ill, and suggests to him that he can "console" her "for all that, if she's stricken, she must see swept away" (229).

Densher asks Kate if Milly has consumption and Kate answers that she doesn't think so:

> "I believe that if she's ill at all she's very ill. I believe that if she's bad she's not a little bad. I can't tell you why, but that's how I see her. She'll really live or she'll really not. She'll have it all or she'll miss it all. Now I don't think she'll have it all."
>
> Densher had followed this, with his eye upon her—her own having thoughtfully wandered—as if it were more impressive than lucid. "You 'think', and you 'don't think', and yet you remain all the while without an inkling of her complaint?"
>
> "No, not without an inkling; but it's a matter in which I don't want knowledge. She moreover herself doesn't want one to want it: she has,

as to what may be preying upon her, a kind of ferocity of modesty, a kind of—I don't know what to call it—intensity of pride."

"What you want of me then is to make up to a sick girl."

"Ah, but you admit yourself that she doesn't affect you as sick. You understand moreover just how much—and just how little."

"It's amazing," he presently answered, "what you think I understand." . . .

"You're prodigious!" (230–32)

We see that Kate, like Milly, like Susan, and like Maud Lowder, has no clear idea of what is the matter with Milly. It is on the basis of this ignorance that she begins to interpret and to create a scenario that will answer both to her own plans and, it would seem, to what she considers will make for Milly's happiness.

Kate explains to Densher, albeit in vague terms, the advantages that might accrue to them if Milly is led to believe that Densher's love for Kate is unrequited (213). She tells him, "I verily believe I *shall* hate you if you spoil for me the beauty of what I see!" (215).

There is no way of knowing what it is that Kate sees, but even if she does not have a fully formulated plan, she is already envisaging the advantage that she and Densher might gain from their association with Milly.[21] Their exchange emphasizes not only the importance that the issue of Milly's health acquires for them, but also the rich unfurling of Kate's consciousness. We see her thinking about Milly's health, and we see her, as it were, thinking on her feet. Typical of both her capacity for complication and of the "intrinsic" ambiguities of Milly's situation is the unfolding of the following dialogue: "She's not a bit right, you know," Kate says.

"I mean in health. Just see her tonight. I mean it looks grave. For you she would have come, you know, if it had been at all possible."

He took this in such patience as he could muster. "What's the matter with her?"

But Kate continued without saying. "Unless indeed your being here has been just a reason for her funking it."

"What's the matter with her?" Densher asked again.

"Why, just what I've told you—that she likes you so much."

"Then why should she deny herself the joy of meeting me?"

Kate had an hesitation—it would take so long to explain. "And perhaps it's true that she *is* bad. She easily may be." (226)

It is impossible to decide whether Kate really thinks that Milly is desperately ill or whether she thinks of her as merely lovesick, or both. In a statement typical of the paradoxes in which Kate deals, she tell Densher:

"I shouldn't care for her if she hadn't so much," Kate very simply
said. And then as it made him laugh not quite happily: "I shouldn't
trouble about her if there were one thing she did have." The girl spoke
indeed with a noble compassion. "She has nothing." (229)

Once again an authorial intrusion at this point emphasizes
Kate's "noble compassion" (229), her concern that Milly, as she
says later, should be given a chance to live while she can, which
is to say a chance to love Densher. "I want . . . to make things
pleasant for her. I use, for the purpose, what I have. You're what
I have most precious, and you're therefore what I use most" (229).
In this perspective, the beauty of what Kate sees is the possibility
of making Milly's short life full. But this aspect of Kate's envi-
sioned "beauty" is inseparable from, indeed shades into, a beauty
of a different sort, namely, the advantage that she and Densher
might reap from a stricken girl who is also "an angel with a
thumping bank-account" (228). Yet another possibility, though, is
that the beauty derives from an imaginative vision which sees no
need for any sacrifice. Perhaps because Milly's mysterious health
is understood by Kate as Milly's doom, she can imagine a future
in which everyone can be satisfied.[22]

The power of Kate's representation of Milly is such that it seems
to persuade Densher, and possibly the readers, of its validity. In
fact, Kate's representation is a performative act which creates its
own authority. Indeed, Kate's imaginative vigor is what engages
us so intensely with her and leads us to see her as more, and better,
than any of the givens of her situation: "no sum in addition would
have made up the total" (6). Kate and Susan manifestly share a
structure in which they are both interpreters who need to be interpreted, and both can readily be seen in terms of highly stereotypic,
highly reductive categories. Yet the novel makes it virtually impossible for us to reduce Kate to any of the categories into which she
would seem to fall. In the first two books we see her irrevocably
as Lionel Croy's daughter, Mrs. Condrip's sister, a young woman
on the make, even as later we are invited to see her as ruthlessly
ambitious and boldly manipulative in her own self-interest. But we
cannot dismiss her as a predator because we share her consciousness, we participate in her desires and distresses.

Yet, while we cannot reduce her to any of the given terms of her
situation, it is also impossible to lose sight of those terms. Kate
is like her father, "like nothing—more's the pity" (17). Terms of
comparison fail and, like Milly, Kate remains a mystery. More than
anything else, it is the fact that James endows Kate with such a

richly dramatized consciousness that precludes any simple reduction. Our interest in her as a character vies with our interest in Milly, and promotes the tug of war that prohibits the stabilization of a clear center.[23]

* * * * *

Merton Densher figures as largely in the tug of war as Milly and Kate. Initially, his consciousness is not as directly or, on the face of it, as brilliantly dramatized as Kate's and Milly's. Yet his developing role in the novel—the centrality of his consciousness as it unfolds from book 6—vies with that of the other major figures in engaging both our interest and tugging our judgment still further off center.[24]

Though he begins by "shrink[ing] from the complications involved in judging" (245), he becomes by the end of the novel what appears to be the climatic locus or site of choice and judgment. As we are seduced by the authority of Densher's representation, we necessarily become aware that representation ultimately lacks precisely the authority we must grant it in order for it to be effective. Indeed, part of the irony of Densher's position is that from the moment he allows himself to become a manipulated tool in Kate's conspiracy he becomes first the chief actor in the working of the conspiracy and then, when he rejects Milly's money, the chief cause for its failure. Densher starts out "finely passive" and is seen at the outset as malleable, lacking any marks, lacking the stamp of character (35), still awaiting "the pressure that fixes . . . value . . ." (35). By the end, however, so firmly has his character shaped itself or been shaped by his experience that he provides what seems to be the decisive turn, not only of events, but also of judgment. It is through the representation of Densher's feelings and choices that the tragedy implicit in the novel's action is perceived.

Yet, inevitably, given the novel's structure of subversion and its treatment of its own system of absences and displacements, we cannot simply affirm Densher's representation. Even his last word is followed by the ironic and still more climactic view offered by Kate: that "we shall never be again as we were" (457), a view that bristles with complications—such as—is it better or worse that they are no longer what they were? If they are no longer what they were, then what are they now? That is a new mystery, a new "secret" that makes what lies ahead as inscrutable as what lies behind.

The subversion of Densher's representation can be understood as one instance of a more sustained and yet subtle form of subversion at work throughout the novel. While the representations that are suggested by each of the competing centers of consciousness may succeed in persuading readers of their adequacy, in fact, not only are these representations eventually rendered equivocal, but the centers of consciousness themselves are ultimately revealed as less discrete or separate than initially understood. All the characters perceive in the same mode: all of them have their "mysteries," and elements of one character's experience are emphatically repeated in another. The novel opens with Kate renouncing half of her small inheritance from her mother, and it closes with Densher ceding his inheritance from Milly to Kate. The imagery with which the characters are associated further reinforces this process: practically all of them are figured as birds at one point or another. (The first doctor's name is Finch, teal is a species of wild duck, strut[hious] an order of flightless birds; Kate and Maud are often seen as eagles, while Densher, like Milly and Kate, is pictured more than once as perched. And Milly is of course a dove.)

These symmetries and repetitive patterns themselves serve to crystallize a specific dynamic, namely, how mystery provokes representation, which is itself the ground of further mystery and thus further representation. Like Kate, all the characters shape their lives in accordance with their interpretation of the nature of Milly's illness. But Milly's illness is not the only mystery that prompts representation.

The pattern is paralleled as each center recapitulates the dynamic of mystery triggering representation, triggering plot. As each of the characters relates to the mystery of Milly's illness, each character is in relation to his or her own private mystery. The conspiracy involving Kate and Densher and Maud and Susan to get Milly's money and/or make Milly happy is, for example, preceded and accompanied by Kate and Densher's conspiracy against Maud Lowder.

Long before the advent of Milly on the scene, Kate, Densher, and Kate's immediate family are all involved in relationships and actions predicated on secrecy, and consequently on plotting. Maud Lowder herself, like Milly, is not an innocent bystander in the plot set up against her. The novel dramatizes how almost all the characters in their turn act on the basis of some undisclosed or partially disclosed secret. To open the book is to open on the secret of Kate's father, Lionel Croy, and his mysterious dishonor.[25]

Kate thinks of her father's dishonor, in itself as mysterious as Milly's illness, as "the great thing in her life" (48). This secret stigma, which she and Merton agree not to probe, is felt by her to determine the course of her life. The silence that surrounds her father is "a perpetual sound in [Kate's] ears. 'It makes me ask myself if I've any right to personal happiness, any right to anything but to be as rich and overflowing, smart and shining, as I can be made'" (50).

This secret remains unexplored in the novel; it quickly gives way to the secret of Kate's relationship with Densher. It is partly because her family, and primarily her father, are "impossible" (47) that Kate's engagement to Densher has to remain hidden. But this engagement is also kept secret for the simple reason that Kate is under the protection and patronage of her aunt Maud Lowder, who she knows would disapprove of such an inauspicious match. Kate feels that if handled correctly, Maud's approval—and money—may be secured.

When Densher asks how she thinks it possible that they can "square" (52) Aunt Maud, Kate replies, "I don't see why you don't make out a little more that if we avoid stupidity we may do *all*. We may keep her" (51–52). But there seems to be more to it. Kate and Densher speak of temporizing, "to gain time," but in fact, mystery provides its own attraction. Densher says:

> "Yes; no doubt, in our particular situation, time's everything. And then there's the joy of it."
> She hesitated. "Of our secret?"
> "Not so much perhaps of our secret in itself, but of what's repre-sented and, as we must somehow feel, protected and made deeper and closer by it. . . . Our being as we are." . . .
> "So gone?"
> "So gone. So extremely gone." (67)

This conversation is hard to follow: they are "gone" on each other, and their mutual "absence" attests to the strength of the secret that "represents" their intimacy. Like Milly, they construct their lives around a secret. (Amongst the earliest of Milly's impressions of Kate, which she "expressed to Susan Shepherd more than once [was] that Kate had some *secret*, some smothered trouble . . ." [114, my emphasis].)

The inaccessibility of Kate and Densher's shared absence is fur-ther elaborated as their relationship is shown to originate in an unreachable, mythical past:

> It was as if they hadn't known how "thick" they had originally become, as if, in a manner, they had really fallen to remembering more passages

of intimacy than there had in fact at the time quite been room for. They were in a relation now, whether from what they said or from what they didn't say, so complicated that it might have been seeking to justify its speedy growth by reaching back to *one of those fabulous periods* in which prosperous states place their beginnings. (247, my emphasis)

Like Milly, Kate and Densher attempt to establish a "center," but this founding "site" is recessive, an effect of fabulation, of story, of representation. (Note the analogy with Milly and what her doctors "did or didn't say.")

A founding center is inaccessible, it would seem, both in Milly's case and in Kate's and Densher's, and hence both the necessary cause and effect of secrecy. It is secrecy that enables the working of Kate's plan. Were Milly to publicly admit that she is going to die, there would be no question of Densher making love to her, and he clearly could not make love to her if his relationship with Kate was public. It is secrecy, then, that creates the context for the striking displacement already noted. When we are first introduced to her, Kate, like Milly, has recently lost her mother and brother: she is in the process of being taken up by Maud Lowder. Her father and sister explicitly push her into her aunt's arms; they want to use her and her potential to make a good marriage for their own social ambitions and, more particularly, money. The key element in her plot to resist having to make such a marriage of convenience is to have Densher make such a marriage for her: Densher should marry Milly. The analogy is clear: Kate requires Densher to do what she would not.

This involves Densher in the dynamic that is central not only to the plot of the novel and its unfolding but to its informing interest: namely the way the absence of center breeds secrets, which breed plot, which breeds distortion, all of which are woven into the whole cloth of representation and all of which both call for and undermine judgment.[26]

As in a good detective story, moreover, all the characters are given good motives for wanting Densher to marry or at least to make love to Milly.[27] Kate and Densher stand to gain a fortune, Susan to have her romantic imagination confirmed by reality, Maud Lowder to have Kate free to marry Lord Mark, and Milly herself to gain the experience or illusion of a full life. But the novel, besides dramatizing the ultimate failure of this plot, dramatizes the cycle of deceit and distortion that propel it, and it clearly engages the issue, the moral issue, of how to judge such deceit.

The novel dramatizes how each of the characters—even Milly,

nursing her secret—is guilty of some kind of deception. As the plot unfolds, the reader's involvement, like that of the characters themselves, entails continually assessing the particular deception being practiced. Like Susan, Maud, Kate, Densher, and Milly, we continually weigh the characters' actions as they struggle to shape their lives.

We take sides, we enter the tug of war: we condemn Kate's brutality, Densher's passivity, Susan's sentimentality, Milly's manipulative pusillanimity. Alternatively, we might stand in awe of Milly's nobility of spirit or find Kate's vitality irresistible. But as we condemn or commend, we become aware of the spread of our response; we become aware that the categories of good and evil, truth and lie, become difficult to distinguish, lose their capacity to orient our experience.

With no firm sense of what constitutes "truth" in this novel, the category of "lie" also becomes problematic. The question is whether the plot into which all the characters enter is "good" or potentially "good" for both Milly and themselves. When Susan tells her sublime lie (262) and Maud tells her "proper lie" (240), we are left to wonder whether these lies could potentially promote a general "good."

The vacuity of representation cannot short-circuit moral judgment, in fact, it necessarily entails such judgment. In the absence of any center or centering truth about the facts of Milly's illness, representation shades by degrees into dissimulation, suppression, error, and lie. Because each character represents his own and others' secrets with no access to anything like hard facts, the novel dramatizes the difficulty as well as the necessity of distinguishing truth from representation, the founding from the fabulous.

*****

That representation and judgment are the specular focus that derives from the interaction of absent centers is reinforced through the way in which this novel images all its major characters as texts, pictures, scenes from plays, or objects of art and culture that, by definition, require representation.

As noted, Susan Stringham is a writer and "typical" reader of a certain sort of romantic material: a fan of de Maupassant and a reader of "the fiction of the day" (114). We are told that for her everything is "literary material" (113), and Milly in particular could be seen by her as one of her own New England literary heroines (133). She is dramatized as tending to think in stereotypes: Milly is a princess living "on the plane of mere elegant representation" (113), Kate is "a figure in a picture stepping by magic out of its frame . . . as the wondrous London girl in person" (113).

This imagination of the pigeon-hole variety[28] is in sharp distinction to Densher's. He too tends to literary metaphors, but his lay bare the problematics of reading and writing. At one point in the novel we are told he feels that

> [h]is full parenthesis was closed, and he was once more but a sentence, of a sort, in the general text, the text that, from his momentary street-corner, showed as a great grey page of print that somehow managed to be crowded without being "fine." The grey, however, was more or less the blur of a point of view not yet quite seized again; and there would be colour enough to come out. (202)

A journalist, Densher finds the thought of "publicly para-graph[ing]" (219) Milly repulsive, just as he dreads reading an account of his own experience in a "cheap edition" (310). Possibly at the opposite end of the writer's spectrum from Susan, Densher's literary self-consciousness expresses a sense of the danger, the potential distortion of representation, at the same time that, in distinguishing between "cheap" and "expensive" art, he suggests some hope that representation need not necessarily distort. Densher tells Kate, "The women one meets—what are they but books one has already read? You're a whole library of the un-known, the uncut. . . . Upon my word, I've a subscription!" (236).

Kate herself, at the prospect of being put in a book, says: "'Chop me up fine or serve me whole'—it was a way of being got at that Kate professed she dreaded" (225). Of course, James is doing precisely that—putting Kate in a book—and the question again is: are there different kinds of books? James's conception of writing is suggested by the narrator's description of Kate at the beginning of the novel: "She hadn't given up yet, and the broken sentence, if she was the last word, *would* end with a sort of meaning" (7). Presumably the notion of discourse here attributed to Kate, namely, that representation can "mean," is something shared, al-beit in a complicated fashion, by James himself. In making both Stringham and Densher writers, and in proliferating references to art and to texts, James seems to call our attention to the nature of writing and its possibilities. Representation as exemplified in this novel is an art that can reflect not the illusory, idealized perfection of completion, but one that can represent the ongoing process of interaction and interpretation that issues in judgment, which in turn issues in action.

Lord Mark takes Milly to see a Bronzino portrait and asks her to recognize herself. She says, "I don't know—one never knows one's self" (145), but she does recognize the unmatchable perfection and completion of the portrait and that, for this very reason, the picture was "dead, dead, dead."[29] She says, "I shall never be better than this" (144).

The art of *The Wings of the Dove* utterly lacks the finality that Milly finds in the art of the Bronzino. At the end of the novel, soon after Milly's death, Densher brings Kate an unopened letter written to him by Milly from her deathbed. He has some kind of instinctive sense of its contents, as does Kate (443). They both assume that the letter announces that Milly has left Densher a large amount of money. Kate "positively decline[s]" (443) to break the seal, open, and read the letter. Densher insists—Kate yet again refuses. Finally, saying "Trust me," Kate jerks the thing into the fire with a quick gesture (445).[30]

For Densher, his thoughts about the letter become his "secret . . . handl[ed] as a father, baffled and tender, might handle a maimed child" (450).

> But so it was before him—in his dread of who else might see it. . . . that he should never, never know what had been in Milly's letter. The intention announced in it he should but too probably know; but that would have been, but for the depths of his spirit, the least part of it. The part of it missed forever was the turn she would have given her act. That turn had possibilities that, somehow, by wondering about them, his imagination had extraordinarily filled out and refined. It had made of them a revelation the loss of which was like the sight of a priceless pearl cast before his eyes—his pledge given not to save it— into the fathomless sea, or rather even it was like the sacrifice of something sentient and throbbing, something that, for the spiritual ear, might have been audible as a faint, far wail.[31] (450–51)

When, two months later, Kate and Densher learn through her lawyers that Milly had indeed left Densher her fortune, the letter, the "unrevealed work of [Milly's] hand . . . was made present to them . . . only by the intensity with which it mutely expressed its absence" (445). The burnt letter becomes a controlling metaphor for James's art in this novel. Present only by the muteness with which it expresses its absence, precious, sentient and throbbing—wailing—the letter is maimed and can only be extraordinarily filled out by the imagination, by representation. The present/absent letter is a metaphor for the necessity of fiction and the anxiety that it provokes within the frightening, fabulous liberty it confers. Whether we trust them or not, Kate and James *do* burn the letter, and thus the novel confronts representation as it issues in action. Densher and Kate do not marry. Representation, not an end in itself, is interminable, but it nevertheless lays the complex ground on which conduct is organized and must be judged. Since, like Densher, we readers are denied her final word, we too are left having to imagine the "truth" of Milly's situation and of *The Wings of the Dove.*

5

Such Abysses of Confidence:
The Golden Bowl

In *The Wings of the Dove,* Milly's letter to Merton Densher, her last will and testament, is burnt unread, and the novel ends.[1] Toward the conclusion of *The Golden Bowl,* Maggie fantasizes receiving a blank letter which then becomes the basis for the resolution of the future action of the novel.

The context for this imaginary text is a conversation between Maggie and her father in which Maggie attempts to establish whether and just how much her father suspects about what she herself already knows—about the affair the Prince, her husband, is conducting with Charlotte, her father's wife. As part of the strategy designed to keep both her husband and the peace, Maggie upbraids her father for his magnanimity, and he replies that if she persists he will ship himself and Charlotte back to America.

> Ah, then it was that the cup of her conviction, full to the brim, overflowed at a touch! *There* was his idea, the clearness of which for an instant almost dazzled her. It was a blur of light, in the midst of which she saw Charlotte like some object marked, by contrast, in blackness, saw her waver in the field of vision, saw her removed, transported, doomed. And he had named Charlotte, named her again, and she had *made* him—which was all she had needed more: it was as if she had held a blank letter to the fire and the writing had come out still larger than she hoped. The recognition of it took her some seconds, but she might when she spoke again have been folding up these precious lines and restoring them to her pocket.[2]

The issues raised through the description of Maggie's receipt of this "would be" letter concentrate what I take to be the concerns of this novel. Whereas in *The Wings of the Dove* a "real" letter is burnt and then imaginatively reconstructed—leading to renunciation of desire, marriage, etc.—the letter in *The Golden Bowl* is imaginary but nevertheless provides the basis for action that will confirm marriage, desire, etc. Whereas in *The Wings of the Dove* the movement might be described as from presence to absence, in *The Golden Bowl* the move is from absence to presence. It is as if James in the previous novels has worked through the problems inherent in his understanding of the mediated nature of reality, and here accepts the insights afforded him by his own work as a basis, no matter how problematic, for being in the world.

Putting aside for a moment the many issues raised by the mode or form of the letter—whom it might be from, the self-deceit involved in this pretended receipt, the fact that it is not a letter at all but a product of Maggie's responsive imagination—we see that what Maggie "recognizes" in the letter is that Charlotte is "doomed." Maggie understands this letter, which ostensibly comes from her father, as an indication that he intends to transport Charlotte to America. In many of James's works, removal to America is the ultimate punishment, and here Maggie recognizes that, in transporting her, Adam is explicitly condemning Charlotte to her doom. His "letter" is her sentence. But whose "writing" is this? Who has passed sentence?

It is far from clear to the reader that Adam *is* the source of the sentence of doom on Charlotte: the curious emphasis on "*there* was his idea" draws attention to Maggie's own perception of Adam's unstated intention: *where* indeed is an idea? In *Maggie's* consciousness? While Maggie might be convinced that she has successfully manipulated her father into revealing *his* idea, the reader has good reason for believing that Charlotte's "removal" would be very much to Maggie's taste. It is no wonder that "the cup of her conviction" would overflow; after all Charlotte is her husband's mistress, and Maggie has been working hard to maintain her marriage. The desire to put some distance between Charlotte and herself and between Charlotte and her husband is understandable, to say the least, under the circumstances as we perceive them.

The difficulty of deciding on the source for this idea is further complicated by the fact that not only these circumstances but everything in the second book of *The Golden Bowl* is given to us through the medium of Maggie's necessarily partisan consciousness. The significance of James's handling of narrative point of view in *The Golden Bowl* will be discussed later but, insofar as anything is firm in this novel, the grounds are firm for thinking that Maggie ascribes her own idea to her father—she projects her own desire for Charlotte's removal. And grounds become proportionately firmer as the text dramatizes the way in which Maggie not only writes herself a letter but fills in the blank of interpretation in a manner that cannot avoid being considered tendentious.

The very fact that this climactic "idea" takes the form of an imaginary letter suggests that writing has authority, or else why imagine a letter? And authority derives from the existence of an "author." Yet this letter, the fruit of Maggie's imagination, posits a fictitious author in Maggie's father—a stratagem that serves many functions. Not only does it allow Maggie to avoid taking responsibility for the awful thought of condemning Charlotte, but it allows her to avoid confronting her own role in the situation, which has led to the need for the condemnation. Her guilt is displaced to a parental "author."

The difficulty of pinning down the source of Charlotte's sentence is compounded by the fact that the letter Maggie holds to the fire is "blank." Since there is no letter from her father, and since even the nonexistent letter is "blank," when filling in the blanks the reader must confront the possibility that Maggie herself is projecting as she interprets, fills in the blank. That the letter is blank undermines its authority no less than does the fact that it is imaginary. The letter provides her with carte blanche to do and think—read—what she likes. It is as though her tremendously wealthy and doting father has given her a blank check to be filled out as she will. But in order for her to fill it out it has to come from him. This gesture of blank writing at once establishes authority and effaces it; the "writing" in this passage cannot be distinguished from projection. It is the nature of the writing under discussion to obscure the source of its own authority.[3]

The problem of attribution is further intensified when the act of "naming" acquires an importance that hovers just beyond interpretation. "[Adam] had *named* Charlotte, *named* her again [my emphasis], and [Maggie] had *made* him." "Naming" itself establishes the authority of writing, and it is through this act that Charlotte herself is somehow transformed from magic, invisible ink to text, to writing; this "blur of light" is reduced to text "like some object marked, by contrast, in blackness." Authority here disappears into writing, magic writing, an absent blank text that authorizes the sentence as it obscures its authority.[4]

The very characteristics of writing dramatized here suggest that there is no escape from the tension of not knowing where this sentence, this doom, originates. Maggie's interpretation of the blank letter, in addition to being subject to the charge of projection, necessarily involves a sleight of hand, which the readers cannot help but repeat when holding up Maggie's letter to the flame of their imagination. When James's writing itself reinforces the tension of not knowing whether there is an origin outside of representation, it is as though James is suggesting that the impossibility of establishing origin is not merely a question of psychology but, more radically, is connected with the nature of experience, the nature of the world. What makes this unbearable is that, whatever the origin, the sentence remains the same: doom.

The letter in *The Wings of the Dove* is consumed by fire; the letter in *The Golden Bowl* is conjured into existence by fire. The absence of the first versus the presence of the second is itself a question of prestidigitation, of the quality of writing itself, a question of juggling absence and presence—and for Milly/Maggie, Kate/Charlotte (especially for Charlotte), a question of the jugular, a sentence of doom.[5]

*****

The nature of writing as prestidigitation is further exemplified in that the scene in which Maggie imagines receiving the blank letter is a close repetition of an earlier scene set in exactly the same place—the same bench under the same shady old oak in the garden at Fawns.[6] As the scene we have just examined is the scene of Charlotte's expulsion, this earlier scene is the scene of her inclusion; and just as we have difficulty pinning down the source of the blank letter, we experience the same difficulty with the first letter in which Charlotte is invited to become one of the Ververs' party.

Although it is Adam who pens the invitation, he does so in circumstances that again make the attribution of authorship problematic. In broad outline, the scene presents Adam reflecting on his changed status as available bachelor. In the absence of the other guests, a certain Mrs. Vance has tracked him down to his lair in the study. He is brought to the realization that since Maggie has married the Prince he himself is once again in the marriage market and will have the bother of dealing with women who pursue him. Up till now it is as though he has been married to Maggie—"she had protected him as if she were more than a daughter" (117). The hint that there is more in their relationship than a "normal" father-daughter intimacy has been much commented upon. But what interests me for the moment is the way the provenance of an invitation (which will issue in Charlotte's marriage to Adam and eventually in the adultery central to the plot of *The Golden Bowl*) again attests to the recurrent preoccupations of the text: the difficulty of pinning down beginnings, or causes, and the ineluctable enigma of communication that this difficulty generates.[7]

In the aftermath of the scene with Mrs. Vance, while discussing the implications of her overtures Maggie tells Adam that she has had a letter from Charlotte apparently indicating Charlotte's desire to join them. Maggie and Adam's exchange of inconclusive mutual questioning foregrounds the difficulty of pinpointing where an idea starts, and constitutes the link with the later "blank" letter. Whose idea is it that Adam write inviting Charlotte to stay with them, Adam's or Maggie's or Charlotte's? We cannot say. If earlier we argued that representation generates yet further representation here, a letter begets a letter—another letter—a sentence. Adam says to Maggie:

> "You've got something up your sleeve."
> She had a silence that made him right. "Well, when I tell you you'll understand. It's only up my sleeve in the sense of being in a letter I got this morning. . . .
> "Charlotte? Is *she* coming?"
> "She writes, practically, that she'd like to if we're so good as to ask her."
> Mr. Verver continued to gaze, but rather as if waiting for more. Then, as everything appeared to have come, his expression had a drop. If this was all it was simple. "Then why in the world not?"
> Maggie's face lighted anew, but it was now another light. "It isn't a want of tact?"
> "To ask her?"
> "To propose it to you."
> "That *I* should ask her?"
> He put the question as an effect of his remnant of vagueness, but this had also its own effect. Maggie wondered an instant; after which, as with a flush of recognition, she took it up. "It would be too beautiful if you *would!*"
> This clearly had not been her first idea—the chance of his words had prompted it. "Do you mean write to her myself?"
> "Yes—it would be kind. It would be quite beautiful of you. That is, of course," said Maggie, "if you sincerely *can.*"
> He appeared to wonder an instant why he sincerely shouldn't, and indeed, for that matter, where the question of sincerity came in. (147–48)

This passage raises the typical difficulty of interpreting Maggie's words, behavior, motives. Are we to understand Maggie as manipulating her father? Is this the first instance of her capacity to manipulate that will only come to the fore in the second half of the novel as a result of the invitation that is now extended? Or is this an instance of an idea genuinely generated between two people? While the intimacy between father and daughter is manifested in the way Adam seems able to read his daughter's mind, this very reciprocity raises questions concerning authority, verifiability, reality. Perhaps Adam's reading of Maggie's mind, rather than interpreting *her* text, creates its own text, which then acquires an authorizing status. Adam seems to be identifying Maggie's unstated wish, but the possibility is raised that, in doing so, he is expressing his own wish. The description of the genesis of this first letter shares with the later letter some quality of the atmosphere of conjuring. In what might seem to be a rhetorical flourish revealing the intimacy of father and daughter, Adam says to Maggie: "You've got something up your sleeve," but read retrospectively, in "the blur of light" shed by invisible writing, both letters seem to suggest the magical quality of writing as sleight of hand.

It is precisely the tension that derives from the delight/anxiety of such uncannily (im)mediate (mis)communication that informs the novel's general structure. This structure is broken up into individual consciousnesses that have difficulty following each other's shifts of mood and understanding.[8] Where this difficulty itself is not dramatized, we seem to get the opposite, namely, that the characters understand one another in so immediate a fashion (to the exclusion of the reader or third party) that the elusive nature of communication is only reinforced. Obfuscation and clarity of communication are seen to be two faces of the same enigmatic process, which at once holds up and buries the possibility of knowing what is being said. The narrative technique implicates readers in the very intimacy that they perforce must penetrate and undo in order to understand the events of the novel, the relation between the effect they perceive and its cause.

When Maggie reveals her plan that Adam write to invite Charlotte, the more natural thing might be for Maggie herself to write; but it will be Adam who writes at Maggie's behest. If later Maggie writes a letter that ostensibly comes from Adam, here Adam writes a letter that seems to have its origins in Maggie's mind, in her plan to marry Charlotte to Adam. This plan would seem to be a response to Mrs. Vance's overtures, . . . which, in turn, we learn, are a response to Adam Verver's changed status, . . . which, in its turn, is a result of Maggie's marriage to the prince and the Ververs' fraught, frayed intimacy. All of these events issue from the Ververs' more general project, their rifling of the Golden Isles (122).[9] The complicated genealogy of the plan to invite Charlotte indicates the general problem of the search for a preceding cause which generates an interminable regressive list.

*****

While the two letters that I have been analyzing play a crucial role in the plot of the novel, they also seem to undermine the very possibility of "plot," if we understand this concept in terms of tracing a neat modulation of cause and effect. The invisible writing of the second letter has its counterpart in the magic reading of the first. More radically, both letters would seem to link and put into question the very concept of writing and the notion of origin, partially through the way they present the mutual transparency of Maggie's and Adam's minds. More and less than a scandal of potential incest, the father-daughter intimacy reflects something of the way in which this novel conceives and presents the problem of relationship between selves.

The result of his reading of Maggie is that Adam writes the invitation to Charlotte, with all its implications for the plot of *The Golden Bowl*.[10] What of the readers reading? As we read Adam reading Maggie, do we too become authors of an interpretation that cannot escape the danger of projection? Whereas the mode of presentation insists on raising these questions, it defeats any satisfactory response and leaves the reader embroiled in the situation of the characters, a situation which makes it impossible to ascertain with any confidence whether the origin of a thought, an interpretation, an understanding, lies within or without his or her own imaginative response. What is the status of the reader's representation? Like the characters, readers may be projecting an origin, a series of causes and effects that *seem* to emanate from the text—from outside themselves—but might well be the fruits of their own imagination.

As in the novels discussed earlier, the narrative structure limiting readers to the characters' consciousnesses makes it difficult for them to verify their own perceptions and to validate the grounds of their response. The implications of this technique have been discussed in relation both to *The Ambassadors* and *The Wings of the Dove*. In *The Golden Bowl* the difficulties of establishing "facts" further dramatizes the problematics of connecting cause and effect, that is of understanding which realities precede and generate the representations that are being confronted.[11]

One clear locus of these difficulties is in the presentation of Adam himself, where the narrative voice—uncharacteristically— does not confine itself exclusively to the character's own consciousness but shifts perspective and lapses into the posture, unlikely for this text, of omniscience. We might expect that an all-wise, all-saying narrator would resolve questions of fact and judgment by apodictically establishing them. Here, however, as in *The Ambassadors,* the problematics of voice, of ironic faceting, and finally, of what is represented in this voice, thoroughly undercut the certainty of what might seem to be established.

Adam is first presented to us about one hundred pages into the first book of the novel, as he is having to face up to changes made in his personal situation due to Maggie's marriage, specifically, his vulnerability to the importunities of Mrs. Vance and her ilk. He is presented to us through the medium of a traditional, external narration, which does not provide us with the character's thoughts but speaks in the first person and observes him "with an interest . . . tender indeed almost to compassion . . ." (111). The grounds for this narrative compassion are immediately stated:

> For it may immediately be mentioned that this amiable man bethought himself of his personal advantage, in general, only when it might appear to him that other advantages, those of other persons, had successfully put in their claim. (111)

As it unfolds, the novel provides considerable grounds for questioning this unqualifiedly sympathetic judgment. Even at the moment of its formulation, however, any judgment is complicated by the way it breaches the narrative stance in all that precedes it and by the dissonance it creates. Suddenly the distanced, ostensibly dispassionate, but also mind-piercing voice modulates into an intimate, avowedly compassionate, but above all, limited mode. Rendering Adam, the narrative voice acquires an almost apodictic presence unlike anything else in this novel. It explicitly refers to itself in the first-person plural: Adam's behavior "invest[s] him with an interest that makes *our* attention"(111, my emphasis). The narrative voice talks of "*our* friend's amiability" (113, my emphasis) and then adopts the tone and distance of an authoritative pedagogue. The departure from the usual tone here provokes unease, as does the content of what is conveyed. The narrator seems to stand in awe of a prodigious wealth it assumes to be the product of "genius." Yet the retreat into a high-toned, authoritative, conclusion-drawing voice suggests unexplored reservations on the part of the narrative voice. Even as we are instructed to accept "our friend's amiability" we are thrown into a generalization, in the mode of Balzacian all-knowingness, that obscures more than it reveals.

Amiability, of a truth, is an aid to success; it has even been known to be the principle of large accumulations; but the link, for the mind, is none the less fatally missing between proof, on such a scale, of continuity, if of nothing more insolent, in one field, and accessibility to distraction in every other. (113)

The more than usually convoluted syntax, and especially the innuendo "of nothing more insolent," might suggest an irony on the part of the narrative voice about Adam Verver's money-making project, about his character.

The possibility that this innuendo implies a reservation and some ironic distance is strengthened when we are told that Adam Verver, having unswervingly devoted himself to the making of money, suddenly discovered in himself "the spirit of the connoisseur" (122). Adam, we are told, finds an image for his newfound activity in Keats' poem "On First Looking into Chapman's Homer"—the image of Cortez discovering the Pacific. Adam's purpose in life is now transformed, and "to rifle the Golden Isles had, on the spot, become the business of his future" (122). Even without recalling Keats' *mistaken* attribution of the discovery of the Pacific to Cortez, a reader can hardly fail to see the irony of the comparison between the spiritual transformation expressed in Keats' poem and Verver's collector's mania. The comparison at once indicates something of the scope of Adam's imagination and hints at the quality of its overarching pretension. It is from the vantage point of hindsight that Adam now conceives of himself as "equal somehow" to the "great seers," the "great producers and creators." We are told that his previous dedication to the mere making of money is transformed for him in the light of this retrospective epiphany, which allows him to transvalue his life's work heretofore. Adam's rewriting of his personal history becomes "a turning of the page of the book of life" (122).

> He had been nothing of that kind before—too decidedly, too dreadfully not; but now he saw *why* he had been what he had, why he had failed and fallen short even in huge success; now he read into his career, in one single magnificent night, the immense meaning it had waited for. (122)

Here James echoes Keats' production of the sonnet in one sitting, in one night, and the allusion surely reverberates with delicate, albeit sympathetic, irony. Meaning is retrospective and a cause is "read" backward from an effect.[12] Here, Adam "reads" his career in business as motivated by the compulsion to collect, which it facilitates, and his reading turns out to be as problematical as all the readings of motive in the novel. This is doubly true because the representation of Adam's reading of his own past and its relation to his present seems arbitrary. As we saw, the questions explored with regard to the authorship of the two letters foreground the impossibility of attribution. In turn, the mode of presenting Adam tends to complicate our sense of the relation between presumed causes in the past and their presumed effects in the present.

We are told from his point of view that, as a young man, he had labored to make money with no ulterior motive. In fact an ulterior purpose would have somehow soiled the immaculate "good faith" of his enterprise (124). We hear that later, in middle age, he was reborn as a connoisseur, and the rebirth is seen to transform his earlier enterprise into a beginning, the condition for the project of collecting. In Adam we see how effect influences, retrospectively creates, and validates cause. This perception is of course of a piece with the larger interests of the novel as a whole, and especially its interest in heightening our consciousness of the distortions involved in establishing fact and causality, in the process of arriving at an adequate representation.

The question of reality, of what lies behind or beneath surfaces, is further problematized in the rendering of Adam's position as a collector. After we learn that Adam has effectively rewritten his early history in the shape of his current consciousness, we are told that "the question of appearance" for Adam only counted in art. "He cared that a work of art of price should 'look like' the master to whom it might perhaps be deceitfully attributed" (126). Deceitful attribution does not matter if the deceit is successful, if the copy looks like the original. This is consistent with Adam's treatment of his own history, which apparently transforms the past to conform to the needs of the present. Given that causes can be posited retrospectively in order to validate specific effects, the issue of causality falls into disrespect and the sole criterion for judgment is reduced to the level of the plausibility of representation.

* * * * *

The difficulty entailed in the unstable chain of causality further exacerbates the inherently problematic nature of representation. This difficulty figures not only in the local effect as characters interpret each other, and as it were interpenetrate each other, but also in the global situation that the novel presents. Any reading of *The Golden Bowl* must engage the question of what destabilizes the (in)famous equilibrium achieved by the characters in the initial stages of this novel—that is, the question of who or what causes the adultery and who can or should be blamed for it. Initially, after Charlotte has married Adam, it seems that everything is arranged and runs as smoothly as a carriage; all the characters act in tandem, and all seem to share common, even communal, needs. The social arrangement presented by the novel purports to arrive at an equilibrium designed not merely for living but for a life in society that will be the best ever. In this arrangement all the characters can fulfill their aspirations to a kind of utopia made possible by huge wealth, intelligence, beauty, tact, sense and enlightened sensibility, based on an appreciation of all that civilization has to offer. But something goes wrong and the reader, like Maggie, is called upon to interrogate the source or cause of the wrong—to ask how it is that things go awry in a world that seems to offer everything, a world (unlike that of *The Wings of the Dove*) in which not merely one character is the "heir of all the ages" but there is enough to go around for everyone.[13]

Through a juxtaposition of two different perspectives on their common situation, Charlotte's in the first book and Maggie's in the second, we acquire a sense of how the multiple narrative perspectives feed the uncertainty at the heart of the novel as to the cause of the moral and emotional tangle on which the action turns. Both Charlotte and Maggie reflect on the source of this dilemma, each from within her own perspective, Maggie blaming Charlotte and Charlotte blaming Maggie. Both women attempt to find a cause for their common situation outside themselves.[14] In order to come to terms with their situation they locate a founding fact in the other and, in the course of doing so, each not only blames the other, but in effect shapes a vision of her situation, and of the other's impact on her situation, in a way that obscures any clear recognition of the cause of the disequilibrium in the emergent situation, or any firm attribution of responsibility for it: blame displaces origin.

Maggie's fireside reverie is a dramatic moment in the process, recalling Isabel's fireside scene in *The Portrait of a Lady*. It underscores the difficulty of pinning down the cause (or causes) of her situation and of grasping the origin of the desires that give rise to it, and all the problems of achieving a sense of a unified and discrete self. We are invited to witness the struggles of a self to understand its experience in terms of how the past shapes the present. The narrative highlights the shifting relation between explanation and motivation, between antecedent action and present awareness.

In the fireside scene we see Maggie reflecting on her marriage, considering the "chain of causes and consequences traceable . . . to her father's marriage and to Charlotte's visit to Fawns" (314).

> But what perhaps most came out in the light of these concatenations was that it had been, for all the world, as if Charlotte had been "had in," as the servants always said of extra help, because they had thus suffered it to be pointed out to them that if their family coach lumbered and stuck the fault was in its lacking its complement of wheels. Having but three, as they might say, it had wanted another, and what had Charlotte done from the first but begin to act, on the spot, and ever so smoothly and beautifully, as a fourth? Nothing had been, immediately, more manifest than the greater grace of the movement of the vehicle— as to which, for the completeness of her image, Maggie was now supremely to feel how every strain had been lightened for herself. So far as *she* was one of the wheels she had but to keep in her place; since the work was done for her she felt no weight, and it wasn't too much to acknowledge that she had scarce to turn around. She had a long pause before the fire, during which she might have been fixing with intensity her projected vision, have been conscious even of its taking an absurd, fantastic shape. She might have been watching the family coach pass and noting that, somehow, Amerigo and Charlotte were pulling it while she and her father were not so much as pushing. They were seated inside together, dandling the Principino and holding him up to the windows, to see and be seen, like an infant positively royal; so that the exertion was *all* with the others. Maggie found in this image a repeated challenge; again and yet again she paused before the fire: after which, each time, in the manner of one for whom a strong light has suddenly broken, she gave herself to livelier movement. She had seen herself at last, in the picture she was studying, suddenly jump from the coach; whereupon, frankly, with the wonder of the sight, her eyes opened wider and her heart stood still for a moment. She looked at the person so acting as if this person were somebody else, waiting with intensity to see what would follow. (315)

This reverie occurs at the point where Maggie has come to suspect that her husband and Charlotte are having an affair, and it becomes an attempt to find an explanation in past events for her present experience and emotion. This attempt to understand the "chain of causes and consequences" is necessarily retrospective. In fact, the entire narrative mode through which Maggie is presented is of a piece with a double focus, where we see Maggie in the present seeing herself both in the present and in the past. One of the effects of James's "free indirect discourse" and the way it purports to situate the reader within Maggie's consciousness (and the bulk of the novel is focalized through Maggie) is to foreground the process of consciousness as it attempts to shape and define itself.

The content of Maggie's thoughts provides many of the themes and motifs that have preoccupied various critics of *The Golden Bowl*, and especially the moral issue of the Ververs' having had Charlotte "in," and having placed her and Amerigo in a position where they do all the work necessary to bolster the Ververs' position in society while allowing them to maintain their own intense intimacy. Maggie fails, however, to move toward the cardinal recognition her situation requires—that is, the recognition of her own and Adam's culpability in placing the "sposi" in a position of great temptation. We may be led to think that this temptation stems as much from their liberation from the demands of their marriages as from their being not only thrown together for long weekends in great houses but placed in roles that prefigure and suggest intimacy, an intimacy that would have been suggested even if they had not enjoyed a prior relationship.

Maggie's reverie clarifies a great number of things about her situation and about her feelings, but it does not lead her to the climactic recognition her situation requires, that is, recognition of her own possible culpability and of the way it is inextricably interlaced with the needs and motives of the others. The form of her reverie would seem at the very least to limit, if not block, self-recognition and reflect a process of representation or image making that distances her from herself as a potentially responsible agent within a dynamic set of reciprocities. Eventually, however, she must, and will assume responsibility.[15] (Maggie's vision of herself jumping from the coach also prefigures her development; toward the end of the novel Maggie tells Charlotte a lie and her passivity becomes a form of activity.)

In her reverie Maggie does seem to recognize herself, but the image shifts and splits as she contemplates it. From being one of four wheels bearing the metaphoric carriage, she becomes, as her consciousness of the moral situation crystallizes, a rider in the carriage, and then a woman who jumps out of it—a woman who is "somebody else" for whom she does not feel, or rather for whom she abnegates, responsibility. Insofar as she does recognize herself in the shifting representations of this "projected vision," Maggie's language suggests that, though Charlotte had been "had in" like extra help and is therefore the one used, Maggie has come to feel herself as the more or less passive victim of Charlotte's machinations, in the sense that once Charlotte was in place, Maggie herself "had but to *keep in her place*" (my emphasis), like a servant or a wheel. Maggie's act of seeing herself acting splits her from herself and underlines her distance from her own experience. This representation provokes the reader to a consideration of her ostensible self-confrontation as a strategy of avoidance, congruent with analogous strategies at other moments of Maggie's experience, and of other characters at various times.

The narrative mode, which precludes authoritative representation, allows James to juxtapose Maggie's and Charlotte's views of the circumstances without giving any indication of what might be the "truth" of the situation. Charlotte's sense of the cause of her situation is almost exactly parallel to Maggie's: whereas Maggie would seem to imply that Charlotte is responsible for her having been "placed" as she is, Charlotte thinks of herself as "placed" by Maggie and her father, "fixed like a pin in a pin cushion" (199). There is a striking symmetry in Charlotte's and Maggie's sense of being defined, as well as controlled, by the other. Charlotte confides in Fanny:

> "It belongs to my situation that I'm, by no merit of my own, just fixed—fixed as fast as a pin stuck, up to its head, in a cushion. I'm placed—I can't imagine anyone *more* placed. There I *am*. . . . I've simply to see the truth of the matter—see that Maggie thinks more, on the whole, of fathers than of husbands. And my situation is such . . . that this becomes immediately, don't you understand? a thing I have to count with." (199)

As Maggie blames Charlotte, Charlotte blames Maggie, and it would seem that the mutual blaming constitutes an avoidance of recognizing culpability. For the *reader,* it is also the ground for or beginning of the recognition—which Maggie eventually reaches— that accepting the reciprocity of placing and being placed within the "system" (Maggie's term) is the only ground of being and acting. The language of "placing," "fixing," and "dooming" is recurrently used to describe Maggie, Charlotte, and many of the other characters. This usage reflects Charlotte's and Maggie's need to blame each other, and constitutes either a displacement or a projection of their own responsibility for generating the woeful situation in which they find themselves. It is only by acknowledging their mutual implication in the play of need and desire that they can find their way out of their dilemma. By employing a narrative technique that precludes privileging one or another version of "blame" and by problematizing any attempt by the narrative voice to establish one authoritative representation, the novel implicates us in the characters' desperate and hopeless struggle to sort out the origin of their predicament. The effect of this mode of representation demonstrates the impossibility of establishing univocal cause while asserting the need for it.

Even when the omniscient narrator once again leaves the confines of free indirect discourse and takes a firm position, as it does when presenting Adam, confusion results (see p. 110). When, for example, Charlotte speaks of her own and the Prince's desire to "take care of [Adam and Maggie]," we learn that:

> [Charlotte] spoke indeed with a nobleness not the less effective for coming in so oddly; with a sincerity visible even through the complicated twist by which any effort to protect the father and the daughter seemed necessarily conditioned for them. (235)

Charlotte *may* feel or be noble, or even sincere, but Maggie's suspicions about the genesis of the Prince and Charlotte's relationship, as well as the fact that the novel begins by establishing their prior intimacy, would seem to disqualify terms like "nobleness" and "sincerity."[16] The intrusion of such terms in the narrative voice generates and feeds our sense of the impossibility of confirming any particular representation of self or situation: of the place one is in, of how one has come to be placed there, and of how one locates oneself, morally and volitionally, within it.

The action of this novel centers on the way in which the social and emotional equilibrium of the characters is disrupted by the Prince and Charlotte's adultery. The adultery is itself embedded in the unusual intimacy of the Ververs, father and daughter. Almost everything in the novel can be seen as a response to this basic situation. The central questions raised by the book have to do with the origins of the Prince and Charlotte's adultery, and the novel dramatizes the process of probing and exploring those origins. In attempting to consolidate an interpretation, the reader, like Maggie, is implicated in providing an account of origin: is it because of the Ververs' high-handed handling of Charlotte and the Prince? Do they treat them too much like objects—precious maybe, treasures even—but *things* nevertheless? Is the Ververs' own relationship unhealthy? Does Maggie think too much of her father, Adam too much of Maggie? Is their treatment of others as museum pieces and their inability to confront their part in the resulting situation a defense against confronting their incestuous desires? Is their treatment of the others as objects a result of these desires? Or should we see Charlotte as rationalizing her desire for the Prince and conversely his for her? Are these two one-time lovers, who were forced to separate for lack of funds, simply looking for an excuse to continue their affair? And is their feeling of being fixed merely a way for them to indulge their "real" desire—for one another? Or does the novel really take an undecidable mixture of erotic desire and mercenary motive for granted, while pursuing its real interest: the representation of the way in which people search for explanations of their situations and desires in origins, causes, beginnings?

The mode of representation in fact forestalls the ascription of origin, and in its search for receding origins the novel presents the self-enclosed and self-enclosing—the essentially solipsistic—nature of the need to find and found self through the construction of some primary ground. This need is informed by the tension between not-knowing and denial. The characters do not know whether there is something out there responsible for their situation or whether the cause of their predicament, although they would assume is out there, is really something they themselves construct and would therefore wish to deny. The novel at once dramatizes the characters' need to discover what has gone wrong and their reluctance to do so. The philosophical consideration of origin, as well as of solipsism and skepticism, is possibly an over-reading of the way in which the characters transform, and thus distance, the pain of desire, a pain so great that it prevents them from recognizing its causes. Perhaps the entire question of tracking down source and apportioning blame should be described in terms of the psychological concept of repression. The tension between these two modes of understanding experience—philosophical and psychological—is what the novel deals with and does not resolve.

In either case, what the novel exhibits is the way its characters negotiate, that is to say, attempt to come to terms with and attempt to avoid their desires. This negotiation is expressed in the way all the characters *look* at all the other characters, *look* for ways to explain and represent their situations. There is a marked emphasis on the motif of "seeing" and not-seeing, and then, as a result, on naming and not naming, on categorizing and not categorizing the things they see or fail to see.

*****

In *The Golden Bowl* the striking emphasis on seeing is one dimension of the need to establish a sense of ground for the self. When everything is awash in the fluidity of an unlimited, indeterminate consciousness, "seeing" would seem to provide a last-ditch attempt to ground representation and hence experience, and to validate for the characters a sense of themselves as coherent, viable subjects. The recurrent emphasis on "seeing" in this novel is the over-determined expression of the desire for some stable fact, phenomenon, or experience. The characters, and like them the reader, look for something that would compensate them for the absence of an orienting principle of stability. The prevailing trope of "seeing" is a direct function of the absence of narrative authority, itself an expression of the absence of a more general authority or transcendental origin that would organize and legislate representation.

When critics stress James's use of the dramatized scene, what they stress is not merely a superficial aspect of drama or of James's technique, but a process that reveals something of the way James conceives and projects his fictional world.[17] What a character (and therefore a reader) "sees" is, by definition, limited. This novel dramatizes how the characters, and perforce the readers, are reduced to a reliance on sight (vision), which would substitute and thus compensate for the experience of loss, of being lost. But as the novel hypostatizes this activity of "seeing," it also exposes its insufficiency, its very blindness, by leading us into a field of conflicting (contradictory) representations that confirm the inadequacy (or impossibility) of authoritative perceptions.

The motif of seeing, and the elusiveness of what can be seen, is vividly established near the beginning of the novel. The Prince, contemplating the Ververs and his difficulty in understanding them, is put in mind of Poe's short story "Gordon Pym" by his sense that there is an "element of the impenetrable" (42) in them. His association links significantly with Adam's epiphany on reading "On First Looking into Chapman's Homer." Whereas Adam compares himself to Cortez and Keats—his adventure is one of utmost transparency and clarity—the salient image for the Prince in the Poe story, which he too recalls as an adventure of exploration and discovery, is of a

> . . . thickness of white air that was like a dazzling curtain of light, concealing as darkness conceals. . . . The state of mind of his new friends [the Americans] . . . had resemblances to a great white curtain. He had never known curtains but as purple even to blackness—but as producing where they hung a darkness intended and ominous. (42)

From this point on, the image of a "white mist" (43) occurs frequently in the novel—sometimes transformed into an image of a cloud of fine dust—and always suggestive of a light that should illuminate but that serves instead to conceal. The above passage, pointing in two directions, suggests a mutual blindness: the Prince, who is used to black curtains, to acknowledged mystery, cannot see "what *was* morally speaking behind [the American's] veil" (43). But the shipwrecked Gordon Pym is *himself* lost in that "dazzling curtain of light." For the Prince, the Ververs' association with the white curtain signifies an "innocence" that blinds him because it is made up of light. Light should facilitate seeing, but in the Prince's eyes the Americans themselves are unaware of their blindness, since their curtain has the quality of "dazzling light."[18]

The importance of seeing becomes paramount when vision is problematic. The European Prince, aware that his difficulties in understanding his American family may derive from the difference between the European and American tradition, tells Fanny that he depends on her "to see [him] through" (45). As in the Poe story, the Prince represents his sense of dependence on her in terms of navigation, ships, sailing, and above all seeing. He says, "I'm excellent, I really think, all round—except that I'm stupid. I can do pretty well anything I *see*. But I've got to see it first" (47). Possibly the Prince projects his own blindness onto the Americans through what for him is the "paradigmatic" American story. Maybe it is only he who is blinded, but as the novel provides no unequivocal guide, it is impossible to attach blame, to track down the source of this experience. What remains is the experience itself—the sense of being lost.

This bewilderment is generalized insofar as "seeing" in this novel is inextricably connected with the problem of some shared ethical code that would orient behavior. The meeting of the European Prince and the American Ververs is a meeting, as in much of James's fiction, between two different cultures. Each has its own tradition, mores, and moral code, and part of what emerges in the dramatization of the cultural confrontation is that there is nothing sufficiently unassailable, nothing basic enough in the culture of either that would allow them to establish some kind of transcendent ground on which to meet.[19]

The novel dramatizes how "seeing" itself is a culture-bound activity, which therefore cannot serve as the basis for communication between the Americans and the Europeans. Steeped in his particular European sense of history, the Prince is aware of the cultural gap and of his consequent dependence on interpreting "American signs."

> He had perceived on the spot that any *serious* discussion of veracity, of loyalty, or rather of the want of them, practically took [Maggie]

unprepared, as if it were quite new to her. He had noticed it before; it was the English, the American *sign* that duplicity, like "love," had to be joked about. It couldn't be "gone into." (37, my emphasis)

For the Prince, the American sign system is not natural, and it is obscured behind what he comes to think of as a "dazzling white curtain." In order for him to penetrate the "American veil," or convention, and read the signs of his newfound family, in order for him to "see" the way they see, he must perform an act of self-imposed blinding, suppressing all that he knows (and knows all too well) about duplicity. The scion of a long line of Italian nobility, the Prince is aware that his European conception of complexity is perhaps inaccessible to his "innocent" American family. In order to see things as his marriage requires him, the Prince will have to learn not to see. In thinking of his, as opposed to the Ververs', relation to history, he recognizes that what he calls their "romantic spirit" (39) is incapable of knowing what the "real thing meant," but

> [*h*]e did—having seen it, having tried it, having taken its measure. This was memory in fact simply to screen out—much as, just in front of him while he walked, the iron shutter of a shop, closing early to the stale summer day, rattled down at the turn of some crank. (39)

The Prince, in short, feels that in order to penetrate the American Gordon Pym mist he has to shutter or screen out his vision of the "real." In this he stands in stark contrast to Adam, who celebrates his own "freedom to see" (128). When Adam compares himself to Cortez, in line with the sonnet he does so in terms of sight. Adam's romantic identification with Keats and Cortez is of a piece with his rewriting of his own history and blinds him to the adultery that is going on under his nose. Amerigo (whose ancestor, in a moment of discovery parallel to that of Cortez, *did* in fact discover America), has to repress his sense of history in order to deal with Adam's putative innocence. Adam's pose of "innocence" is what allows him to repose confidence in the Prince, but the Prince is aware that such confidence is ungrounded, and is therefore an abyss.[20]

For both the Prince and Charlotte the American's innocence opens such *"abysses of confidence"* (41; my emphasis) that it "would demand of them the most anxious study and the most independent, not to say original, interpretation of signs" (220). In the absence of a transcendent signified, the arbitrary nature of these contending systems of signification promotes the emphasis on seeing, on interpretation, on naming, that permeates the novel.

Again and again "seeing" is seen to fall short of the ground it would
establish; again and again, "seeing" gives way to "naming," as
though through a series of displacements "naming" itself could
establish or demolish "facts" and provide a basis for behavior that
"seeing" has failed to do.[21] All of the characters will become adept
in the arts of prevarication, applying "at different times, different
names" (220). As we saw with the Prince, seeing is inextricably
linked with not seeing, and naming is linked with the refusal to
name. The Prince, thinking not-thinking about the fact of his adultery, recognizes "that there were things he could prize, forms of
fortune he could cherish, without at all proportionately liking their
names" (258). In order to save her marriage, which is the same
thing as saving her father from explicit knowledge of both her own
pain and his wife's infidelity, Maggie will manipulate "the forms of
[Adam's] ignorance" (410). Charlotte too promotes the advantages
of ignorance when she says to the Prince: "Ah, for things I mayn't
want to know, I promise you shall find me stupid" (272). Maggie
can tell the Prince on the one hand that she "is not afraid of history" (33) but on the other hand when questioned by her father
about Charlotte's previous relationships, she declares, "I don't
want to know!" (153).

But though the characters take pains to avoid naming pain, the
repressed is implicit in the expressed. In a phrase that foregrounds
the problematics of dissemination, Fanny, aware of the adultery
and of Maggie's manipulations, feels that her activities "were now
bearing fruit that might yet bear a larger crop" (212). In my discussion of the preface to *The Ambassadors,* I suggested that a similar
phrase expressed James's sense of "the co-presence of traces in
every sign," and thus of the impossibility of controlling or limiting
the effects of speech or action: language can only signify as an
effect of relation to that which it excludes.[22] Fanny's statement
here, expresses a similar awareness, further colored by her reluctance to take responsibility for bringing the Prince and Maggie
together. As the exposition of her situation unfolds, it becomes
clear that Fanny's failure to name is in effect related to the uncertainty as to what she sees, part of a deliberate refusal to see that
serves to absolve her from the responsibility that clear sight would
have entailed.

The ethical issue of accepting or avoiding responsibility is seen
here as implicated in the way Fanny conceives and represents human action in terms of the relation between cause and effect. Specifically, we learn that what she is experiencing is "mere blind

terror" but that "on trying . . . she could none the less give it no name" (212).

> The sense of seeing was strong in her, but she clutched at the comfort of not being sure of what she saw. Not to know what it would represent on a longer view was a help, in turn, to not making out that her hands were embrued; since if she had stood in the position of a producing cause she should surely be less vague about what she had produced. This further, in its way, was a step towards reflecting that when one's connexion with any matter was too indirect to be traced it might be described also as too slight to be deplored. (212–13)

Cause and effect are made contingent on naming, naming on "seeing"—and Fanny, like the other characters, and possibly like the reader, would name and not name, see and not see. The colonel's is the most inclusive, radical judgment. We are told that, for him, "Statements were too much like theories, in which one lost one's way" (218–19).

The motif of seeing and naming in a *novel* is, by definition, bound to the act of reading, and this is emphatically the case here. There are countless instances of the use of the motif of reading, both literal reading as in letters and telegrams, and metaphorical reading, as in the interpretation of a wide variety of signs within the "world" of the novel. We saw this with Maggie's reading of Adam's "letter," we saw it in Amerigo's struggle to read the American "signs," and we saw the Prince and Charlotte's problem of "interpret[ing] . . . signs." A clear instance of such reading is to be found when Adam contemplates Maggie's response to the situation created by Mrs. Vance. At this juncture, the scene is described as follows: the exchange between Adam and Maggie is "mute" (130) as he becomes aware of what he takes to be—in his second guessing—his daughter's fear for his future. In this "soundless" interaction, he discovers that their relationship is "altered."

> He *saw*, again, the difference lighted for her. This marked it to himself—and it wasn't a question simply of a Mrs. Vance the more or the less. For Maggie too, at a stroke, almost beneficently, their visitor had, from being an inconvenience, become a sign. They had made vacant, by their marriage, his immediate foreground, his personal precinct—they being the Princess and the Prince. They had made room in it for others—so others had become aware. He became aware himself, for that matter, during the minute Maggie stood there before speaking; and with the sense, moreover, of what he saw her see, he had the sense of what she saw *him*. This last, it may be added, would have been his

intensest perception had there not, the next instant, been more for him
in Fanny Assingham. Her face couldn't keep it from him; she had
seen, on top of everything, in her quick way, what they both were
seeing. (131)

References to signs and tokens requiring "reading" (representation or interpretation) have been discussed in previous chapters.
What in *The Wings of the Dove* is seeing round several corners,
second guessing, is presented here as the dizzying perspectives of
different views, and as the way in which the multiplicity of such
views itself becomes for the characters, in this case for Adam, a
"sign." The characters have to read their situations on the basis
of what they see. The lack of authority of the narrative voice finds
its expression in this overemphasis on "seeing." In an ironic move,
in the rare moments when the narrative voice does express itself
directly—that is, not through a particular focalizer or character—
the erosion of its authority is seen to contaminate the status of the
concept of authority. This is explicit in the passage that directly
follows the one quoted above, where the issues of writing, reading,
and seeing all come together in a vertigo of absent ground and
suspended authority; the narrative voice is itself implicated in the
"vice" of too much seeing, too much reading.

> So much mute communication was doubtless, all this time, marvel-
> lous, and we may confess to having perhaps read into the scene, prema-
> turely, a critical character that took longer to develop. (131)

Is this an abrogation of authorial responsibility? If the narrator or
writer becomes reader, what happens to the "real" reader? It is
not so much that our function has been usurped but that it has
been extended to a point where the authority, the author that would
ground representation, disappears beneath us as reader and writer
are conflated.

Far from having read too much into the scene, as the above
quote implies, the second half of the novel, Maggie's book, reveals
how much she and we read and do not read, see and do *not* see,
as with Maggie we incessantly *look,* searching for a means of controlling and representing our experience.

*****

If there is a single precursor image of Maggie in James that most
captures the imagination, it is the image of Maisie in *What Maisie
Knew,* her nose flattened against a pane of glass, peering at the

activities of the grown-ups. In *The Golden Bowl* Maggie's nose is not always quite as flattened when we see her, time and again, on the other side of a glass barrier looking at her father, her husband, Charlotte, together and apart.

The entire second book of the novel, "The Princess," revolves around Maggie's attempt to see her situation clearly, to assess and come to terms with her suspicions of her husband's adultery, to save her father from explicit knowledge of his wife's infidelity and of his daughter's suffering; and, finally, to save her marriage. Saving her marriage will also save her father's. The form that Maggie's activity takes is to look, and to wait. Readers, situated as they are in Maggie's consciousness, read with her and, like her, attempt to formulate strategies of representation on the basis of what they and she see and do not see.

Through his handling of Maggie's character James exposes the limitations of traditional mimetic fiction. I have therefore chosen in the following section to explore the tortuous path of Maggie's *bildung* and to show how James asserts the possibility of a more open order of representation. Maggie—Adam's daughter, the Prince's wife, Charlotte's friend and rival—is made to cope with desire, adultery, suggestions of incest, deceit, and manipulation in a world no longer underpinned by moral absolutes. James's attempt to reconcile the semiotic and the moral reaches its climax in the character of Maggie who, despite her eventual realization of the absence of grounding essences, successfully asserts the possibility of effective action without jettisoning moral categories. We begin with Maggie as American Innocent, the Maggie—"not afraid of history," characterized by Fanny's statement that she "wasn't born to know evil" (80) who squints at the possibility of her husband's adultery.[23]

The stress on seeing and how it derives from a sense of the absence of any orienting ground or origin has already been examined. We have noted how the motif of looking *is* the search for the compensating fact that would redeem the absence of origin. If at the beginning of the novel Maggie is confident that she can "divide her faith into water-tight compartments" (37), by the opening of her book we feel the leaks, as her confidence in the innate stability of her categories of experience—of her sign system—collapses under the stress of a sign it cannot contain. Sensing that something is amiss, but not quite able to acknowledge that her husband may be betraying her, Maggie finds that an imaginary pagoda rises at "the very centre of the garden of her life" (301).

Maggie walks "round and round" the predominantly "outland-ish" pagoda:

> she had carried on her existence in the space left her for circulation, a space that sometimes seemed ample and sometimes narrow; looking up, all the while, at the fair structure that spread itself so amply and rose so high, but never quite making out, as yet, where she might have entered had she wished. She had not wished till now—such was the odd case; and what was doubtless equally odd, besides, was that, though her raised eyes seemed to distinguish places that must serve, from within, and especially far aloft, as apertures and outlooks, no door appeared to give access from her convenient garden level. The great decorated surface had remained consistently impenetrable and inscrutable. . . . The thing might have been, by the distance at which it kept her, a Mahometan mosque, with which no base heretic could take a liberty; there so hung about it the vision of putting off one's shoes to enter, and even, verily, of one's paying with one's life if found there as an interloper. (301–2)

Maggie understands her vision as "figur[ing] the arrangement—how otherwise was it to be named?—by which, so strikingly, she had been able to marry without breaking, as she liked to put it, with her past. She had surrendered herself to her husband . . . and yet she had not . . . given up her father by the least little inch" (302).[24]

The felicity of Maggie's representation notwithstanding, what she does not quite see is the extent of the threat that her blocked access to this new sign makes her feel. The felt danger of "paying with her life" is both exacerbated and attenuated by the utter strangeness of this "Mahometan mosque," marked by the domestic yet esoteric image of "putting off one's shoes to enter." "Moving for the first time in her life as in the darkening shadow of a false position" (303), the shadow cast by the pagoda hides and highlights Maggie's evasion of what she feels about what she sees. What emerges a few pages later is that Maggie is in the grip of jealousy, suspecting that her husband is having an affair with her father's wife, her best friend.

This jealousy triggers a process. Suspecting—which for Ameri-can Maggie is a new way of seeing—means literally to see under; under-seeing is for Maggie a new mode of under-standing.[25] The pagoda becomes the sign for Maggie of her initiation into a mode of awareness that will confront her with the limitations of her previous understanding. Her previously unitary perception of her secure domestic life is split by this unstable figure of her imagination.

From this point on she will gradually come to replace her perception of the world as made up of stable essences with a growing sense of how representations are constructed within a system of unstable signs. Maggie is now initiated into a consciousness of a system of signs that frees her to act, to establish "a new basis and something like a new system" (462). As her anxiety surfaces, things are no longer necessarily what they seem. Insofar as she dis-covers and re-covers the gap that underlies and separates the sign from the thing signified, she is now able, through various acts of dissimulation, to manipulate appearances.[26] The pagoda is a sign of Maggie's new consciousness signifying the "arrangement" and also its breakdown. It becomes a floating signifier which figures, both her inclusion and exclusion in the, for her, new world where signs are not essentially linked to stable essences.

Maggie, like Strether in *The Ambassadors,* has understood something of the arbitrary nature of appearances, has established a new relation to the "precious equilibrium," and, like Strether, has learned to dissimulate through what I call the "enabling lie." Unlike Strether, however, whose initiation issues in renunciation, Maggie feels that her "readjustment of relations" (326) puts her in touch with "history" (306). She learns the meaning of fear. She reminds herself of an actress who suddenly begins "to improvise, to speak lines not in the text" (322). Freedom as well as its anxiety is a function of separation—of line from text, of sign from signified, of daughter from father. Becoming free and asserting her validity in her own eyes is, for Maggie, a protracted process:

> . . . to be free, to be free to act, other than abjectly, for her father, [Maggie] must conceal from him the validity that, like a microscopic insect pushing a grain of sand, she was taking on even for herself. (396)

The process entailed in separation is literally portrayed as we see Maggie on the other side of the glass windows of the terrace at Fawns, herself unseen, watching the others. Suspecting leads to its cognate—spying. In becoming suspicious, Maggie has escaped the trap of her cozy "arrangement." The process, however, is as yet incomplete—as she spies on the others she is at once inside and outside. Adam, the Prince, Charlotte, and Fanny are playing cards, and she watches her father and "her father's wife's lover facing his mistress" (456). This is the paradigmatic image of Maggie, her nose not quite pressed against the pane of glass, watching the others play an adult game and wondering about "the secret behind every face" (457).

Fixing the scene before her, Maggie finds her sign, her orientation, in the doubleness of her response. Her feelings alternate between power and impotence: as the others hold cards in their hands, she holds *them* in hers (456). In phrases that echo the imaginary letter and the Poe story, blinding light turns to darkness, and Maggie ponders passing a sentence of doom.

> There reigned for her, absolutely, during these vertiginous moments, that fascination of the monstrous, that temptation of the horribly possible, which we so often trace by its breaking out suddenly lest it should go further, in unexplained retreats and reactions.
> After it had been thus vividly before her for a little that, springing up under her wrong and making them all start, stare and turn pale, she might sound out their doom in a single sentence, a sentence easy to choose among several of the lurid—after she had faced that blinding light and felt it turn to blackness . . . (456–57).

Maggie's sense of power provokes in her a corresponding fear of retaliation. She can sentence them to doom, yet she feels as though "a beast might have leaped at her throat"(458).[27] The others "might have been figures rehearsing some play of which she herself was the author," (458) but she feels like "the scapegoat of old gone forth into the desert to sink under his burden and die" (457). Positioned outside on the terrace looking in, Maggie is aware of the horror of her situation but resists the temptation to experience herself either as classical avenger or as classical victim. Were she to take herself seriously as either she would lose her Prince. The world of scapegoats and avengers is a world of moral absolutes, a biblical world of tragedy and catharsis. Maggie chooses to reject such a world since accepting it would mean exile:

> . . . she saw as in a picture, with the temptation she had fled from quite extinct, why it was she had been able to give herself so little, from the first, to the vulgar heat of her wrong. She might fairly, as she watched them, have missed it as a lost thing; have yearned for it, for the straight vindictive view, the rights of resentment, the rages of jealousy, the protests of passion, as for something she had been cheated of not least: a range of feelings which for many women would have meant so much, but which for *her* husband's wife, for *her* father's daughter, figured nothing nearer to experience than a wild eastern caravan looming into view with crude colours in the sun, fierce pipes in the air, high spears against the sky, all a thrill, a natural joy to mingle with but turning off short before it reached her and plunging into other defiles. (459)

On the terrace Maggie's situation cuts her off from a "natural" response to her own vision whose power, however, is attenuated by the order of representation, by syntax and proliferating negatives, by the imposition of the mediating phrase "as in a picture." Maggie's epiphany, her emotion—like the traditional scapegoat—is sunk at the bottom of a long concessive paragraph, buried beneath a heap of language. Maggie's epiphany is the expression of the impossibility of epiphany. She intuits the "natural joy" of mingling but is separated as the caravan plunges "into other defiles" before reaching her. The image of the caravan, like that of the pagoda, becomes a figure of Maggie's exile from an order such as the biblical, in which signs necessarily signify fixed references. However, the exigencies of her situation, her desire for the Prince and her desire to belong, initiate her into a new order of representation.

Her freedom to interpret the sign inheres in the autonomy of the sign, in its arbitrary nature; it can be buried, changed, held up, or put down. Maggie can feel the horror and its insufficiency.

> She saw at all events why horror itself had almost failed her; the horror of finding evil seated, all at its ease, where she had only dreamed of good; the horror of the thing hideously *behind,* behind so much trusted, so much pretended, nobleness, cleverness, tenderness. It was the first sharp falsity she had known in her life, to touch at all, or be touched by; in one of the thick-carpeted corridors of a house of quiet on a Sunday afternoon; and yet, yes, amazingly she had been able to took at terror and disgust only to know she must put away from her the bitter-sweet of their freshness. The sight, from the window, of the group so constituted, *told* her why, told her how, named to her, as with hard lips, named straight *at* her, so that she must take it full in the face, the other possible relation to the whole fact which alone would bear upon her irresistibly. It was extraordinary: they positively brought home to her that to feel about them in any of the immediate, inevitable, assuaging ways, the ways usually open to innocence outraged and generosity betrayed, would have been to give them up, and that giving them up was, marvellously, not to be thought of (459).[28]

The language of the above passage holds horror as firmly as horror can be held—and puts it away. The bittersweet of hypostatized evil, falsity, tenderness, even terror, is realized, actualized—and put away. Maggie's "sight" has "*told*" her that to think of these concepts as inhering *behind* appearances and language, although "assuaging," fixes the "inevitable," the im-mediate. Lacan's concept of the gaze provides an interesting perspective on the scene of Maggie's spying and the way in which the clash between the unconscious and the conscious shapes and subverts the looking subject.[29] To accept the notion of inevitability is to lose the freedom conferred by domesticity, by "thick-carpeted corridors," connecting a language that cannot be pinned or fixed to metaphysical abstractions.[30] For Maggie to accept evil as immanent, *behind,* is to accept the identity of the sign and the thing signified, is to accept non-freedom and eschew the possibility of relation, social relation opened by a differentiating non-immediate language.[31] Maggie can't give them up—Adam, Amerigo, Charlotte, even Fanny. How could she? To do so would be to completely isolate herself in some metaphysical realm of what, for this novel, is American romanticism. And what use are concepts like trust and tenderness, or even falsity, if they don't implicate relationship?

Maggie thus comes to accept language and relation based on difference; if she will not accept "Evil," she recognizes that she has no choice but to rename evil, to accept what seems amazing, extraordinary, marvelous. She accepts being implicated in a social system and signifies this acceptance by telling her lie.[32]

Charlotte comes out to the terrace in search of Maggie where they walk side by side until Charlotte stops Maggie "and ma[kes] her stand where the party at cards would be before her" (464).

> Side by side, for three minutes, they fixed this picture of quiet harmonies, the positive charm of it and, as might have been said, the full significance—which, as was now brought home to Maggie, could be no more, after all, than a matter of interpretation, differing always for a different interpreter. As she herself had hovered in sight of it a quarter of an hour before, it would have been a thing for her to show Charlotte—to show in righteous irony, in reproach too stern for anything but silence. But now it was she who was being shown it by Charlotte, and she saw quickly enough that, as Charlotte showed it, she must at present submissively seem to take it. (464)

Given her decision not to cut herself off from the others, Maggie has to "seem to take it." But given her new-found awareness that "significance . . . could be no more than a matter of interpretation, differing always for a different interpreter," what is the status of the "seem" in her acknowledging Charlotte's interpretation? If Maggie has relinquished the security of grounding metaphysical terms, on what basis can she now distinguish appearance from reality, "seems" from "is"? (Note the distance she has traveled in the space of the few minutes since her last look through this window.)

The "dramatic irony" of this repeated window image would seem to undo the relative stability of Maggie's recently hard-won sophistication. The scene on the terrace blurs the conventional boundaries of the concept of "dramatic irony." In uncanny resonance with James's project throughout the novel, a chain of infinite regression subverts the audience-actor hierarchy. Maggie is both actor and spectator, and when Charlotte joins her there are two spectators, Charlotte suspicious, Maggie divided. How can the reader, the third spectator, decide which of them has the privilege of knowledge? What does this spectral structure do for the reader's own knowledge of the abyss of knowledge? Especially since we learn, as we look at the two of them looking at Adam, that

Not yet, since his marriage, had Maggie so sharply and so formidably known her old possession of [her father] as a thing divided and contested. She was looking at him by Charlotte's leave and under Charlotte's direction; quite in fact as if the particular way she should look at him were prescribed to her; quite, even, as if she had been defied to look at him in any other. (464)

Maggie's particular focus on her father at this juncture of recantation and her consequent sense of loss and division suggest that she is aware of the plurality of interpretation.

If we have been discussing her initiation into a system of deferred signification—a mode of thought and perception that tends to erase hard and fast categories, that accepts division and the split in the sign—here Maggie accepts a degree of separation from her father that will allow her to maintain a degree of intimacy. As Maggie senses it, Charlotte's interdiction—when she "defied" Maggie to look at Adam in "any other" way—might be a pale reflection of a taboo: not *that* way. The scene of spying suggests emotional issues having to do with social relations—such as permissible degrees of intimacy between father and daughter and, by extension, between husband and wife, husband and lover—but also philosophical questions concerning language, ontology, epistemology, the nature of good and evil in the world. Just how open is interpretation? Freed of the isolating constraints of American romanticism, of faith in the sanctioning moral categories of experience, what happens to the concept of "truth"?

Charlotte tells Maggie, "I'm aware of no point whatever at which I may have failed you . . . nor of any at which I may have failed anyone in whom I can suppose you sufficiently interested to care" (467), stressing the tension between *duplicity* and what might be a *sincere* expression of how Charlotte perceived the exigencies of the famous "equilibrium."[33]

But in the second half of this novel the reader shares *Maggie's* consciousness, and with her, her awareness of falsehood. When she tells Charlotte, "I've *not* felt at any time that you've wronged me," she is lying, but she is not necessarily lying when she says, with a strategic pause, indicated by the sign of a space (—) and presumably held long enough to encompass a new concept of truth: "I accuse you—I accuse you of nothing" (468).[34]

This space acquires a specific content when we learn that "truth" for Maggie is no longer tied to any transcendent category but to what purports to be a sense of expedience matching Charlotte's own, and elevated in the name of love and loyalty.

> Maggie had to think how [Amerigo], on his side, had had to go through with his lie to [Charlotte], how it was for his wife he had done so, and how his doing so had given her the clue and set her the example. He must have had his own difficulty about it, and she was not, after all, falling below him. It was in fact as if, thanks to her hovering image of him confronted with this admirable creature even as she was confronted, there glowed upon her from afar, yet straight and strong, a deep explanatory light which covered the last inch of the ground. He had given her something to conform to, and she hadn't unintelligently turned on him, "gone back on" him, as he would have said, by not conforming. They were together thus, he and she, close, close together—whereas Charlotte, though rising there radiantly before her, was really off in some darkness of space that would steep her in solitude and harass her with care. The heart of the Princess swelled, accordingly, even in her abasement; she had kept in tune with the right, and something, certainly, something that might be like a rare flower snatched from an impossible ledge, would, and possibly soon, come of it for her. The right, the right—yes, it took this extraordinary form of her humbugging, as she had called it, to the end. It was only a question of not, by a hair's breadth, deflecting into the truth. (468–69)

The sophistry involved in opposing "the right" to "truth," in conflating "the right" with humbugging, would seem to justify, for Maggie, her "transvaluation of values."[35] And yet it leaves some readers, including myself, unsatisfied. Not only has Maggie "conformed" and resisted the danger of her own potential isolation by condemning Charlotte to "some darkness of space that would steep her in solitude," but she has done so by retaining the categories that sanction such behavior, thus consolidating her power.[36]

The justification of Maggie's "lie" might be seen as a gross rationalization. Aware that she cannot possibly maintain her previous intimacy with her father, she erects an elaborate construction in order to avoid contending with the implications of that intimacy or with the horrors of unspeakable, unnamed desire. Alternatively, Maggie's lie might be understood as a recognition of the value of fiction. Her enmeshment in a social system based on difference and not on positive "truths" requires the creation of fiction, whose value can only be assessed in terms of the responses that meet it. Maggie's self-consciously generated fiction, her lie, allows her to manipulate appearances and to engage her self through her desire for the other, her Prince.[37] It is through her fiction that Maggie achieves separation from her father and intimacy with her husband, marking the end of her initiation into a different order of representation.[38]

*****

The novel ends as Charlotte leaves to begin her exile; Maggie and the Prince embrace and Maggie says of Charlotte: "Isn't she too splendid? . . . That's our help, you see . . ." (547). The Prince responds:

> "'See'? I see nothing but *you*." And the truth of it had, with this force, after a moment, so strangely lighted his eyes that as for pity and dread of them, she buried her own in his breast. (547)

No matter how the characters or the reader conceive of the status of sign, the availability or not of an origin that is or is not deferred, the orienting potential of "seeing," the freedom or anxiety of interpretation, the fact or fiction of repression—it seems that the last words in this novel, which ends with the traditional comic topos of a restored marriage, are "pity and dread," as Maggie "buries" her eyes in her husband's breast.[39]

Although the burial is metaphoric and Maggie's eyes are not quite Oedipus's eyes, the classic Aristotelian tragic formula of pity and dread is not easily laid to rest. In the world of *The Golden Bowl,* what *is* literally buried? There are no funerals *in* the novel, but there *is* a death which precedes the dramatized events and creates the conditions for their possibility. Maggie's mother, Adam's first wife, is dead. Were she in the novel, Maggie's relationship with her father would surely be very different, and clearly, Charlotte's role in the plot impossible. Maggie, represented as a young woman, must have been even younger at the time of her loss. We learn surprisingly little about the first Mrs. Verver, and her loss is nowhere directly represented; what the novel does represent abundantly is other sorts of loss—loss of certainty, stability, freedom, loss of confidence in the capacity of language to adequately reflect experience, loss of confidence that traditional social forms such as marriage can contain and not constrain individual expression, loss of comfort in that most basic social relation, the relation between father and child.[40]

The most obvious as well as the most "worked" motif in this novel of collecting reduces people to things, mere commodities. In another version of the same motif, characters think of other characters as hunters or rampant beasts of prey. In a separate but related cannibal motif Adam and the Prince are seen as species of fowl; Charlotte associates marriage with being eaten (174); and for Fanny, to *think* about the other characters is to make a meal of them (201). Even Maggie images the form of her life as "the pretty mould of an iced pudding, . . . into which, to help yourself you didn't hesitate to break with the spoon" (318). The "form" that dominates *The Golden Bowl* is the golden bowl itself as it proliferates into images of all sorts of containers—among them, carriages, cups.[41] The cup of consciousness overflows into an expanding series of images of water, boats, transport, jumping; implicit in the stream is the explicit poison of the cup of the Borgias.[42]

These images of violence proliferate to such an extent that they become part of the novel's texture, and, as such, create an atmosphere of muted, diluted menace rather than point a specific threat. Even the first Mrs. Verver's absence—we don't even have her given name—makes itself felt throughout this novel in displaced images of primal, but not quite focused, danger. It is this quality (through quantity) of unobtrusive metaphorical density that intrudes sufficiently on the reader's consciousness to make him feel the need for air. Many readers complain of the claustrophobia of *The Golden Bowl,* and I would argue that the overelaborate quality of the writing serves to control and camouflage—not quite close out—what in James is a never-direct confrontation with death.

The closest the novel can come to confronting the absence that is death is through images of strangulation, simulated suffocation. The second half of *The Golden Bowl* is bound by the image of a cord that stretches in Maggie's mind to Adam's hand, to Charlotte's neck, to her own neck, to the Prince.

Maggie's memory of her last days at Fawns is the extraordinary vision of her father and Charlotte in the gallery reviewing Adam's possessions. Adam went ahead, while "Charlotte *hung* behind" (my emphasis);

. . . their connexion would not have been wrongly figured if he had been thought of as holding in one of his pocketed hands the end of a long silken halter looped round her beautiful neck. He didn't twitch it, yet it was there; he didn't drag her, but she came; and those indications that I have described the Princess as finding extraordinary in him were two or three mute facial intimations which his wife's presence didn't prevent his addressing his daughter. . . . They amounted perhaps only to a wordless, wordless smile, but the smile was the soft shake of the twisted silken rope. . . . Maggie's translation of it . . . came out only, as if it might have been overheard. . . . "Yes, you see—I lead her now by the neck, I lead her to her doom, and she doesn't so much as know what it is. . . . (493–94)

The "faint, far wail" of the maimed child that concludes *The Wings of the Dove* echoes in "the shriek of a soul in pain" (497). This is what Maggie and the reader hear now and again and again as, with "her nose fairly flattened" against the glass behind which "lurked the *whole* history of the relation . . ." (520), Maggie hears the "strange wail of the gallery . . . repeat its inevitable echo" (499). The wail—ostensibly Charlotte's—is in Maggie's and the reader's ear; it is the wail of desire, of mourning for lost unity, the price to be paid for the "knowledge" of self and otherness.

6

The Looped Garland

IN a little-noted scene toward the end of *The Golden Bowl* Maggie remembers watching Charlotte functioning as cicerone for the visitors at Fawns and describing Adam's treasures[1]:

> "The largest of the three pieces has the rare peculiarity that the garlands, looped round it, which, as you see, are the finest possible *vieux Saxe,* are not of the same origin or period, or even, wonderful as they are, of a taste quite so perfect. They have been put on at a later time, by a process of which there are very few examples, and none so important as this, which is really quite unique—so that, though the whole thing is a little *baroque,* its value as a specimen is, I believe, almost inestimable." (496)

This is all we learn about the objet d'art Charlotte is describing. It seems that the garlands have been made in Saxony, but as for the rest of the piece—we do not know. Maybe it's a piece of china, but it could well be any artifact colored with Saxe blue. The object remains mysterious. Because of the addition of the garlands to the largest of the three pieces its provenance is unclear. Genealogy is suggested, but so is the difficulty of pinning down origin. Neither the lost secret of the process with which it was made nor the mystery of its origin detracts from the mysterious piece; rather, each adds to its "inestimable"—because unique—value.

The imagery used to describe this "inestimable" specimen suggests its association with the golden bowl where, like the garlands, the gold was also added, "put on . . . by some beautiful old process" evocative of "a lost art . . . [and] also of a lost time" (105). But whereas the flawed bowl lies shattered in three pieces, the unknown imperfect object Charlotte describes seems to be composed of three pieces and owes its "unique" integrity to bricolage.

I see this tripartite treasure as an emblem of *The Golden Bowl* and of James's art in the three novels of the major phase discussed in this study. We are not given Charlotte's description of the piece directly, but filtered through Maggie's consciousness as she watches. The very mode of representation distances us from the piece, and representation itself emphasizes its unknowable origin, the problem of its uniqueness, and the problem of unity in heterogeneity. The "looped" garlands in the context of this scene inevitably evoke the "long silken halter looped round [Charlotte's] beautiful neck" (493), and the cord that binds and bonds the characters evokes, for me, the thread that binds the three novels of James's major phase.

James's highly embellished "baroque" art in the late phase, as exemplified in the image of the Saxe china, represents a layering, an intricately worked surface which has alternately baffled and attracted readers. Readers have been confused by the novels' complex style, their dense and elusive form, and the equivocation implicit in the ethical situations they project.

Over the last forty years, much of the criticism on James has attempted to absorb him into the mainstream novelistic tradition by tracing links between the opacity of his syntax and form on the one hand, and the complexity of his characters' ethical and existential struggle on the other. In this book I have attempted to show that the novels of the late phase transform the novelistic tradition by problematizing the classical novel and the basic assumptions of its traditional design. These works stand between the classical and the modern and postmodern novel. While successfully creating a mimetic "world," these novels cast doubt on the very existence of the "world," and of fiction itself as a stable, unmediated representation of "reality." In this perspective, the seemingly unusual dimensions of these works can be seen as highly effective ways of projecting the *weltanschauung* characterizing James's late phase.

In *The Tragic Muse*, a relatively early work set explicitly in the world of the theater, James explores the self-subverting nature of representation in a novel, that, broadly speaking, adheres to a more traditional nineteenth-century format. Through the interactions between Nick Dormer, Gabriel Nash, Peter Sherringham, and Miriam Rooth, James dramatizes the difficulty of distinguishing representation from any "truth" that might give rise to that representation.

By the time he comes to write the novels of the late phase, James is generating a fictional world that provides the reader with a sense of how his centers of consciousness process their experience in an atmosphere where the very possibility of doing so is problematic. He uses either one center of consciousness or more than one, and uses them in a way that both denies and grants every center such authority as is possible in the fictional world being depicted. In *The Ambassadors* we find only one center of consciousness, and since it is the only one, the reliability of its representations is both unavoidable and suspect. We can question the validity of Strether's representations but have no means of testing them against the authority of either an omniscient narrator or against other centers. In *The Wings of the Dove,* where we have access to Milly's, Kate's, and Densher's thoughts, we miss the authority of some narrative voice that would instruct us on how to shape an interpretation able to encompass the different points of view. In *The Golden Bowl* the narrative is focalized through three major characters, the Prince, Maggie and James's ficelle, Fanny. Each has a particular slant on the dramatized events, and the absence of an omniscient narrator, coupled with the limited perspective of each of the characters, implicates readers in the dizzying project of representation, despite their awareness of the necessary partiality and distortion implicit in this activity. Readers cannot tell, and there is no narrator with sufficient authority to instruct them, which of the characters to trust, how much to trust, or indeed, how to trust.

Writing and reading are dramatized as aspects of representation, and in the late works scenes of writing are presented as structured by the absence of fixed points, the "stars" of my opening, which would allow writing and reading to signify in anything like the way the various authors and readers would like. Mrs. Newsome in *The Ambassadors* figures as such a "star," and Strether's writing is seen to be structured by her absence; Milly's death in The *Wings of the Dove* is what provokes Densher to read/fantasize what he imagines she has written him; Maggie in *The Golden Bowl* writes herself (and reads) an imaginary letter in invisible ink. In all three novels, writing and reading are seen to be structured by the absence of some grounding term that could allow the signifying system to function unambiguously, to clearly represent what it is suggested that the characters might want to represent. The characters themselves have no choice but to communicate through a system of signs that are ultimately unable to guarantee direct, unambiguous communication. Readers are brought to realize that what they read is necessarily part of this very system, and that the author's text and the readers' interpretations are subject to the same difficulty. The characters interpret and act on the basis of their own interpretations, which, in turn, rest on other characters' interpretations. The result is that, although representation is seen as illimitable, and thus problematic, it remains the only basis for action.

The proliferation of representations, then, raises the dilemma of freedom in all its gravity. An unbridled succession of possible alternative representations, all equally plausible, is hard to square with the attempt to maintain the frame of a mimetic world, where real characters interact and are hence inevitably confronted with ethical choices. It is through the figure of the aesthete/spectator that James explores the ostensible opposition between ethics and aesthetics.

The spectator in James is, as we have seen, always a version of the aesthete. The very word "aesthetic" is cognate, via its Greek root, with the verb "to perceive," but part of what distinguishes the late novels of the major phase from earlier works is James's growing interest in creating the kind of narrative which foregrounds, in Gelley's terms, his spectators' "specular investment" in the scenes they witness. While in the earlier novels James's spectators are confined to the margins of the central action—in terms of the reader's interest in them, if not in terms of the consequences of their actions—their descendants become the central protagonists of James's late work.

Ralph in *The Portrait of a Lady* is an example of an early reflector, whose involvement in the action of the novel is precisely that of the spectator who watches from the side and occasionally intervenes critically to tip the scales of action in a particular direction, such as manipulating Isabel's endowment. In contrast, the spectators in the late novels are included, brought onto the main stage of James's action. Strether, Milly, and Maggie all share the generic qualities of the aesthete/observer, and they too stand somewhat apart from what seems to be the ongoing action, yet their development toward and involvement in the action, through their status as spectators, is the focus of attention. Furthermore, from *The Ambassadors* through *The Wings of the Dove* to *The Golden Bowl*, the level of involvement of these reflectors in the events they observe follows a sequence culminating in Maggie who, in *The Golden Bowl*, is both spectator and actor.

In *The Ambassadors* the action, on a superficial view, might be seen to revolve around Chad's illicit relationship with Madame de Vionnet and his dilemma about whether or not to return to America. But the chief source of interest in the novel is the way in which Strether reflects these issues, and what happens to him in the course of his observation of Chad's Paris. His climactic observation of the lovers on the river, with his consequent sense of their intimacy, is exemplary of this structure. Milly, in *The Wings of the Dove,* only makes her first appearance some hundred pages after the novel begins, and because she is, in a certain reading, the victim of Kate's and Densher's conspiracy, she is of course excluded from this part of the action. Like Ralph's, Milly's ill health provides a partial explanation for her separation from everyday life, but whereas Ralph suffers and dies from a specific disease, a mystery surrounds Milly's illness and eventual death. She is dramatized as wanting to engage life, but for some enigmatic reason is unable to do so. It is precisely her desire for experience and for life that is stressed in those moments that seem to characterize her as a typically remote Jamesian spectator as, for instance, when she inadvertently comes upon Kate and Densher in the National Gallery. The growing complexity of James's handling of the aesthete who is also involved in life and its complexities is further brought out in that, at certain points, we have access to the consciousness of both Kate and Densher. Clearly motivated by their desire for each other, they too, nevertheless, share the characteristics of the observer as, for example, they watch Milly and make their plans during the party she gives at the Palazzo Leporelli.

Finally, in *The Golden Bowl* all the figures share something typical of the character of the removed reflector, while at the same time each is engaged in the struggle to achieve selfhood and satisfy his or her desire in the context of the unusual situation presented in the novel. Adam is the possible exception, seemingly more fixed in the position of the earlier, remote, acquisitive aesthete, whose freedom consists in seeing. Maggie is the most interesting figure, however, since it is ultimately through her that James suggests how the aesthetic involves a system of seeing and interpreting that entails the ethical.

Associated on the one hand with Osmond and his deadening reification of all that is vital, and on the other with the activity of observing, aestheticism separates a concern with appearances, with the way things look from the ethical struggle of the engaged self to generate codes of behavior through which to recognize its own desire and the desire of others. By the time he publishes *The Ambassadors,* however, at the beginning of the major phase, James can be understood to be moving toward a form of narrative that undoes the ethics/aesthetics opposition.

In *The Ambassadors* Strether is dramatized as having a consciousness of both the aesthetic and the ethical. It is through his aesthetic appreciation of Chad's Paris that Strether becomes aware of his implication in a system of signification that he cannot morally accept. In dramatizing the limitations of the fixed categories in terms of which Strether organizes his experience, James exposes the problem(atic)s of mimetic representation. Strether is slowly initiated, through his capacity for aesthetic appreciation, into a mode of signification best described in terms of a theory of semiosis that accepts values as being the product of differences: he recognizes the absence of an absolute concept of virtue able to validate his response to his experience. The scene on the river, where he sees Chad and Madame de Vionnet together, is what Gelley calls "a scene of desire." That this scene includes the spectator's fantasy becomes evident when Strether, with an expanded sense of the meaning of virtue, knowingly acquiesces in the lie that describes Chad's and Madame de Vionnet's relationship as "virtuous": his newly acquired sense of the value of the aesthetic expresses itself in his recognition of the limitations of a purely moral response.

His moral sense is expressed, however, when he urges Chad to be faithful to his lover. Strether recognizes, but is unable to resolve, the conflict between his aesthetic and his moral sense. Both are implicated in his sense of Paris, which can be understood as expressing Strether's notion of the semiotic. The novel ends with his return to America and his renunciation of further involvement in the lives of those around him; his "only logic" will be, as he formulates it, "not, out of the whole affair, to have got anything for myself" (365). Strether's renunciation, whether explained in terms of his insistence on a moral code or in terms of his retreat to the safety of a spectator's distance, suggests his disengagement from ongoing life, and further suggests James's difficulty in reconciling his own protosemiotic awareness with a more traditional moral sense.

A similar problem(atic) informs the structure and the dramatized action of *The Wings of the Dove*. Whereas in *The Ambassadors* Strether *learns* to lie, in *The Wings of the Dove* each of James's centers of consciousness is seen to manipulate the other on the basis of hiding what in this more self-consciously semiotic novel may be the truth. The "truth" in this novel is inaccessible, or more radically, unavailable in terms of a present/absent dichotomy. Milly hides the secret of her illness so successfully that even after she dies neither the reader nor the other characters can be sure of what caused her death. It is on the grounds of this mysterious illness that she looks on, with distance and yearning, at the life she thinks she is destined to miss. She looks primarily at Densher, but also at Densher and Kate, in the Gallery scene, for example, where her fantasy of a lover's tryst is much more self-evident than that of Strether's in James's previous novel. For their part, Kate and

Densher hide their engagement, and may be lying to Milly when they encourage her to think that Densher is attracted to her.

All three are concerned with maintaining fictitious appearances that will hide their secrets, so that in this context the idea of Densher marrying Milly in order to make what might be her short life happy is not unequivocally immoral. That Milly's money might eventually make Kate and Densher happy together is not necessarily a reason for depriving Milly of her desired husband. Whether the money is onus or bonus is difficult to say, since when Milly finally dies, Densher might well be in love with her memory. Like Strether in *The Ambassadors,* Densher renounces desire at the end of *his* story: he renounces both Kate and the money Milly has left him. And as in the case of *The Ambassadors,* it is impossible to determine here whether this renunciation stems from a moral scruple or an aesthetic retreat. Milly's death might be taken as an ultimate retreat, but in leaving Densher her money she might be understood to affirm the beauty of an aesthetic design from which she, by definition, is excluded. The secrets of the novel are seen to generate situations that simultaneously express truth and falsehood, and thus prohibit any disentanglement of the moral from the aesthetic.

Finally, in *The Golden Bowl,* although Maggie tells a lie as do her fictional forebears of James's major phase, the novel does not end with renunciation but with Maggie's affirmation of her desire for the Prince and of her engagement in the life of desire. Having discovered that her husband and her stepmother are lovers, Maggie spies on them through the window of the terrace at Fawns. Parallel to Strether, Maggie also experiences the limitations of her previous mode of perception; like Strether, her confidence in the absolute presence of categories like "good" and "evil" is shattered. She too recognizes, in this scene, her implication in a system of signification that cannot be reduced to simple opposites. Charlotte, the Prince, and Adam are only playing cards, but the way James represents this scene highlights its connection with the scenes of desire in the two previous novels, and explicitly foregrounds the desire that structures the spectator's participation. In looking at the others, Maggie constructs and recognizes herself through her desire for her husband and her love for her father. Her gaze is interrupted when Charlotte, her husband's mistress, emerges to challenge her. This is the moment of Maggie's lie: she publicly embraces Charlotte and disavows any knowledge of the adultery. Dramatized as being a direct result of the preceding scene of spying, Maggie's lie is seen as her self-conscious generation of a fiction that will enable her to manipulate appearances, and thereby manipulate Charlotte, her husband, and her father. The word "fiction" in fact shares its Latin origin with the infinitive "fingere," to form or to figure, and with the word for counterfeiting. Maggie's lie is a species of fiction generated from her experience as an outside observer. This specular experience is what enables her to move inside the area of conflict and struggle, and to engage her self through her desire for the other, her Prince. Whereas the characters in *The Ambassadors* and *The Wings of the Dove* remain encapsulated within their own consciousness, where they thus remain subject to the dangers of skepticism, in *The Golden Bowl,* through Maggie, James dramatizes the possibility of mutual recognition and acknowledgment of the other, thus suggesting an escape from what amounts, in Cavellian terms, to radical skepticism.

The ethical moment lies in the very capacity of a Milly or a Maggie, or even a Kate (imaginative descendants of Madame Merle and James's earlier corrupt aesthetes), to generate fictions that become the grounds of their ethical action. These characters of James's late novels succeed in crossing, and crossing out, the lines of demarcation between melodramatic villain and hero.

Through an exploration of the issue of representation, then, James exposes the problematics implicit in the traditional assumptions of the mimetic novel. Not only does he subvert the given forms of the work of art as an imposed coercive structure, an irreducible frame, or even as a copy or imitation of something else but, through the aesthetic/ethical moment, he also reaffirms the necessity for social engagement and thus social form. The whole tissue of selfhood (and the self's relations with the other) is seen as an interlocking set of relations characterized by the lack of an organizing essence. The spectating self emerges through its enmeshment in this network and through the ethical moment of its relation to others. The touchstone of this relation is the reading of others in ways that are least solipsistic, namely, in ways that most recognize and acknowledge the desire of the other. Such recognition takes place within a field of fiction that can take into account the fictions of the other, and the desire of the other that generates such fiction. The scene of desire is the scene of fantasy, and James recognizes and acknowledges the presence of unconscious desire that disrupts the self and can never be directly recognized or acknowledged.

The fictional worlds of *The Ambassadors, The Wings of the Dove,* and *The Golden Bowl* are generated from within an awareness of the inescapability of the problematic intrinsic to representation, and their conclusions are organized by an enabling lie, which in *The Golden Bowl* finally celebrates the capacity to tell or accept an untruth, a fiction. In all these works, the ethical is implicated in the aesthetic in that the terms and forms of social life have to be generated and regenerated through the creative activity of representation, the activity of fiction making.

Notes

Chapter 1. Representation in the Late Novels

1. The phrase "the ordeal of consciousness" is taken from James's preface to *The Wings of the Dove*. He is describing Milly Theale: "the case prescribed for its central figure a sick young woman, at the whole course of whose disintegration and the whole ordeal of whose consciousness one would have quite honestly to assist" (Henry James, *The Art of the Novel: Critical Prefaces* [New York: Charles Scribner's Sons, 1962], 289).

2. In his essay "Henry James" Ezra Pound writes of James's work as expressing "the rights of the individual against all sorts of intangible bondage!" in *Literary Essays of Ezra Pound* (London: Faber and Faber, 1963), 296.

3. Dorothea Krook, *The Ordeal of Consciousness in Henry James* (Cambridge: Cambridge University Press, 1967). This influential study is part of a long and distinguished tradition that situates James's fiction in an ethical, and ultimately redemptive, context.

4. Merle A. Williams, *Henry James and the Philosophical Novel: Being and Seeing* (Cambridge: Cambridge University Press, 1993), provides a succinct account of recent studies that consider James's achievement in terms derived from different philosophical schools. Williams attempts to avoid the pitfalls of reducing literature to "the subordinate role of clarifying, extending and supporting philosophical enquiries" (20) by tracing the overlapping nature of James's fiction and philosophy. Her claim is that "James's novels enact a predominantly phenomenological approach to human phenomena, but one tempered by Derridean reservations, and interspersed with deconstructive digressions. This subtle admixture becomes the characteristically Jamesian enterprise of fiction as philosophy" (11).

5. The selection of papers in *Allegory and Representation: Selected Papers from the English Institute, 1979–80* (n.s, no. 5., ed. Stephen J. Greenblatt [Baltimore and London: Johns Hopkins University Press, 1981]) presents a wide range of different contemporary theoretical approaches to the subject of representation. Stephen Greenblatt's preface (vii.xiii), offers a lucid and succinct summary of the main issues at stake.

6. Jeanne Campbell Reesman, *American Designs: The Late Novels of James and Faulkner* (Philadelphia: University of Pennsylvania Press, 1991), characterizes the late novels thus: "At issue is the philosophical preference for knowledge defined as hermeneutics, or knowledge as a group of interpretations, over epistemology, or knowledge as a single truth" (x). While I find her definition of epistemology somewhat narrow, I agree with her formulation that what James seems to be calling for is a "hermeneutic moral community" (82).

7. This problem is perhaps most acutely encountered in *The Sacred Fount* (1901).

8. Stanley Cavell, *The Claim of Reason* (Oxford: Oxford University Press,

1979). Cavell's strategy for escaping the dangers of radical skepticism involves the recognition and acknowledgment of the other, and is relevant for my discussion of the late James.

9. In 1901, Harry Thurston Peck expressed his outrage at James's circumlocutions in *The Sacred Fount* with the following memorable statement: "[James] really seems to be sinking into a chronic state of periphrastic perversity," in *Henry James: The Critical Heritage*, ed. Roger Gard (London: Routledge & Kegan Paul, 1968), 308. Roger Gard's collection of contemporary reactions to James's work provides many further adverse contemporary responses to his late style.

10. F. O. Matthiessen identifies the last three completed novels, *The Ambassadors, The Wings of the Dove,* and *The Golden Bowl,* as belonging to what he calls James's "major phase," in *Henry James: The Major Phase* (New York: Oxford University Press, 1963).

11. Peter Brooks, *The Melodramatic Imagination: Balzac, Henry James, Melodrama, and the Mode of Excess* (New Haven: Yale University Press, 1976), 15.

12. Shlomith Rimmon, *The Concept of Ambiguity: The Example of James* (Chicago: University of Chicago Press, 1977), is the most rigorous contribution to an understanding of Jamesian ambiguity. In the theoretical part of her study she aims at a "delimitation of the term *ambiguity* to cover only the relation obtaining between mutual exclusives" (xi). She writes that "'double meaning' or 'multiple meaning' do not call for choice, while 'ambiguity' simultaneously calls for choice and makes it impossible" (14). While Rimmon emphasizes both the necessity and the impossibility of choosing between mutually exclusive meanings (17), and thus contributes a theory which illuminates a central aspect of the Jamesian text, the question of meaning itself remains intact within an overall albeit problematicized mimetic framework.

13. For a fuller explication of this problem, see J. Hillis Miller, "The Figure in the Carpet," *Poetics Today* 1.3 (spring 1980): 106–109; the reply, Shlomith Rimmon-Kenan, "Deconstructive Reflections on Deconstruction: In Reply to Hillis Miller," *Poetics Today* 2 (1980): 185–88; and the response to that reply, J. Hillis Miller, "A Guest in the House: Reply to Shlomith Rimmon-Kenan's Reply," *Poetics Today* 2.1 (1980): 189–91. All references to James's texts are to editions in the list of primary sources.

14. Adrian Poole, *Henry James* (New York and London: Harvester Wheatsheaf, 1991), suggests this connection with the later works.

"'Representation' is a key word in the novel (along with 'exhibition'). Nick jokes about its different senses when he remarks on the unlikelihood of his constituents appreciating his representing them on canvas as much as his representing them in Parliament. There seems an absolute incompatibility between the two kinds of activity. Yet the novel does propose a term that stands half-way, as it were, between the 'public life' pursued by a politician or a diplomat and the 'artistic life' pursued by a painter. The term is 'theatre', and it is here that the novel conducts its wittiest examination of the boundaries that supposedly separate the practices of public and private or political and artistic life." (75)

15. In *The Golden Bowl* the finger-post that should provide orientation in fact fails to do so. It is interesting to note Dickens's similar use of the image of the finger-post. In *Great Expectations,* rather than provide direction, the finger-post is hidden in mist and confuses Pip.

16. Howells is credited with coining the phrase "international novel." See Wil-

liam Dean Howells, "Mr. Henry James, Jr. and His Critics," *Literary World* 13 (14 January 1882): 10.

17. James expresses his sense of America's lack of tradition in his comments on Hawthorne. For a very interesting selection of James's discursive writing on the problematic relationship between America and Europe see the section "The Writer and His Culture," in *Theory of Fiction: Henry James,* ed. James E. Miller, Jr. (Lincoln: University of Nebraska Press, 1972), 45–61.

18. For a review of the history of this criticism, see Tony Tanner, "Introduction," in his *Henry James: Modern Judgements* (London: Macmillan, 1968), 11–41.

19. Phillip Rahv would appear to disagree with such a view: "Europe is romance and reality and civilization, but the spirit resides in America," but his use of the concept of "spirit" might in fact support my claim that America is associated with concepts invoking essences ("Attitudes Toward Henry James," in *The Question of Henry James,* ed. F. W. Dupee [New York: Henry Holt, 1945], 280).

20. This would seem to be a standard romantic trope or topos. In Wordsworth's "Ode to Duty," duty—imaged as "Stern Lawgiver"—"doth preserve the stars from wrong," and we are told by the editor of the Norton Anthology that this is a reference to Kant's imaging of the categorical imperative: "Two things fill the mind with ever new and increasing admiration and awe . . . the starry heavens above and the moral law within" (*The Norton Anthology of English Literature,* vol. 2, 3rd ed. [New York: Norton, 1974], 183). It is interesting to note that in German, Stern means star, so that Wordsworth's figure of the "Stern Lawgiver," which "preserves the stars from wrong," would appear to undermine its desired authority in a self-reflective turn.

21. Providing a full account of Derrida's thought is beyond the scope of the present book. The implications of logocentrism, found everywhere in Derrida's work, are clearly formulated in Jacques Derrida, *Of Grammatology,* trans. Gayatri Chakravorty Spivak (Baltimore: Johns Hopkins University Press, 1982).

22. This figure, already known to classical rhetoric, is given the name *occupatio praeterito.* For a lucid discussion of the strategy of writing under erasure and its origins in Nietzsche and Heidegger see Gayatri Spivak's preface to *Of Grammatology.* She describes Derrida's notion of *sous rature* as "the mark of the absence of a presence, an always already absent present, of the lack at the origin that is the condition of thought and experience" (xvii).

23. For Derrida, logocentrism, the ascription of "presence" or an originary status to the word, is neither a mistake nor an accident. In his critique of logocentrism, Derrida stresses the unavoidability of constructing a notion of origin without which interpretation would be impossible.

24. Mary Cross describes *The Ambassadors* in terms appropriate for Charlotte's situation: "*The Ambassadors* is a story of signifiers, a narrative of the process of denomination by which words categorize the world. The names for things, especially for his experiences, give Strether . . . great trouble. . . . It is his triumph, eventually, 'to find the names,' only to discover that they do not settle anything; the signifiers are in motion and the process of denomination keeps coming undone." *Henry James: The Contingencies of Style* (London: Macmillan, 1993), 100.

25. Jacques Derrida, "Differance," in *Speech and Phenomena And Other Essays on Husserl's Theory of Signs,* trans. David B. Allison (Evanston: Northwestern University Press, 1973), 129–30. In this essay Derrida attempts to describe the strategy that would do away with the untenable hierarchical duality of pres-

ence and absence. He coins the term "differance"—among others such as "itera-tion," "supplement," and "dissemination"—to suggest the way presence is always deferred and different from itself. In *Positions* (trans. Alan Bass [Chicago: Univer-sity of Chicago Press, 1981], 27), he says: "Differance . . . is a structure and a movement no longer conceivable on the basis of the opposition presence/absence."

26. In her wonderful chapter on *The Golden Bowl*, Susan Winnett offers an insight on Charlotte's status as a stand-in artist. "When James constructs a novel-istic world whose code of behavior excludes those incapable of obeying its laws, he is endorsing the cohesive and generational power of a fiction of closure within the world he is creating without necessarily condoning its code. . . . On the other hand, however, its compositional necessity does not diminish its arbitrariness, and James's prose repeatedly documents the disjunctions between his chosen medium of representation—an artificial world of artifice—and the more properly natural passions that play themselves out within its boundaries." *Terrible Socia-bility: The Text of Manners in Laclos, Goethe, and James* (Stanford, CA: Stanford University Press, 1993), 173.

27. de Man formulates the problem thus: "Language is not an instrument or tool in man's hands, a submissive means of thinking. Language rather thinks man and his 'world'." Harold Bloom, Paul de Man, Jacques Derrida, Geoffrey Hart-man, J. Hillis Miller, *Deconstruction & Criticism* (New York: Continuum, 1979), 224. Michel Foucault in "What is an Author?" addresses the status of the author and sees him as a function of the discourse in which he is situated: "it is a matter of depriving the subject (or its substitute) of its role as originator, and of analyzing the subject as a variable and complex function of discourse," *Textual Strategies: Perspectives in Post-Structuralist Criticism*, ed. Josué V. Harari (London: Meth-uen, 1979), 158.

28. Percy Lubbock, *The Craft of Fiction* (New York: Viking, 1973); F. W. Dupee, *Henry James* (New York: Doubleday, 1956); Matthiessen, *Henry James*.

29. Charles R. Anderson, *Person, Place, and Thing in Henry James's Novels* (Durham, NC: Duke University Press, 1977), agrees that James "salvaged from his disaster [in the theater] the method of scenic construction" (175).

30. Gerard Genette, *Narrative Discourse* (Oxford: Basil Blackwell, 1980), ar-gues with Booth's conception of the Jamesian technique of showing (in *The Rheto-ric of Fiction*) when he discusses the problematics of mimetic narrative: "the very idea of *showing*, like that of imitation or narrative representation . . . is com-pletely illusory: in contrast to dramatic representation no narrative can 'show' or 'imitate' the story it tells. All it can do is tell it in a manner which is detailed, precise, 'alive,' and in that way give more or less the *illusion of mimesis*—which is the only narrative mimesis for this single and sufficient reason: that narration, oral or written, is a fact of language, and language signifies without imitating" (163).

31. Genette denies "internal focalization": "Indeed, the very principle of this narrative mode implies in all strictness that the focal character never be described or even referred to from the outside, and that his thoughts or perceptions never be analyzed objectively by the narrator," *Narrative Discourse*, (192). Although conceding that it is rarely total, Genette cites Strether in *The Ambassadors* as an example of internal focalization (189), and cites Roland Barthes's approach to what the latter calls the *personal* mode of narrative: "According to Barthes, this criterion is the possibility of rewriting the narrative section under consideration

into the first person . . . without the need for 'any alteration of the discourse other than the change of grammatical pronouns'" (193).

As I argue in my chapter on *The Ambassadors*, it might be that *The Ambassadors* cannot be considered to employ a personal mode of narration even in Barthes's seemingly liberal sense. However, what seems to be important is that the reader does not have access to an authority outside of Strether's represented consciousness. See David Carroll, *The Subject in Question: The Language of Theory and Strategies of Fiction* (Chicago: University of Chicago Press, 1982), for a discussion of the dramatic scene and its implications for the concept of point of view and the issue of the subject. He devotes an entire chapter, entitled "The (Dis)Placement of the Eye ('I'): Point of View, Voice, and the Forms of Fiction," to an extremely thorough discussion of the problem of point of view in James. Carroll shows how point of view is organized in James by centers of consciousness; Carroll uses Derrida to deconstruct this concept. His strategy is to move from a discussion of James himself in the prefaces, on to Lubbock and Booth to show how "James's point of view on point of view can hardly be considered a point at all" (66). For an extremely nuanced and wide-ranging discussion of narrative techniques see Dorit Cohn, *Transparent Minds: Narrative Modes for Presenting Consciousness in Fiction* (Princeton: Princeton University Press, 1978).

32. Moshe Ron provides a definition of the structure of *mis en abyme* and examines the way this figure problematizes mimetic narrative. He describes *mis en abyme* "as an iconic figure peculiar to narrative" and defines it as follows: "Any diegetic segment which resembles the work where it occurs, is said to be placed *en abyme*." "The Restricted Abyss: Nine Problems in the Theory of *Mise en Abyme*," *Poetics Today* 8 (1987): 436. See Shoshana Felman, "Turning the Screw of Interpretation," *Literature and Psychoanalysis: The Question of Reading Otherwise*, ed. Shoshana Felman (Baltimore: Johns Hopkins University Press, 1982), 94–207, for an analysis of how the motif of reading and writing produces the problematic structure of *mis en abyme* in "The Turn of the Screw."

33. Aware of the impossibility of any interpretation not being "interested," John Carlos Rowe writes: "An *interested* reading is what we would teach; we ought to learn how we might use Henry James in our own acts of understanding, focused not merely on the pyramidal outlines of his monument but on the color, tone, and animation of our images," *The Theoretical Dimensions of Henry James* (Madison: University of Wisconsin Press, 1984), 16.

34. Many of James's late stories, such as "In the Cage" and "Papers," revolve around different aspects of the problematic of writing. In the opening chapter of *Theoretical Dimensions*, Rowe deals extensively with this issue in terms of a semiotic theory similar to that suggested here. Susanne Kappeler, *Writing and Reading in Henry James* (New York: Columbia University Press, 1980), devotes a full-length study, informed primarily by structuralist theory, to this motif in James.

35. In a deconstructive mode, J. Hillis Miller affirms the ethical dimension in reading in general, and in James's late work in particular. See *The Ethics of Reading: Kant, de Man, Eliot, Trollope, James and Benjamin* (New York: Columbia University Press, 1987), 120–22. In his examination of the problem of ethics in James, with a particular emphasis on *The Ambassadors*, Myler Wilkinson shows how his reading of *The Ethics of Reading* helps him conclude: "The ethical moment in James . . . is simply the determination to go on reading and make meaning as carefully and truthfully as is humanly possible," "Henry James and the Ethical Moment," in *The Henry James Review* 11.3 (fall 1990): 172.

36. For instance, Ross Posnock associates James's notion of reification with

that of the critical theorists of the Frankfurt School and combines this with a Lacanian concept of the subject. Posnock writes that in James, "the absolute subject has already been demystified. Consistent with his indifference to origins, James neither believes in a moment prior to reification, from which man is exiled and nostalgic for return, nor does he imagine the self triumphing over alienation. Rather identity itself is bound up with alienation," "Henry James, Veblen and Adorno: The Crisis of the Modern Self," *Journal of American Studies* 21 (1987): 31. In his discussion of *The American Scene,* Posnock addresses the issue of aestheticism and ethics as he writes: "I don't read that work as evidence of a nervous aesthete's flight from modernity but rather as a sustained and sympathetic engagement that at once explores, accepts and critiques the 'ravage' of the American scene" (32).

37. In 1926, Ezra Pound identified the paramount importance of the theme of freedom in James's work: "Yet I have heard no word of the major James, of the hater of tyranny; book after early book against oppression, against all the sordid petty personal crushing oppression, the domination of modern life . . . human liberty, personal liberty, the rights of the individual against all sorts of intangible bondage. . . . What he fights is 'influence,' the impinging of family pressure, the impinging of one personality on another; all of them in highest degree damn'd, loathsome and detestable" (*Literary Essays,* 296). Echoing Pound, Maurice Beebe writes that "for James, the worst of crimes was the aggressive exploitation or appropriation of another human being," "The Turned Back of Henry James," in *Henry James: Modern Judgements,* ed. Tony Tanner 87. Even a work such as *The Princess Casamassima,* which explicitly deals with a cell of underground revolutionaries bent on liberating the working classes, is in fact concerned with the individual struggle of one of its members, Hyacinth Robinson, to achieve the freedom to shape his own life. In *The Bostonians,* where the subject is ostensibly the women's movement in Boston, much of our interest is in the way Verena Tarrant's life is subordinated to the conflicting desires of Olive Chancellor and Basil Ransome.

38. Ruth Bernard Yeazell notes that "Madame Merle, Kate Croy, and Charlotte Stant all share a striking family resemblance," but she distinguishes this group from a second group of victims that includes Isabel Archer, Milly Theale, and Maggie Verver. *Language and Knowledge in the Late Novels of Henry James* (Chicago: University of Chicago Press, 1976), 4. Leo Bersani's understanding comes closer to my own: "Throughout James's career . . . we find an almost necessary deduction of dishonesty from the art of appearances. The problem . . . is to find an alternative to Isabel Archer different from Madame Merle. Or, to put it another way, James has to recuperate Madame Merle morally by incorporating her into Isabel." *A Future for Astyanax: Character and Desire in Literature* (Boston: Little Brown, 1976), 136.

39. As early as 1882, William Dean Howells compared James to George Eliot in these terms: "with George Eliot an ethical purpose is dominant, and with Mr. James an artistic purpose." W. D. Howells, "Henry James Jr." (*Century Illustrated Monthly Magazine,* November 1882, iii, 25–29), in Gard, *Henry James: The Critical Heritage.* The opposition that Howells found is concisely formulated in Krook's *The Ordeal of Consciousness.* In her chapter on *The Golden Bowl* she writes: "the aesthetic and the moral, though intimately bound up with each other, are yet not the same; indeed they can even, in certain circumstances, be mutually exclusive" (243). For Krook, the Prince is "James's quintessential Aesthetic Man," defined as such by his thinking of himself as "the touchstone of taste"

(241). Krook views the aesthetic/moral opposition as one of the principal themes of the novel (271), which "is finally transcended [when the touchstone of taste is] incorporated into the moral . . . by Maggie Verver's love" (276). Stuart P. Sherman, "The Aesthetic Idealism of Henry James," in *The Question of Henry James,* (ed. F. W. Dupee [New York: Holt, 1945]) is one of many critics who would argue with Dorothea Krook. He thinks that the ethical becomes absorbed in the aesthetic. For him the problem is one of "noblesse": "The controlling principle is a sense of style, under which vice . . . loses half its evil by losing all its grossness" (87). A similar idea is suggested by Joseph Warren Beach who claims that the Ververs' obligation is "to translate the moral concept into the language of simple good taste." "The Figure in the Carpet," in *The Question of Henry James,* ed. Dupee 102. Hochman also sees an opposition between these two categories in James, which he formulates in terms of surface and depth. For Baruch Hochman, the categories remain distinct: "The ultimate limitation of [James's] art is his need to treat the world as sheer spectacle, to cleave to surfaces, to eschew the passional and therefore the moral depths." *The Test of Character: From the Victorian Novel to the Modern* (Rutherford, NJ: Fairleigh Dickinson University Press, 1983), 128–29. All the above critics construe the relation between aesthetics and ethics, no matter how problematic, in terms of a clash of essential categories.

40. In her basically Marxist approach, Carolyn Porter reinforces my sense of the significance of Maggie's status as spectator, although in her discussion of *The Golden Bowl* she generalizes the implications of this position: "Thus the romantic triumph of the visionary imagination to which Maggie's career testifies is achieved at the cost of exposing a world in which it is not merely the artist who is confined to the posture of a spectator; everyone is reduced to that position." *Seeing and Being: The Plight of the Participant Observer in Emerson, James, Adams, and Faulkner* (Middletown, CT: Wesleyan University Press, 1981), 136.

41. See two articles by Martha Craven Nussbaum for a profound discussion of the problem of ethics in James: "'Finely Aware and Richly Responsible': Literature and the Moral Imagination," *Literature and the Question of Philosophy* (Baltimore and London: Johns Hopkins University Press, 1987), 169–91, and "Flawed Crystals: James's *The Golden Bowl* and Literature as Moral Philosophy," *New Literary History* 15, no. 4 (1983); 25–50. See also Bersani, *A Future for Astyanax,* 132–33, for a discussion of James's emphasis on the issue of freedom as involving the generation of fiction.

42. Alexander Gelley, *Narrative Crossings: Theory and Pragmatics of Prose Fiction* (Baltimore: Johns Hopkins University Press, 1987), 159. In elaborating on the scene of desire that mobilizes the spectator's fantasy, Gelley notes his indebtedness to Freud's concept of primal scene, which he defines as "[the] term designated as a traumatic experience in the genetic development of the infant. The content of the experience might be variable—for example, viewing of parental coitus, seduction by an adult, threat of castration. But what is characteristic in every instance is the unstable position of the subject, both (or alternately) inside and outside the scene, as actor and viewer, as victim of a terrifying act and producer of the scene. It is through the analysis of this double structure of the scene that Freud developed his theory of fantasy. The fantasy is the product of an ongoing transformation of infantile traumatic experience, a process that makes this repressed psychic data available to consciousness in various figured or staged forms" (160).

43. ibid., p. 158.

44. ibid., p. 159. In a feminist argument that asserts Maggie's achievement, Chery B. Torsney rings further changes on the notion of the "specular." Maggie "moves from a position as an object, a commodity exchanged between men, a mystifying position indeed, to *the* subject of the novel." "Specular(riza)tion in *The Golden Bowl*," *The Henry James Review*, 12 (spring 1991): 145.

45. In his brilliant discussion of the late novels, David McWhirter notes: "Having found a way to liberate Milly Theale from the prison-house of desire, James can now allow Maggie Verver to consummate her predecessor's dream of loving and being loved," *Desire and Love in Henry James: A Study of the Late Novels* (Cambridge: Cambridge University Press, 1989), 147. In contrast, Alfred Habegger's study of James's attitude to women would seem to deny the possibility of any development in James's handling of his heroines. "Behind James's narratives there is found the ancient theory that women are weaker than men. . . . [They] have been lamed in secret by their author." *Henry James and the "Woman Business"* (Cambridge: Cambridge University Press, 1989), 26.

Chapter 2. Artist as Audience: *The Tragic Muse*

1. In Henry James, *The Art of the Novel: Critical Prefaces* (New York: Charles Scribner's Sons, 1962), 79.

2. Michael Anesko, *"Friction with the Market": Henry James and the Profession of Authorship* (New York and Oxford: Oxford University Press, 1986), notes that *The Tragic Muse* is "a lineal descendant of James's other large novels of the eighties—*The Bostonians* and *The Princess Casamassima*. Despite their dissimilar settings and subjects, all three books portray the conflict (as James said in *The Bostonians*) between the individual's 'genuine vocation' and society's 'hollow and factitious ideal'" (119). My approach in this chapter is to show how this novel prepares for the books of the major phase.

3. For an interesting discussion of the possible implications of James's phrase "I never 'go behind,'" see Eve Kosofsky Sedgwick, "The Beast in the Closet: James and the Writing of Homosexual Panic," in *Sex, Politics, and Science in the Nineteenth-Century Novel*, ed. Ruth Bernard Yeazell (Baltimore and London: Johns Hopkins University Press, 1986), 148–86.

4. The composition of *The Tragic Muse* (1890) comes between James's writing of such stories as "The Liar" (1889), "The Lesson of the Master" (1892), and "The Real Thing" (1893), stories that explicitly treat the theme of representation in art and literature and the equivocal nature of the artist's and novelist's role.

5. In the chapter entitled "The Scene is Primal," Philippe Lacoue-Labarthe, analyzes Freud's "Psychopathic Characters on the Stage" in order to explore "the relationship of psychoanalysis to theatricality, or more generally to *representation*" (99). The author posits that "there is a *reality* 'outside of representation'" (101) but insists on relating the "analytic *necessity* of the representational mechanism . . . exclusively to *desire* . . . ." (102). *The Subject of Philosophy,* ed. Thomas Trezise, trans. Thomas Trezise et al., (Minneapolis and London: University of Minnesota Press), 1993.

6. For a wide-ranging discussion of the problem of radical skepticism, its connection to solipsism and the issue of community, see Stanley Cavell, *The Claim of Reason.*

7. Reader-response has been theorized by many critics, chief among them Wolfgang Iser, Hans Robert Jauss, Norman Holland, and Stanley Fish. For an interesting account of reader-response criticism see Elizabeth Freund, *The Return*

of the Reader: Reader-Response Criticism (Methuen: London and New York, 1987).

8. In the context of examining James's developing response to the relation of fiction and history, which is to say his changing conception of the claims and status of fiction, Roslyn Jolly traces the connection between *The Tragic Muse,* on the one hand and *The Ambassadors* and *The Golden Bowl* on the other. "Through Miriam, James explored ways in which the historical contract set out in his early criticism, but challenged by the behavior of the characters in his early novels, could be replaced by a fictional contract resting on very different attitudes towards experience and imagination." *Henry James: History, Narrative, Fiction* (Oxford: Clarendon Press, 1993), 80.

9. For a comprehensive summary of the plot of *The Tragic Muse,* see Dorothea Krook, *The Ordeal of Consciousness,* 63–64. Krook writes: "The central theme of *The Tragic Muse* turns upon the conflicting claims of the world of art on the one side, the world of affairs on the other" (63).

10. Nick's statement about art—"any ground that's gained by an individual, any spark that's struck in any province, is of use and of suggestion to all the others. We are all in the same boat"—anticipates T. S. Eliot, "Tradition and the Individual Talent," in *Selected Essays* (Harcourt, Brace & World: New York, 1964).

11. I find support for my approach to *The Tragic Muse* in William R. Goetz, "The Allegory of Representation in *The Tragic Muse," Journal of Narrative Technique* 8 (1978). The entire essay (151–164) argues convincingly that *The Tragic Muse* is "an allegory *of* representation: a story about the different senses of 'representation' and their relevance to what the novel itself can do" (152). Goetz focuses on the allegorical dimension of James's novel, whereas I want to stress that James's approach albeit schematic, nevertheless exposes the problematics of representation and presents this as an existential issue.

12. Krook notes that *The Tragic Muse* "is the first of James's major works to deal almost exclusively with Englishmen, Englishwomen and English life. . . . The main emphasis throughout falls upon the English theme" (62). In *Henry James: The Critical Heritage,* Roger Gard provides a mixed selection of contemporary reviews, some of which confirm the novel's acuity in "getting" English life, and many others which suggest that James does not understand the English at all. Edwin Sill Fussell's book, *The French Side of Henry James,* (New York: Columbia University Press, 1990), as its title indicates, stresses the contribution and the significance of James's French experience. In his chapter on *The Tragic Muse* he notes: "The treatment of the English in *The Tragic Muse* is finally to be understood in the light of its being James' most French novel, hence in its range of reference his most aesthetic, aesthetic here meaning, anti-Philistine, anti-bourgeois" (126).

13. This sets up the motif of "sinful" Paris which James will develop considerably in *The Ambassadors.*

14. In his recent book, *Professions of Taste: Henry James, British Aestheticism, and Commodity Culture* (Stanford, CA: Stanford University Press, 1990), Jonathan Freedman suggests that "James's response to aestheticism had considerable impact on aestheticism itself, remaking or remodeling it in such a way as to prepare it for full entry into the cultural mainstream under the sign of modernism, negating its subversive play with a multitude of irresolute possibilities by—ironically enough—fulfilling its desire to achieve resolution through the valorizing of art" (xxvi); "James builds on the structures of British aestheticism to produce

the great work of aestheticist art that the aestheticist movement itself conspicuously failed to create—*The Golden Bowl*—and thence to help fashion the more austere aestheticism we call modernism" (170).

15. ibid., 168.

16. Nash's emphasis on "tone" finds an echo in James himself who in his preface insists on, and admits the difficulty of, addressing such a subject. "I may well be summoned to say what I mean in such a business by an appreciable 'tone' and how I can justify my claim to it—a demonstration that will await us later" (81). At the end of the preface James does indeed return directly to this subject albeit via a discussion of Nick Dormer: "No, accordingly, Nick Dormer isn't 'the best thing in the book,' as I judge I imagined he would be, and it contains nothing better, I make out, than that preserved unity and quality of tone, a value in itself" (97).

17. I will argue in the succeeding chapters that part of what characterizes James's development in the major phase is his capacity to conceive of the observer as a participant as well. In the later novels the very category of "observer" or "reflector" will be somewhat undone, as the observer is seen to play an increasingly active role in the events of the fiction he observes.

18. In the late novels, the violent rupturing of human relationships in history underlies the action of the novels. When in his final interview with her in Paris, Strether goes to see Madame de Vionnet, he notices the flagstones and considers how they might be stained with the blood of the French Revolution. In *The Wings of the Dove* Milly imagines a head bobbing at the window and thinks of the guillotine. In *The Golden Bowl* Maggie imagines that her head is on the block and identifies with the scapegoats and martyrs of history. None of these scenes is central to the works in which they appear but the potential violence of human relations is never far from the surface of James's work and often resonates through the theme of the French Revolution.

19. In *The Princess Casamassima* (1886), the anarchist Hyacinth Robinson's apostasy—he has sworn an oath to assassinate a noble—is dramatized as deriving from the sensitivity of his response to Parisian art and architecture. James emphasizes on the one hand the difficulty of appreciating (to the point of worship) the beauty of the achievements of the *ancien régime,* and on the other, the difficulty of dismissing the social system, no matter how unjust, that gave rise and expression to such beauty.

20. Mark Seltzer describes *The Tragic Muse* as "virtually an inventory of aesthetic and political modes of representation, and their entanglement." *Henry James and the Art of Power* (Ithaca: Cornell University Press, 1984), 155.

21. In the next chapter I show how this pun becomes part of the basis for exploring the problematic issue of representation in *The Ambassadors*.

22. Nick's language indirectly echoes Gloucester in *King Lear* 4.1.: "As flies to wanton boys, are we to th' gods/ They kill us for their sport." Later in the same paragraph Nick characterizes himself in the following words: "I'm a wanton variation, an unaccountable monster" (125–26). To my ear, in the context of Nick's feeling of victimization, there is an uncanny echo combining both *King Lear* and *King Oedipus*.

23. Adeline R. Tintner affirms Nick Dormer's status as James's spokesman: "*The Tragic Muse,* 1890, meets the typically British objection to art as something 'pardonable as long as it's done at odd hours' by proving that it represents the most serious and productive activity." "The Museum World," in *Henry James: A*

Collection of Critical Essays, ed. Leon Edel (Englewood Cliffs, NJ: Prentice Hall, 1963), 148.

24. Replying to his sister Alice's favorable response to *The Tragic Muse,* James does indeed seem to echo Nick's attitude to his public. "I have no illusions of any kind about the book, and least of all about its circulation and 'popularity.' . . . One must go one's way and know what one's about and have a general plan and a private religion—in short have made up one's mind as to *ce qui en est* with a public the draggling after which simply leads one in the gutter. One has always a 'public' enough if one has an audible vibration—even if it should only come from one's self." *Henry James: The Critical Heritage* (Gard, ed.), 194.

25. In her chapter on *The Tragic Muse,* Marcia Jacobson does not sufficiently distinguish between the different conceptions of representation that underlie James's characterization of Miriam and Nick. The result is that in her reading "the claims of art in the parallel plot are not adequately realized." *Henry James and the Mass Market* (Tuscaloosa: University of Alabama Press, 1983), 73.

26. William Macnaughton, in an article that examines the effects of the changes James made for the New York Edition of *The Tragic Muse,* emphasizes a similarity between Nick's and Miriam's attitudes to art: "In a way analogous to the actress Miriam Rooth, when Nick is captured by his talent it is impossible to separate the real from the spurious." "The New York Edition of Henry James's *The Tragic Muse,*" in *The Henry James Review* 13, no. 1 (winter 1992): 24. For a biography of Rachel Felix, the acclaimed actress who served as the model for James's fictional portrait of Miriam, see Rachel M. Brownstein, *Tragic Muse: Rachel of the Comédie-Française* (New York: Alfred A. Knopf), 1993.

27. There is a striking similarity between this description of the presentation of Miriam Rooth and the presentation of Milly Theale in *The Wings of the Dove.* In his discussion of Milly Theale in the preface to the New York Edition of *The Wings of the Dove,* among many cognate formulations James writes of his "instinct everywhere for the *indirect* presentation of his main image." *The Art of the Novel,* 306.

28. In the preface to the New York Edition, James writes: "I never 'go behind' Miriam; only poor Sherringham goes, a great deal, and Nick Dormer goes a little, and the author, while they so waste wonderment, goes behind *them*" (91). Kaja Silverman refers to this passage in the context of engaging Eve Kosofsky Sedgwick's article on James's homosexuality in "The Beast in the Closet." Silverman focuses attention on James's presentation of versions of "the primal scene" and claims that "[t]he Jamesian phantasmatic can . . . be said to enclose homosexuality within heterosexuality, and heterosexuality within homosexuality." She insists on the "sexual import" of this passage and thus links James's narrative technique with his sexuality. "Too Early/Too Late: Subjectivity and the Primal Scene in Henry James," *Novel* 21 (1988): 183; also in *Male Subjectivity at the Margins* (New York & London: Routledge, 1992), 167. In this more recent study, Silverman explicitly connects the *The Tragic Muse* with the dramatic scene and the primal scene. I find support in this argument for my more general assertion of the connection between this novel and the later work. I return to the issue of the "primal scene" in my final chapter.

29. H. E. Scudder—a brilliant, and favorable, contemporary reviewer—notes the felicity of James's presentation of the actress as though she were on stage: "It is a striking illustration of Mr. James's power of handling his material that from first to last Miriam Rooth is always seen *en face.* That is to say, though their author indulges in an analysis of his other characters, he gives the reader only a

front view of his heroine. When she appears she is on exhibition"; quoted in *The Critical Heritage*, (Gard, ed.), 216.

30. Dorothea Krook *(The Ordeal of Consciousness)* remarks a different dimension of James's use of the indirect method when she notes that Nick's election is described, "none of it directly, all of it by its effects" (73). However, Krook is careful to distinguish *The Tragic Muse* from James's later work as "not at all 'difficult'" (62). For Krook, *"The Tragic Muse, like The Bostonians* and *The Princess Casamassima,* is much more directly in the mainstream of the contemporary English tradition—the fictive art practiced by Thackeray, Dickens, George Eliot—than are the works of James's late period" (64n). Alan W. Bellringer, *Henry James* (London: MacMillan, 1988), does not appreciate James's experiment in the handling of his narrative: "Using the omniscient-author technique in *The Tragic Muse,* James is inclined to be defensive and evasive as he declines to follow his characters out of view into their jobs and other essential activities" (77).

31. At least one contemporary reviewer of *The Tragic Muse* is not taken in by James's "indirect" presentation of Miriam Rooth. "It is the actress who has the most body . . . who is, in fact, the most human of the party. She has some force, and above all some *directness,* which is not given to the others." *The Critical Heritage*, (Gard, ed.), 195.

32. The problem of what constitutes the "real" is repeated in *The Ambassadors,* when Miss Barrace laughs at Strether's insistence on reaching an underlying truth. "Oh, I like your Boston 'really's'" (132). See the next chapter for a fuller analysis of this issue.

33. In his brilliant discussion of a characteristically American concern with the theater and theatricality and how this bears on the idea of stable selfhood, Ross Posnock, using *Henry James: Autobiography* (ed. F. W. Dupee [New York: Criterion, 1956] (452), notes that James "is less concerned with role playing organized by a centered self than with putting in question the notion of this anchoring self. Because this core self, what Henry James calls 'prime identity,' begins and ends 'with itself' and has 'no connections and suggests none,' it remains static and homogeneous. In contrast, a heterogeneous, theatrical self 'bristles' with the mobility and impurity of internal difference, of something not wholly itself but infiltrated by 'a different mixture altogether'." *The Trial of Curiosity: Henry James, William James, and the Challenge of Modernity* (New York and Oxford: Oxford University Press, 1991), 58.

34. I find widespread confirmation for this point in Joseph Litvak's brilliant chapter on *The Tragic Muse:* "just as Miriam's spectacularly inclusive orbit conjoins the aesthetic with the journalistic and the commercial, so her transgression of the line between the stage and the audience figures the power of theatricality to render problematic the very division between art and 'the world' that the counterplot seeks to maintain." *Caught in the Act: Theatricality in the Nineteenth-Century English Novel* (Berkeley: University of California Press, 1992), 260.

35. This would seem to be James's restatement of Keats's "negative capability."

36. In *Deceit, Desire, and the Novel: Self and Other in Literary Structure,* trans. Yvonne Freccero (Baltimore and London: Johns Hopkins University Press, 1965), René Girard uses a Freudian model to show how desire is mediated through a third party. Sherringham's desire for Miriam is often dramatized as emerging when he becomes aware of how others value her, in this instance Madame Carre, but both Basil Dashwood and Nick Dormer are cast in similar roles.

37. Miss Tressilian, a minor character, gives expression to this thought most

directly when, with a degree of incredulity, she asks: "You don't mean to say that Mr Sherringham wanted to *marry* her!" (527). Miss Tressilian is referring of course to the fact that Miriam Rooth is an actress.

38. It might be possible, in a crude formulation, to imagine that Miriam is simply exploiting Peter. A similar ambiguity might be thought to organize the plot of *The Wings of the Dove,* where the question of love is inextricably connected to the question of self-interest.

Chapter 3. The Story of the Story: *The Ambassadors*

1. An earlier version of this chapter was published as "*The Ambassadors:* The Story of the Story," in *Hebrew University Studies in Literature and the Arts* 12 (1984): 85–115.

2. For an essay that focuses on the "visual and diplomatic representation of a character or appearance to another" see Joanna A. Higgins, "The Ambassadorial Motif in *The Ambassadors*," *The Journal of Narrative Technique* 8 (1983): 165–75.

3. Julie Rivkin adopts a position similar to my own when she writes that an examination of Strether's role "requires a shift in the ground of critical discussion from questions of morality or character . . . to questions of representation or delegation." "The Logic of Delegation in *The Ambassadors*," *PMLA* 101 (1986): 819. Rivkin's essay, like my own, is indebted to Derridean theory, and her strategy of exposition is much like mine; she gives no indication of having read my essay. For a more traditional approach to the question of embassy see William Goetz, *Henry James and the Darkest Abyss of Romance* (Baton Rouge: Louisiana State University Press, 1986): "The title of the novel already indicates that Strether appears not in his own capacity but one in a series of substitutable representatives of another agent. This agent is specifically Mrs. Newsome, though sometimes it is designated by extension as 'Woollett.' Later in the novel, Woollett is represented by the Pococks. . . . Strether must now be replaced because he has failed to represent the interests and intentions of Woollett, as embodied in Mrs. Newsome, faithfully. Strether must serve two masters at once, as it were: he represents James as well as Mrs. Newsome, and only by misrepresenting the latter's intentions can he loyally serve the author by achieving the dramatic tension and irony on which the novel is based" (193). Carren Kaston's view of the "ambassadorial mission" comes closer to my own. She writes: "In *The Ambassadors* (1903), James continued to explore the connections between consciousness, selfhood, and authorship by developing . . . the metaphor of ambassadorial mission. Through the metaphor of the ambassador, the novel encompasses a study of substitutive or second-hand agency, a type of unoriginal relation to the world in which Strether's absence from himself inevitably traps him." *Imagination and Desire in the Novels of Henry James* (New Brunswick, NJ: Rutgers University Press, 1984), 82–83.

4. Philip Grover writes: "Throughout *The Ambassadors* we are given experiences, not in the form that *anyone* would receive them, but in the form that they are perceived by a specially sensitive and consciously articulate mind. What is there *could* be perceived by others than Strether, but the important fact is that for the most part it is not. Only Maria Gostrey—and to a lesser extent Little Bilham—help him and save him from solipsism." *Henry James and the French Novel: A Study in Inspiration* (London: Paul Elek, 1973), 174.

5. In *The Notebooks,* James recalls a conversation between Jonathan Sturges

and William Dean Howells, who had exhorted Sturges: "Oh, you are young, you are young—be glad of it: be glad of it and *live*." (226)

6. This is Jonathan Culler's formulation of the deconstructionist application of Saussure's theory, in *Saussure* (Glasgow: Fontana, 1976), 111.

7. In his article "The Figure in the Carpet," J. Hillis Miller addresses this problem. He writes: "The infinity and hence impossibility of the narrator's task reforms itself, then, within the arbitrarily closed line which was drawn to make the infinite finite" (106–109). Note in this connection James's well-known remark in the preface to *Roderick Hudson:* "Really, universally, relations stop nowhere, and the exquisite problem of the artist is eternally but to draw, by a geometry of his own, the circle within which they shall happily *appear* to do so." *Roderick Hudson* (New York: Harper & Brothers, 1960), 8. See also Shlomith Rimmon-Kenan's response in "Deconstructive Reflections on Deconstruction" (185–88).

8. For a brilliant discussion of *The Ambassadors* that stresses that "[t]he fact of difference is the one positive term" in this novel, see Ross Posnock, *The Trial of Curiosity* (222). Cautioning her readers against the dangers of reading too much into James's use of the word "difference," Millicent Bell writes that "It is tempting, though not at all necessary, to give 'difference' . . . a deconstructive sense that James could not have intended, as a pun upon deferral indefinitely prolonged." *Meaning in Henry James* (Cambridge, MA, and London: Harvard University Press, 1991), 327. Nicola Bradbury explicitly reads James's late novels under the sign of *differance;* she seeks to show how "James's technique, shifting from *The Ambassadors* into *The Wings of the Dove* . . . explores the possibilities of balancing closure (the sense of an ending) against *differance* (endless change) in the celebration of absence as a positive joy through the text." "'Nothing that is not there and the nothing that is': The Celebration of Absence in *The Wings of the Dove*," in *Henry James: Fiction as History,* ed. Ian F. A. Bell (London: Vision Press and Barnes & Noble, 1985), 87.

9. E. M. Forster, *Aspects of the Novel* (London: Edward Arnold, 1958), 140.

10. Julie Rivkin uses Derridean theory to formulate the same point: "The supplement, like the ambassador, is a stand-in supposed to alter nothing of that which it stands for; it is defined as an addition having no effect on the original to which it is being joined. Yet the existence of the addition implies that the original is incomplete and in need of supplementation; the paradoxical logic of supplementarity is that what adds onto also subtracts from this example to all representation and argues that there is no original presence outside supplementation." "The Logic of Delegation," 819.

11. James's success in "employing but one centre" has been the subject of much critical debate. Joseph Warren Beach, Percy Lubbock, and Richard P. Blackmur, for example, all argue for James's success in creating a single fictional point of view, whereas others such as John E. Tillfor and Joan Bennett take issue with the above and note instances of authorial omniscience. Franz K. Stanzel points out several passages of free indirect style that "[suggest] the author rather than the character as its source." F. K. Stanzel, *A Theory of Narrative,* trans. Charlotte Goedsche (Cambridge: Cambridge University Press, 1984), 35. A representative sample of this debate has been included in *Twentieth Century Interpretations of "The Ambassadors,"* ed. Albert E. Stone, Jr. (Englewood Cliffs, NJ: Prentice-Hall, 1969).

12. John Carlos Rowe makes a similar point in *The Theoretical Dimensions of Henry James* (Madison: University of Wisconsin Press, 1984). In his discussion of Heidegger he writes that "Heidegger provides an excellent philosophical justi-

fication for a power (political or metaphysical) that would claim its authority by virtue of its dispersion and displacement. Henry James's writings both anatomize the subversive power of this sort of social artistry and are implicated in the general rhetoric of such artistry by virtue of their appeal to literary ambiguity. Many of James's fictional donnés depend upon the absence or effacement of the actual social and economic authorities. Mrs. Newsome's authority in *The Ambassadors* is a function not only of her absence from the dramatic action but also of Strether's insistence upon his independence from her ambassadorial charge" (123).

13. It is interesting to note that words like "presence," "difference," and even "plentitude," used here in connection with James's critique of the primacy of the spoken voice, all become key terms in Jacques Derrida's critique of what he takes to be the logocentrism underlying Western metaphysics. (Derrida's term is "plenitude.")

14. "The long convoluted sentences also reflect this desire for plenitude, for there is seemingly no gap in the continuity of the psychological scene in the late James: cause and effect are endlessly analyzed in the effort to achieve some knowledge of a particular situation, although actual comprehension or decisive action on the part of the central consciousness is rare." Donna Przybylowicz, *Desire and Repression: The Dialectic of Self and Other in the Late Works of Henry James* (Tuscaloosa: University of Alabama Press, 1986), 296.

15. In his story "In the Cage" (1898), published three years before he finished writing *The Ambassadors*, James explores the subject of telegraphy via his protagonist, a young woman working in a post-and-telegraph cage; her experience of life is primarily via the telegrams she sends for others. Eventually disappointed with her vicarious life, the girl decides to marry.

16. In *The Golden Bowl* the association of writing with tricks and magic is further strengthened. See my discussion in chapter 5.

17. In his preface to *The Golden Bowl* James asserts the connection between writing and doing: "the whole conduct of life consists of things done, which do other things in their turn, just so our behaviour and its fruits are essentially one and continuous and persistent and unquenchable, so the act has its way of abiding and showing and testifying, and so, among our innumerable acts, are no arbitrary, no senseless separations. The more we are capable of acting the less gropingly we plead such differences; whereby, with any capability, we recognize betimes that to 'put' things is very exactly and responsibly and interminably to do them. Our expression of them, and the terms on which we understand that, belong as nearly to our conduct and our life as every other feature of our freedom; these things yield in fact some of its most exquisite material to the religion of doing" (25). J. Hillis Miller, in *The Ethics of Reading* (102–22), uses James's explicit reading of himself in this preface to argue for the connection between writing and reading and ultimately to argue for the way that reading can produce ethics.

18. For a description of what can be understood by this Lacanian phrase, I recommend Anika Lemaire, *Jacques Lacan* (London: Routledge & Kegan Paul, 1977). She writes: "Lacan will insist upon the fact that socio-cultural and linguistic symbolisms impose themselves with their structures as orders which have already been constituted before the *infans* subject makes his entry into them. The young child's entry into the symbolic order will fashion him in accordance with structures proper to that order" (6).

19. I quote in full a passage from Richard P. Blackmur's "The Loose and Baggy Monsters of Henry James," which argues for James's concern with personal rela-

tions: "The extremes with which Henry James was obsessed had largely to do with the personal human relations and almost nothing at all to do with public relations except as they conditioned, marred, or made private relations. It may be said that James wooed into being—by seeing what was there and then going on to create what might be there in consciousness and conscience—a whole territory of human relations hitherto untouched or unarticulated. I do not say not experienced, only unarticulated. So excessive is this reach into relation, there is no escape possible for the creatures caught in it except by a deepening or thickening of that relation until, since it cannot be kept up, it must be sacrificed." In *Twentieth Century Interpretations of "The Ambassadors,"* ed. Albert E. Stone, Jr. (Englewood Cliffs, NJ: Prentice Hall, 1969), 51.

20. William Veeder, *Henry James—The Lessons of the Master: Popular Fiction and Personal Style in the Nineteenth Century* (Chicago: University of Chicago Press, 1975), analyzes this passage to describe James's late style and to show how he succeeds in "sustaining the illusion of mental processes in *The Ambassadors.*" Veeder's argument, which I find persuasive, is that James can create the illusion of Strether thinking "only if he can generate an analogous process in us. The very presence of an initial metaphor or negation will impel us farther into the passage for elucidation. The eventual literal or positive statement does not, in turn, function as a simple authorial explanation. We can escape our initial puzzlement only by joining the metaphoric and literal or negative and positive elements together in our minds. Our minds are made to move, to jump like a spark across a dark gap. We ourselves create that relationship, that connection, which is meaning" (213–14).

21. Kaston comments on this passage: "Through verbal conundra, among the most sophisticatedly indefinite of the arts of conversation, Maria Gostrey, little Bilham, and Chad teach Strether to postpone his need for fixed knowledge. Evading him without precisely lying to him, they put forward a form of truth that Strether has later to acknowledge is only a "technical lie." To put it another way, artful, even deceptive, speech and manners may enlarge the possibilities of the real and the right. *The Ambassadors* thus represents a . . . stage of reconciliation of the dialectic in James between style and substance, artfulness and trustworthiness, surface and depth." *Imagination and Desire,* 84–85.

22. For an excellent discussion of the dialogue in this novel see Ruth Bernard Yeazell, *Language and Knowledge.*

23. Peter Smith traces James's development from *The Princess Casamassima* to *The Ambassadors.* "Like Hyacinth Robinson, Lambert Strether is lured by the beauty of a foreign lady—this time a countess, Mme de Vionnet—whose attractions are again the human form of the general beauty of Paris. Strether also feels the constraining tug of morality. Indeed, the struggle waged between his developing taste and his preconceived duty is just as fierce as it had been for Hyacinth, but the most telling aspect of its presentation is no longer a buried and symbolically conceived fable. Now the struggle informs a humourous surface, one which remains humourous and is still connected to the whole even when the depths of seriousness have been disclosed. Once more we see a man being undone by beauty, and once more we are witnesses to an erosion of moral content which leaves only a pleasant-seeming husk behind." *Public and Private Value: Studies in the Nineteenth-Century Novel* (Cambridge: Cambridge University Press, 1984), 149.

24. Lyall H. Powers thinks that James's metaphor of the stage "expresses . . . the distressing fact that Strether will not see life for what it really is, will see it—

prompted with all the good will in the world—as a picture or a play upon a stage." *Henry James and the Naturalist Movement* (East Lansing: Michigan State University Press, 1971), 176.

25. I find partial support for this in Rowe: he finds that James's criticism of Trollope applies as much to James as to Trollope. In "Anthony Trollope" James is critical of Trollope's "suicidal satisfaction in reminding the reader that the story he was telling was only, after all, a make-believe," in *The Future of the Novel: Essays on the Art of Fiction,* ed. Leon Edel (New York: Random House, 1956), 258. But Rowe says of James himself that he "always exposes his fiction. . . in the fundamental assumption of the *textuality* of experience. . . . James's social dramas are built on the basic philosophical assumption of a world in which the only objects for understanding are the always already interpreted texts of social convention. James supersedes romantic pictorialism by substituting his 'portraits' and 'objects d'art,' whose formal coherence and visual immediacy would seem to be tokens of art's substitution of human forms for the sheer facticity of nature. Following unwittingly and unwillingly in the footsteps of Emerson and American transcendentalism, James goes further to expose these 'objects' as mere masks, which betray the complex process of composition and signification that lurk behind their self-evident and seemingly uncomplicated surfaces." *The Theoretical Dimensions of Henry James,* 71–72. Whereas I agree with Rowe about James's "assumption of the *textuality* of experience," I think that James is reacting to American transcendentalism. Rowe's use of the word "lurk" with all its negative connotations suggests unexamined assumptions, on his own part, of counterpossibilities.

26. Ian Watt, "The First Paragraph of *The Ambassadors:* An Explication," in *Twentieth Century Interpretations,* 75–87.

27. George E. Smith, "James, Degas, and the Modern View," adds an interesting dimension to our understanding of James's awareness of what will later be conceptualized as "intertextuality" when tracing Degas's influence on James: "And as James matured and moved closer to his preoccupation with psychological narrative, he would surely be alive to Degas' continued use of the centre of consciousness, which, as Degas matured became extreme, as evidenced in the later pastel nudes, known for their "keyhole" effect. So what I am suggesting is that in Degas James recognized the full range of possibilities for his own narrative technique (including . . . that of the voyeur)." *Novel* 21 (1987): 64. See Rowe's interesting discussion of this scene in *The Theoretical Dimensions,* 198–99.

28. My formulation suggests a possible affinity between James and Wilde. Although an exploration of this subject is beyond the scope of this study, I refer the reader to Stephen Donadio's excellent book, *Nietzsche, Henry James, and the Artistic Will* (New York: Oxford University Press, 1978), in which the connection between all three writers is elaborated through the figure of Emerson; and to Jonathan Freedman's *Professions of Taste,* which explores the connection between Wilde and James in the context of modernism.

29. Baruch Hochman, *The Test of Character,* 128. Veeder comments on this passage to argue for a particular quality of the reader's involvement in the language of *The Ambassadors.* I quote him at length in order to do justice to his brilliant analysis of the process of reading.

"Here . . . our viewpoint is the character's. We move down through the passage, word by word, moment by moment, as Strether moves through Paris, event by event, day by day. Paris is cumulatively defined for us in our passage through the language as it is for Strether in his European sojourn. Initially we find our Puritan assumptions confirmed:

Paris is Babylon. This a priori notion soon begins to erode, however. After Paris has become an 'object' and then a 'jewel,' we discover that the jewel evinces not only the 'hard'ness which we expect but also the opposite traits of evanescence and amorphousness. What is 'hard' is not *hard,* and so becomes hard to define. Since what we are reading is itself a definition, we recognize that knowledge is less an a priori entity than an accretive process—Paris-Babylon-object-jewel-hard-not—and that even this process is not fully reliable because it remains open-ended and tentative. Nor does the next sentence restore convenient limits. After 'twinkled . . . trembled . . . melted' indicate that even so apparently undifferentiated a thing as evanescence can entail differences upon differences, we then experience the opposite lesson. Differences fail to occur where we might expect them: 'surface' interchanges with 'depth,' antonyms become synonymous. And our Puritan equation of Paris and Babylon seems simplistic indeed. By not merely presenting us with statements of a character's thought, by making us instead experience a mind ticking, James's style sets our minds in motion too. We are moved by Strether's situation because his words are our Paris. (*Henry James,* 2–3)

30. In his historicist study, Ian F. A. Bell situates James and his relation to the problem implied by "spectacle" in James's contemporary commodity culture: "Human assets become cultural commodities whose value resides in the transactions of social exchange: what are produced above all are modes of display and spectacle. . . . James's great achievement in the marketplace is to recognise the tensile relation between the prison *and* the liberation of the spectacle: his Romance recognises its own formal historicity by its witnessing and registration of consumption's practices at their early stages. James, in effect, advertises the advertisement of the history he lives through, the Romance of display, surface and performance." *Henry James and the Past: Reading into Time* (New York: St. Martin's Press, 1991), 13.

31. In a recent historicist essay that draws on Ian Bell's *Henry James and the Past,* Richard Salmon writes: "*The Ambassadors* is a novel that challenges our understanding of surfaces. Lambert Strether's sensory impressions of objects and social manners construe 'Paris' as the phenomenal site of a fraught epistemological venture. But this phenomenal vision, which registers the world as a spectacle, a self-conscious *mise en scène,* reproduces, at the same time, forms of commodity display that allow us to grasp the historical contingency of perception." In "The Secret of the Spectacle: Epistemology and Commodity Display in *The Ambassadors,*" *The Henry James Review,* 14.1 (winter 1993): 43.

Chapter 4. The Story of the Fabulous Center: *The Wings of the Dove*

1. Representative of those critics who argue for James's connection with melodrama are Peter Brooks, *The Melodramatic Imagination,* and Jacques Barzun, "Henry James, Melodramatist," in *The Question of Henry James,* ed. F. W. Dupee, 261–73. See my discussion of this point in chapter 1.

2. The imagery used to describe Milly connects her with the "dove" of the title of the novel. Krook attempts to establish the connection between James's choice of title and Psalm 55: "My heart is sore pained within me: and the terrors of death are fallen upon me. Fearfulness and trembling are come upon me, and horror hath over-whelmed me. And I said, Oh that I had wings like a dove! then I would fly away, and be at rest." For Krook, Milly is the tragic heroine of the novel who descends into the world in order to redeem it (*The Ordeal of Consciousness in Henry James,* (195). Quentin Anderson is another critic who sees Milly

as the redeeming dove of the title: "Milly Theale's case is that of the domesticated, the naturalized, the explicable redeemer." For Anderson, the central experience of the novel has to do with the way Milly the dove effects Densher's redemption. *The American Henry James* (New Brunswick, NJ: Rutgers University Press, 1957), 233.

3. Whereas critics like Krook and Anderson identify Milly as the heroine of the novel, for F. R. Leavis the central protagonist is Kate. In his essay "The Later James," Leavis says that "[Milly] isn't there, and the fuss the other characters make about her as the 'Dove' has the effect of an irritating sentimentality." For Leavis, Kate's "resoluteness . . . appears to us as partly admirable: the pressures driving her—her hateful outlawed father, the threatening fate represented by her married sister's overwhelming domestic squalors, the inflexible ambition of her magnificently vulgar aunt, Mrs. Lowder—are conveyed with such force as to make them seem, for a person of such proud and admirable vitality, irresistible. Henry James's art, that is, has a moral fineness so far beyond the perception of his critics that they can accuse him of the opposite." *The Great Tradition: George Eliot, Henry James, Joseph Conrad* (London: Chatto & Windus, 1962), 159–60.

Daniel Mark Fogel is representative of those critics who see Densher's transformation as "the central dramatic action in *The Wings of the Dove*. He moves, in Blakean terms, from innocence to organized innocence, and his journey follows the Romantic paradigm of spiral return. Densher begins in the refreshing but too-simple innocence of his first love for Kate Croy, passes through a period of complicity in Kate's plot against Milly Theale, and at last, under the spell of Milly's forgiveness, rises in a mood of blessedness and renunciation to a transcendent, informed innocence." *Henry James and the Structure of the Romantic Imagination* (Baton Rouge: Louisiana State University Press, 1981), 57.

In his excellent article, Lee Clark Mitchell also attempts to avoid designating a central character but rehabilitates what he takes to be Kate's bad reputation. He argues "that censure of Kate misrepresents the novel, which achieves a suspended vision of her." "The Sustaining Duplicities of *The Wings of the Dove*," *Texas Studies in Literature and Language* 29 (1987): 188. Leo Bersani stands out in his refusal to designate a hero. "*The Wings of the Dove* [is] a drama of blurred identities in which the real hero is a narrator-center responsible to other people only in his appreciations." *A Future for Astyanax*, 145.

4. For an example of how contemporary narrative theory can illuminate the complexities of James's use of centers of consciousness, see Linda Raphael, "Levels of Knowing: Development of Consciousness in *The Wings of the Dove*," in *The Henry James Review* 11.1 (winter 1990): 58–71.

5. Yeazell writes: "Never knowing to what literal disease Milly Theale succumbs, we may assume that she dies of betrayal; almost as easily, however, we may choose to believe that what kills Milly in the end is not the lovers' ambiguously kind deception, but Lord Mark's brutal truth. We might in fact go even further, and question how deceptive Kate and Densher finally are—especially since Densher does genuinely fall in love with the American girl. It is a measure of the fluidity of James's world that we find it so difficult to know where we stand, either morally or epistemologically. In such a world, to see Kate Croy's language solely as lies would indeed be a failure of vision." *Language and Knowledge in the Late Novels*, 84.

6. Virginia C. Fowler also recognizes the ambiguous status of Milly's health in the unfolding of the novel: "although the novel's very plot can be enacted only by virtue of the other characters' conviction that Milly does suffer from a fatal

illness, equal importance is placed, in part through the mysterious and ambiguous treatment of her disease, on the spiritual deficiency that unfits Milly for life." "Milly Theale's Malady of Self," in *Novel* 14 (1980): 58.

7. I agree with Paul Armstrong when he writes that with Conrad and Ford, James helps "inaugurate the self-consciousness of the modern novel about signs and interpretation by shifting the focus of the genre from constructing lifelike worlds to exploring the dynamics of world construction." *The Challenge of Bewilderment: Understanding and Representation in James, Conrad and Ford* (Ithaca: Cornell University Press, 1987), ix.

8. James, *The Art of the Novel,* 294.

9. Sheila Teahan also deals with the images of James's preface to *The Wings of the Dove,* focusing specifically on the medallion image. In a more radical reading she claims that this image suggests that "the work of art is paradoxically founded on a necessary blindness to its own way of being." "The Abyss of Language in *The Wings of the Dove,* in *The Henry James Review* 14.2 (spring 1993): 212.

10. See James, *The Art of the Novel,* 288. (Page numbers in the following quotations refer to this work.)

11. Jacques Derrida addresses the problematic concept of center in "Structure, Sign, and Play": "Henceforth, it was necessary to begin thinking that there was no center, that the center could not be thought in the form of a fixed locus but a function, a sort of nonlocus in which an infinite number of sign-substitutions came into play. This was the moment when language invaded the universal problematic, the moment when, in the absence of a center or origin, everything became discourse—provided we can agree on this word—that is to say a system in which the central signified, the original or transcendental signified, is never absolutely presented outside a system of differences. The absence of the transcendental signified extends the domain and the play of signification infinitely." *Writing and Difference* (London: Routledge and Kegan Paul, 1978), 280. John Carlos Rowe, "Structure," in *Critical Terms for Literary Study,* eds. Frank Lentricchia and Thomas McLaughlin (Chicago and London: University of Chicago Press, 1990), 23–38, examines the concept of structure in a historicist perspective, finally emphasizing its exchange value in an industrial economy. For a discussion of Derrida's "Structure, Sign, and Play," in a study that attempts to reconcile deconstruction and aestheticism, see Jonathan Loesberg, *Aestheticism and Deconstruction* (Princeton: Princeton University Press), 1991, 89–91.

12. James, *The Art of the Novel,* 306.

13. Fowler argues for a connection between Milly and James's cousin Minny Temple through an emphasis on what is unusual in both: "a close analysis of the text reveals that Milly Theale is doomed as much by her own psychology as she is by her illness; furthermore, this psychology which renders her in some way unfit for life and yet which also reflects a spiritual purity that has redemptive effects on others actually and accurately points to James's ambiguous feeling about Minny Temple." "Milly Theale's Malady," 59.

14. Elizabeth Allen comments on Susan Shepherd's romantic vision in the following: "The temptation to 'interpret' Milly, to search for a meaning in her wealth and freedom, is epitomized by Susan, with her literary and aesthetic approach to life, her tendency to label, to generalize and to see the likeness/portrait more clearly than the person." *A Woman's Place in the Novels of Henry James* (London: Macmillan, 1984), 159.

15. In the course of a discussion of James's shorter fiction, Tzvetan Todorov,

The Poetics of Prose (trans. Richard Howard [Ithaca: Cornell University Press, 1977]) argues that

> The Jamesian narrative is always based on *the quest for an absolute and absent cause.* Let us consider the terms of this phrase one by one. There exists a cause: this word must here be taken in a very broad sense; it is often a character but sometimes, too, an event or an object. The effect of this cause is the narrative, the story we are told. It is absolute: for everything in this narrative ultimately owes its presence to this cause. But the cause is absent and must be sought: it is not only absent but for the most part unknown; what is suspected is its existence, not its nature. The quest proceeds; the tale consists of the search for, the pursuit of this initial cause, this primal essence. The narrative stops when it is attained. On one hand there is an absence (of the cause, of the essence, of the truth), but this absence determines everything; on the other hand there is a presence (of the quest), which is only the search for an absence. Thus the secret of Jamesian narrative is precisely the existence of an essential secret, of something not named, of an absent and superpowerful force which sets the whole present machinery of the narrative in motion. The motion is a double and, in appearance, a contradictory one (which allows James to keep beginning over and over). On one hand he deploys all his forces to attain the hidden essence, to reveal the secret object; on the other, he constantly postpones, projects the revelation—until the story's end, if not beyond. The absence of the cause or of the truth is present in the text—indeed, it is the text's logical origin and reason for being. The cause is what, by its absence, brings the text into being. The essential is absent, the absence is essential. (145)

In my reading of *The Wings of the Dove* the state of Milly's health becomes equivalent to what Todorov calls the present absence. Frank Kermode's *The Genesis of Secrecy: On the Interpretation of Narrative* provides me with further support for such an interpretation in that Kermode argues—to my mind successfully—that secrets breed narrative and narrative breeds further narrative (Cambridge: Harvard University Press, 1979).

16. In an extremely interesting study of *The Wings of the Dove*, Allen (*A Woman's Place*) argues for a reading of Milly similar to my reading of Maggie in *The Golden Bowl:* she begins by comparing Milly to Hester in Hawthorne's *The Scarlet Letter.* Hester is "alienated from and marked by her society [and] develops her own resisting subjecthood in response to the awareness this alienation provokes. This subjecthood leads not to her rejecting the A she wears, but ultimately to her insisting on it to the extent that its significance is transformed" (146). In Allen's view "Milly moves from feeling that her subject existence is . . . obscured by her visibility as a sign" to sustaining the attention Densher bestows upon her "not through rejecting her function as a sign, but by reworking and augmenting it, and by letting him see that this is what she is doing. She presents herself as manipulating meaning for his benefit. Having accepted the determining factor of social naming, that what she is called she must in some sense be, . . . Milly becomes even *more* of a dove, of an American girl, so that her spectators are pulled further in than they intended to go" (146–7).

Rowe's essay on *The Wings of the Dove* is informed by a similar emphasis on post-structuralist linguistics but rather than focusing on Milly, as Allen does, he points to the more general problem of language in the late James.

> James's later novels announce not only the ambiguous world in which his characters are forced to live but the unstable nature of the linguistic signs as well. Trapped by conventional truths or acceptable realities, James's characters not only surrender their own individuality but also threaten the arbitrariness of the sign that assures the vitality of language. Thus, in the same sense that Milly Theale uses her life and death to disillusion

Kate and Densher about London society, James's later novels are concerned with the deconstruction of habitual modes of signification. Yet James does not offer his own discourse as an alternative for the reader, because his language is too intimately tied to the subject of his critique. By opening up the dead categories of social language, James offers the possibility of interpretative thought and renewed meaning. Thus he deftly skirts the dogmatism and didacticism he condemns so vigourously in many of his characters. (*Henry Adams and Henry James: The Emergence of a Modern Consciousness* [Ithaca: Cornell University Press, 1976], 168–69).

17. James, *The Art of the Novel*, 292.

18. In his preface to *The Wings of the Dove*, James discusses the difficulties of making his protagonist "sick" (ibid., 289); Charles R. Anderson seems to accept James at face value. He sees the lack of information on Milly's illness as a means of creating ambiguity in order to emphasize Milly's living rather than dying. *Person, Place, and Thing*, 190. Rimmon's formulation of this ambiguity is more fruitful: "The prospect of a mortal disease is necessary for the flowering of Kate's design, while the possibility of a 'psychological' illness is essential for the impact of Milly's tragedy, of her turning her face to the wall as a result of the betrayal. Hence an ambiguity 'resolved' only by the postulation of a psychosomatic disease *avant la lettre.*" *The Concept of Ambiguity*, 94.

19. Although Allen formulates this question of mystery in terms of a feminist critique, I do not see why the same dynamic should not apply to men: "in her relation to a reader, or male subject, if woman cannot discard the reading process altogether she can at least set up her own puzzle, make the man look at her on her own terms, even withhold or mystify the answer. Milly attempts to do this on a complex and powerful level. By making the puzzle personal, and suggesting that the clue to decipherment is personal, the attention is focused back on to the woman as signifier, rather than to easily determined meanings." *A Woman's Place*, 147. A further reservation about Allen's formula is the volitional aspect she attributes to the concealing or revealing of mystery. If woman is to be seen as signifier, then surely the process of signification would depend on a relationship to a system of signs that itself structures the signifier woman.

20. Daniel Schneider notes this image and shows how it is connected with "the motif of showing," which in *The Wings of the Dove* promotes the difficulty of distinguishing between appearances and reality. *The Crystal Cage: Adventures of the Imagination in the Fiction of Henry James* (Lawrence, KN: Regents Press, 1978), 110.

21. Yeazell formulates this problem in the following way: "to decide that Kate Croy is simply a hypocrite and a liar is to ignore her power as an artist—her power to reshape the world according to the demands of her imagination. By proclaiming Milly's desire to live 'wonderful' and 'beautiful,' Kate suppresses much that is sinister, but she also draws attention to all the wonder and beauty that may indeed be found in Milly's situation. Speaking so strongly of the 'beauty' which she sees, Kate almost makes her vision truth." *Language and Knowledge*, 82.

22. Mitchell supports my interpretation when he argues that "judged by consequences alone, [Kate] clearly does enrich others' experience—most notably in the extraordinary gift of life that results from her deception of Milly. Indeed, from this perspective, deceit appears less a tool of self-interest than a mode of artful generosity, and disapproval of Kate . . . seems far less appropriate than praise." Mitchell's argument focuses on how "mutual deceptions are made to appear at once noble and self-serving." "Duplicities of *The Wings of the Dove*," 188. Yeazell

makes the same point when she writes that "insofar as the lovers' plot encourages [Milly's] desire for life, it too may be called beautiful. For if Milly is irrevocably doomed to die, Kate and Densher have at least granted her the illusion of love—have allowed her to 'live,' as Strether would say, as long as she is able." *Language and Knowledge*, 83.

23. For a different view of the function of deception in *The Wings of the Dove* see Janet Gabler-Hover's article, "Truth and Deception: The Basis for Judgement in *The Wings of the Dove*," *Texas Studies in Language and Literature* 29 (1987), 170–71. Gabler-Hover argues that "a primary theme in *The Wings of the Dove* is a concern . . . for the underlying moral determinacy of language. . . . There is an expected organic relationship between language and the reality it reveals. . . . Indeed, *The Wings of the Dove* constitutes a rhetorical battle between two principal heroines for the love of a man. Both Kate and Milly use language to their own persuasive ends. The outcome of their battle reveals that for rhetorical eloquence, the truthful and persuasive functions of language must be compatible, in fact interchangeable: the most persuasive language is one that does not violate the truths of reality, for linguistic truth promotes both trust—the basis for meaningful relationships—and epistemological growth. . . . *The Wings of the Dove* presents a struggle between higher and lower forms of rhetorical art and argues profoundly for the humanistic necessity of truthful language."

24. Bersani notes Densher's transformation but understands the problems this involves: "Densher's paroxysm of moral scruples affects us as the creative strategy meant to veil the fact that we are no longer in the kind of novelistic world where such scruples would be relevant." *A Future for Astyanax*, 144.

25. In her brilliant and provocative chapter "Is the Rectum Straight?: Identification and Identity in *The Wings of the Dove*," Eve Kosofsky Sedgwick (*Tendencies* [Durham, NC: Duke University Press, 1993], 73–103), writes "with and against" Kaja Silverman's "Too Early/Too Late," arguing that the subject of this novel "is precisely the difference made by damaged origins—origins damaged by homophobia" (74). Kosofsky Sedgwick makes a convincing case for thinking that the cause for Lionel Croy's unnamed dishonor is his homosexuality, and goes on to argue that "the unexpected rhetorical possibilities . . . which specify the homosexual secret by failing to specify anything, . . . form a crux between starkly alternative, semantically 'full' and modernistically 'empty' readings of a single linguistic figure" (75). Her reading of the "medallion" image is used to support the same point (102–3). Kosofsky Sedgwick engages the question of origins to offer "one model for nonseparatist and at the same time antiheterosexist interpretations of sexual identity" (75).

26. Peter Brooks, *Reading for the Plot: Design and Intention in Narrative* (New York: Vintage Books, 1985), 144, suggests an interesting dimension that I do not deal with: "It would be worth making the argument that Henry James's heroines create a far more erotic bodily presence than has usually been allowed, especially those such as Kate Croy . . . and Charlotte Stant, . . . who use the body as power, and by that power indeed create the deviation of plot."

27. Kumkum Sangari's article, written with the concerns of post-colonialist discourse in mind, supports such an interpretation: "the question of the distribution of guilt and responsibility in *The Wings of the Dove* comes to revolve around "the similarity of the different" and the "possibility that *the ostensibly different is actually the same.* All the major characters . . . urge the conspiracy along because it fits in various ways with their own designs." "*The Wings of the Dove:*

'Not Knowing, But Only Guessing'," *The Henry James Review* 13, no. 3 (fall 1992): 293.

28. See chapter 2 for a discussion of Maria Gostrey's "pigeon-hole" imagination.

29. Adeline R. Tintner, *Henry James and the Lust of the Eyes: Thirteen Artists in His Work* (Baton Rouge and London: Louisiana State University Press, 1993), agrees with received opinion that "James meant the reader to think of Bronzino's portrait of Lucrezia Panciatichi" (95) as the portrait closely resembling Milly, and argues: "the portrait serves as both a mirror for Milly—making her aware of the possibilities of life and the almost courtly position she holds in her London set—and a prediction of her doom" (100).

30. In *The Insecure World of Henry James's Fiction: Intensity and Ambiguity* (London: Macmillan, 1982), Ralf Norrman focuses on aspects of James's style in the belief that "the style reflects the man" (1). He sums up the picture of the world that James presents in the word "uncertainty." In his brief and heavily ironic comments on the motif of letters in James he argues that James's use of ambiguity expresses this uncertainty. "Utterances in James should preferably not be uttered. Wills should not be read, instead one should speculate over their contents (*The Ivory Tower*). Letters should not be opened and read; it is much better to throw them unopened into the fire (*The Wings of the Dove*) or give them unopened to a friend ('Eugene Pickering'). That way one knows their contents much better than by reading them. Or does one?" (129). In "Proust, James and Le Désir de Venise," Tony Tanner deals with the issue of ambiguity in his analysis of the place of Venice in James's consciousness. He argues that James, after considering alternatives, chose Venice as the setting for Milly's death because "for James [Venice] was pre-eminently the city or two cities, of the great extremes—of all the hope and beauty of life, of the possibilities of art and passion; and all the sense of loss and despair, waste and belatedness. The city of ambiguous transformations, and degenerations—of the physical and the moral and spiritual world: of mortality and mercy." In *Journal of American Studies* 21 (1987): 25.

31. William W. Stowe sees this scene as expressing Milly's redemptive qualities: "Milly's nature and her value in the text and in Densher's life are defined not only by her actions and her intentions, not only by the observable effect of her words, but by her unknowable words themselves. Milly makes a difference, a difference Kate is beginning to understand and Merton can so far only feel. She does this not by fitting into the argument of the text, by providing a third alternative to two unsatisfactory views of the world, but by focusing the words and the images the text and its characters use, by paradoxically embodying freedom and servitude, life and death, by personifying the abyss, the holy spirit, even love itself, by being a princess and representing those 'two things' to which the text so often almost interchangeably refers, *everything* and *nothing*." *Balzac, James, and the Realistic Novel* (Princeton: Princeton University Press, 1983), 169.

Chapter 5. Such Abysses of Confidence: *The Golden Bowl*

1. In *The Wings of the Dove* we learn that in Milly's burnt and thus blank letter she left Densher her fortune. In the introduction to his book, *The Theoretical Dimensions*, Rowe notes the importance and the prevalence of the motif of letters which in James's work are, for one reason or another, inaccessible. Rowe sees this motif as part of James's problematizing of the very project he is engaged in—writing. In her discussion of the burnt letter in "The Turn of the Screw," Shoshana

Felman writes an interesting footnote concerning "the crucial importance of fire in Henry James's life, and its recurrent role, both real and symbolic, as a *castrating agent:* just as James's father lost a leg in attempting to put a fire out, James himself believed he had injured his back in the course of a fire, as a result of which he was afflicted for the rest of his life with a mysterious, perhaps psychosomatic back ailment." "Turning the Screw of Interpretation," 148.

2. The motif of cups and containers and the motif of light are discussed below.

3. "A literary text simultaneously asserts and denies the authority of its own rhetorical mode." Paul de Man, *Allegories of Reading: Figural Language in Rousseau, Nietzsche, Rilke, and Proust* (New Haven and London: Yale University Press, 1979), 17.

4. In an interesting analysis in his book on Thomas Eakins and Stephen Crane, Michael Fried addresses the "problematic of the *materiality* of writing" which he finds to be "simultaneously elicited and repressed: elicited because, under ordinary circumstances, the materiality precisely doesn't call attention to itself—in fact we might say it effaces itself—in the intimately connected acts of writing and reading; and repressed because, were that materiality allowed to come unimpededly to the surface, not only would the very possibility of narrative continuity be lost, the writing in question would cease to *be* writing and would become mere mark." *Realism, Writing, Disfiguration: On Thomas Eakins and Stephen Crane* (Chicago: University of Chicago Press, 1987), xiv. Maggie's invisible letter is hardly "ordinary" and does indeed both "call attention to itself" and "effac[e]" itself, thereby raising the general problematic of the status of writing.

5. In the context of a discussion of the "domination of linguistic form," Derrida writes: "To question the origin of that domination does not amount to hypostatizing a transcendental signified, but to a questioning of what constitutes our history and what produced transcendentality itself." He then discusses *differance* and the necessity of writing under erasure: "The necessity of passing through that erased determination, the necessity of that *trick of writing* is irreducible." *Of Grammatology*, 23–24. Maggie's trick writing is in this perspective expressive of the nature of writing itself.

6. Fawns is the summer home rented by the Ververs which is presented in the novel as the concrete embodiment of the English tradition that the Americans have come to Europe to acquire. For a discussion of the significance of the imagery of art and architecture in the novel, Laurence Bedwell Holland's chapter on *The Golden Bowl* is excellent; see his *The Expense of Vision* (Princeton: Princeton University Press, 1964), 331–37.

7. In his notebook, James wrote of his intention to write a story about a father and daughter who both became engaged, the father, a youngish widower, to a girl the same age as his daughter. The father marries "to console himself in his abandonment—to make up for the loss of his daughter, to whom he has been devoted." The basis for the subsequent complications would be the "intense and exceptional degree of attachment between the father and daughter—he peculiarly paternal, she passionately filial." The marriage would take place and the father and daughter would maintain their old interest while the husband of the one and young wife of the other would in turn be thrown together, with the father's second wife becoming "much more attractive to the young husband of the girl than the girl herself has remained." *The Notebooks of Henry James,* ed. F. O. Matthiessen and Kenneth B. Murdock (New York: Oxford University Press, 1961), 130–31.

8. In his preface to *The Golden Bowl* James notes "the endless worth for 'delight,' of the compositional contribution" of having two centers of conscious-

ness. "It is the Prince who opens the door to half our light upon Maggie, just as it is she who opens it to half our light upon himself." For James the very quality of illumination depends on this compositional structure. *The Golden Bowl*, 10–11.

9. Acquiring a prince is part of the Ververs' general project. For a fuller discussion of the ambiguity implicit in Adam Verver's acquisitive nature, see Edwin T. Bowden, *The Themes of Henry James: A System of Observation through the Visual Arts* (London: Archon, 1956), 101–104. For my discussion of the implications of aestheticism in James see chapter 1.

10. In his chapter on James, J. Hillis Miller *(The Ethics of Reading)* stresses the interpenetration of reading and writing as we read James himself writing about the experience of reading (109).

11. Tony Tanner identifies *The Golden Bowl* as a novel that subverts the conventions "by which the author pretended to know his gentle or not so gentle reader. . . . *The Golden Bowl* offers an exemplary case of how those same conventions are dissolved in a flow of metaphors that recognize no constraints." *Adultery in the Novel: Contract and Transgression* (Baltimore: Johns Hopkins University Press, 1979), 86–87.

12. In *The Pursuit of Signs: Semiotics, Literature, Deconstruction* (London: Routledge & Kegan Paul, 1981), in a chapter entitled "Story and Discourse in the Analysis of Narrative" (169–87), Culler uses the story of Oedipus to posit the following: "Instead of the revelation of a prior deed determining meaning, we could say that it is meaning, the convergence of meaning in the narrative discourse, that leads us to posit this deed as its appropriate manifestation. . . . [W]e can say that the crucial event is the product of demands of signification. . . . [M]eaning is not the effect of a prior event but its cause" (174). In a paragraph strikingly reminiscent of Derrida's paragraph from "Structure, Sign and Play in the Discourse of the Human Sciences" (quoted in chapter 1), Culler writes: "This logic by which event is a product of discursive forces rather than a given reported by discourse is essential to the force of the narrative, but in describing [*Oedipus Rex*] in this way we have certainly not replaced a deluded or incorrect model of narrative by a correct one. On the contrary, it is obvious that much of the play's power depends on the narratological assumption that Oedipus's guilt or innocence has already been determined by a past event that has not yet been revealed or reported. Yet the contrary logic in which Oedipus posits an act in response to demands of signification is essential to the tragic force of the ending. These two logics cannot be brought together in harmonious synthesis; each works by the exclusion of the other; each depends on a hierarchical relation between story and discourse which the other inverts. In so far as both these logics are necessary to the force of the play, they put in question the possibility of a coherent, noncontradictory account of the narrative. They stage a confrontation of sorts between a semiotics that aspires to produce a grammar of narrative and deconstructive interpretations which in showing the work's opposition to its own logic suggest the impossibility of such a grammar" (176).

13. Maggie in particular is clearly in some way a parallel—in others a development—of Milly, who is "heir of all the ages" in *The Wings of the Dove*.

14. For a discussion of what in Stanley Cavell's terms is the recognition of otherness, see chapter 1.

15. In what I judge to be too vague a formulation, Sallie Sears describes the reverie in which Maggie sees herself jumping from the coach as deriving from "the interlocking machinery of human guilt." *The Negative Imagination* (Ithaca: Cornell University Press, 1968), 169. See chapter 1, note 38, for Yeazell's and

Bersani's differing viewpoints on the importance of Charlotte's and the Prince's past relationship.

16. The parallel between Charlotte and Kate is brought out here; in *The Wings of the Dove* it is also an uncharacteristic intrusion by the narrator that established Kate's nobility. See chapter 4.

17. See my discussion of the dramatic scene in chapter 1.

18. In *Of Grammatology*, in the course of a discussion of writing, Derrida notes: "We are thus not blind to the visible, but blinded by the visible, dazzled by writing" (37). Although it would seem that it is not writing that blinds the Prince, he *is* blinded by the visible: his reference is to Poe's writing.

19. In the absence of such ground, morality becomes merely a function of intelligence. Fanny says that "stupidity pushed to a certain point *is*, you know, immorality. Just so what is morality but high intelligence?" (87). Fanny Assingham says of herself that she is a "double-dyed donkey." In equating morality with intelligence is she not acting, as a *triple*-dyed donkey, as her name implies: 1)Fanny; 2)Ass[ing]; 3)ham or ass?

In a discussion of Fanny Assingham's function in the novel, and her connection to the international theme, Ora Segal's chapter on *The Golden Bowl* makes the case that Fanny as the "*'usurping* consciousness'" (210) is "the true centre of interest" (209). *The Lucid Reflector: The Observer in Henry James's Fiction* (New Haven: Yale University Press, 1969), 170–210. For a discussion of the international theme and James's sense of America's lack of tradition see chapter 1.

20. Note that the Prince is bewildered by what for him is the "grotesque" capacity of the Ververs to conceive of him and his relationship with Charlotte as innocent: "as if a galantuomo, as *he* constitutionally conceived galantuomini, could do anything *but* blush to 'go about' at such a rate with such a person as Mrs Verver in a state of childlike innocence, the state of our primitive parents before the Fall" (252–53).

21. Mary Cross describes *The Ambassadors* in terms appropriate for Charlotte's situation: "*The Ambassadors* is a story of signifiers, a narrative of the process of denomination by which words categorise the world. The names for things, especially for his experiences, give Strether . . . great trouble. . . . It is his triumph, eventually, 'to find the names', only to discover that they do not settle anything; the signifiers are in motion and the process of denomination keeps coming undone." *Henry James: The Contingencies of Style,* 100.

22. See the discussion in chapter 3 of this image from James's preface to *The Ambassadors*.

23. Maggie's fictional relation to Isabel is clear here. In *The Portrait of a Lady* Isabel is also characterized, time and again, as wanting to experience at the same time that she is afraid of suffering.

24. The issue of fantasy is discussed in chapter 1.

25. In "Turning the Screw" Felman's discussion of seeing emphasizes the split sign: "*Seeing*, in other words, is of the order of the *signifier* (that which is perceived as a *conveyer* of signification, in the very *process* of signifying), while *knowing*, on the other hand, is of the order of the *signified* (that which *has been meant*: the accomplished meaning which, as such, is mastered, known, possessed). 'Knowing,' therefore, is to 'seeing' as the signified to the signifier: the signifier is the *seen*, whereas the signified is the *known*. The signifier by its very nature is ambiguous and obscure, while the signified is certain, clear, and unequivocal. Ambiguity is thus inherent in the very essence of the act of seeing. . . ." (156). At this point Felman uses Lacan's terms which claim that the

concept of knowledge is always in and of the Other, so that while knowing is not ambiguous in the ordinary sense, it is necessarily an alienated construct.

26. In her discussion of "The Turn of the Screw," Felman notes the opposition between a naive belief in the transparency of the sign, associated with Mrs. Grose who doesn't know how to read, and the "school of suspicion" associated with psychoanalysis (Felman ascribes this formula to Paul Ricouer). For Felman the school of suspicion is "*a school of reading*" (188) that teaches interpretation of signs, not by looking at them but by seeing through them. "'[S]uspicion' is directed . . . toward the non-transparent, arbitrary nature of the sign; it feeds on the discrepancy and distance which separates the signifier from its signified. . . suspicion constitutes, thereby, the very motive of the process of interpretation." (189–90).

27. Note that this image is from "The Beast in the Jungle" (1903), published in the same year as *The Ambassadors*. In this story John Marcher spends his life waiting for "[s]omething or other [which] lay in wait for him . . . like a crouching beast in the jungle. It signified little whether the crouching beast were destined to slay him or to be slain. The definite point was the inevitable spring of the creature" (497). In *Henry James: Selected Fiction,* ed. Leon Edel (New York: E. P. Dutton, 1964), 482–536. While in this story Marcher remains a passive subject of his fantasy and therefore misses life, Maggie in *The Golden Bowl,* written a year later, actively intervenes and does the springing herself. Jean Laplanche and Jean-Bertrand Pontalis, *The Language of Psychoanalysis* (trans. Daniel Lagache [London: Karnac Books, 1988]), define the term "Phantasy (or Fantasy)" as "an imaginary scene in which the subject is a protagonist, representing the fulfillment of a wish (in the last analysis, an unconscious wish) in a manner that is distorted to a greater or lesser extent by defensive processes" (314). In their discussion of phantasy, Laplanche and Pontalis point out that "phantasies are . . . scripts (scenarios) of organised scenes which are capable of dramatisation—usually in visual form." They conclude their discussion with the following: "In so far as desire is articulated . . . through phantasy, phantasy is also the locus of defensive operations: it facilitates the most primitive defense processes, such as turning round upon the subjects' own self, reversal into the opposite, negation and projection" (318). Maggie's "lust of the eye," her need to see, is the sign of unresolved primal scene fantasies, but unlike Marcher, she succeeds in engaging her fantasy.

28. Krook, in her chapters on *The Golden Bowl,* adduces much evidence to support her contention that it is the quality of Maggie's innocence that allows her to redeem a corrupt society through the transforming power of love (*The Ordeal of Consciousness,* (232–34). In contrast, Tony Tanner writes "there are those—many—who see Adam and Maggie as almost allegorical saviours and restorers of the crumbling relics and structures of European civilization, but that to me is too happy and facile a reading. There is too much awareness of the ambiguity of those forms which may be as ghastly as they are necessary . . . ; too much awareness that the new rearrangement rests on a felicitous deceit and a potentially ruthless power; too much sense of concealed evil, 'the horror of the thing hideously *behind*,' behind so much pretended, nobleness, cleverness, tenderness." *Henry James: The Writer and His Work* (Amherst: University of Massachusetts Press, 1985), 121.

29. Since Lacan's discussion of the gaze takes the split in the subject for granted, I shall use Gelley's formulation of Lacan's notion of the mirror stage, and its connection to the gaze, to recap material covered in my first chapter.

Gelley describes Lacan's theory thus: "the individual's awareness of self and world derives from a specular act whereby control and dependence, self-identity and objectification are inextricably linked. The child, in Lacan's model, sees itself seeing (in the mirror). It has before it the image of its sovereign gaze and at the same time of the dependent object of that gaze." *Narrative Crossings*, 166. Based on this theory of the mirror stage Jacques Lacan explains his idea of the gaze:

> the interest the subject takes in his own split is bound up with that which determines it—namely, a privileged object, which has emerged from some primal separation, from some self-mutilation. . . .
> In the scopic relation, the object on which depends the phantasy from which the subject is suspended in an essential vacillation is the gaze. Its privilege—and also that by which the subject for so long has been misunderstood as being in its dependence—derives from its very structure. . . . From the moment that this gaze appears, the subject tries to adapt himself to it, he becomes that punctiform object, that point of vanishing being with which the subject confuses his own failure. Furthermore, of all the objects in which the subject may recognize his dependence in the register of desire, the gaze is specified as unapprehensible. That is why it is, more than any other object, misunderstood, and it is perhaps for this reason, too, that the subject manages, fortunately, to symbolize his own vanishing and punctiform bar in the illusion of the consciousness of *seeing oneself see oneself*, in which the gaze is elided. (*The Four Fundamental Concepts of Psycho-Analysis*, trans. Alan Sheridan [Harmondsworth: Penguin, 1979]), 83.

In this scene we see Maggie *looking* at her father and her husband and her husband's mistress, who is also her father's wife, and trying to place herself in the scene she sees; instead she is positioned by her gaze and the fantasies it provokes of her own disappearance in the mirror she contemplates. In her brilliant book, *The Historical Eye: The Texture of the Visual in Late James* (Boston: Northeastern University Press,1991), Susan M. Griffin reexamines "the stock figure of the Jamesian perceiver" (3). Her analysis of Maggie in these terms supports a Lacanian reading. "Maggie's sights, whether structured domestic scenes or mental images that appear and reappear, reveal her growing awareness of herself as both creature and creator of her social environment. When the identity of the self is a function of the social environment, when knowledge is both visually acquired and displayed, seeing and being become strategies in the struggle to survive. Maggie's visual power demonstrates that the gaze is not exclusively male in James" (20).

30. John Alberti, "The Economics of Love: The Production of Value in *The Golden Bowl*," *The Henry James Review* 12, no.1 (winter 1991) citing James's preface to *The Princess Casamassima* (11), shares my emphasis on the social dimension of *The Golden Bowl*. "Aesthetically, James is interested in how consciousness shapes experience, and he defines experience as 'our apprehension and our measure of what happens to us as social creatures'; what is finally important for the characters in *The Golden Bowl* is not making an impossible separation of love, money, and art, but understanding how value systems in general are created and the economics of the risks and sacrifices they demand" (1).

31. My view of the meaning of the "horror of the thing hideously *behind*" is to be sharply distinguished from that of critics like Judith Woolf, who fix univocal interpretations. Woolf understands Maggie's sense of horror as a response to her husband's incest. *Henry James: The Major Novels* (Cambridge: Cambridge University Press, 1991), 142.

32. Dupee exonerates Maggie from moral censure in a well-turned phrase: "Maggie's fault does not make Charlotte's justification: it merely makes her op-

portunity." *Henry James*, (New York: Doubleday, 1956), 229. Despite the felicity of the formulation Dupee's remark remains within too simplistic a moral context. In discussing *The Golden Bowl* in *Adultery in the Novel*, Tanner writes that "almost everything takes place at the level of 'image' . . . which is the level at which the failed contracts have to be reconstructed and renegotiated; it is a level also of consciously fabricated lies both of utterance and repression—and this is the level at which the book has to be 'read.' I use quotes to indicate that reading has become interpretation in a new way" (86).

33. In his discussion of Maggie, J. A. Ward notes that "Maggie discovers that a form is preserved only as it is strained." *The Search for Form: Studies in the Structure of James's Fiction* (Chapel Hill: University of North Carolina Press, 1967), 219. Crews would seem to agree with Ward; he writes in connection with Maggie: "to observe decorum is tacitly, although often hypocritically, to admit that others are worthy of one's consideration. . . . There is no reason why social forms cannot be worked for good ends as well as evil ones." *Tragedy of Manners*, 83.

34. Tanner, writing of James's *A London Life* (1888) in *The Reign of Wonder* (Cambridge: Cambridge University Press, 1965) focuses on the motif of seeing and connects this both with James's "epistemological scepticism" and "a new morality of vision." I give the passage in full: "In concentrating on *A London Life* I have wanted to suggest that although James continually uses the innocent, the candid outside eye as a strategy he is not necessarily using it to enforce a facile condemnation of society. He took the untutored eye—so revered by the Transcendentalists—and subjected it to a dynamic, unprogrammed education. And watching the naive person assimilating, misconstruing, digesting, regurgitating, concentrating, omitting, as he or she was faced with the task of visually appropriating the world, James learnt something profound about the whole question of veridical knowledge, about the whole problem of verifying impressions. His study took him towards epistemological scepticism and towards a new morality of vision. . . " (277).

35. The term "humbug" appears in *The Wings of the Dove* in the context of Kate and Densher "humbugging" Mrs. Lowder. The derivation of this colloquial expression is unclear but since the word also refers to a particular kind of striped candy it would seem an attempt to sweeten the deceit it denotes.

36. Hugh Stevens, in "Sexuality and the Aesthetic in *The Golden Bowl*," *The Henry James Review* 14, no.1 (winter 1993), 63, argues: "Maggie's eventual assumption of agency involves an assertion of the sexual bond between her and her husband and a banishment of Charlotte, not only to American City but also, in a series of revealing fantasies, to the position of a savage, primal femaleness, the place of the 'other woman.'"

37. In what she describes as a "post-structuralist feminist perspective," Priscilla L. Walton sees Maggie as a "textual reviser . . . whose revisions constitute her means of opening the closed text of Book I. . . . Indeed, her methodology is in accord with the tenets of post-structuralist feminism since her revisions disrupt the masculine referentiality of Book I by privileging the pluralizing nature of the feminine Other in Book II." I share Walton's sense of Maggie's function as a "textual reviser," but remain unconvinced that this is solely a feminist prerogative. "'A mistress of shades': Maggie as Reviser in *The Golden Bowl*," *The Henry James Review* 13, no. 2 (spring 1992): 144.

38. As I note in chapter 1, the endings of all three of the novels discussed in this study are organized by lies of one sort or another. In his extremely illuminat-

ing chapter on *The Golden Bowl,* Crews understands the novel to be concerned with the subject of power and emphasizes "the problem of social causality." *The Tragedy of Manners,* 84. Crews is interesting on the subject of the struggle for power that occurs between the characters: Maggie's ability to impose her fiction on the others is an expression of her power. Sears describes Maggie's new awareness and her new tactics thus: "She has come full circle from faith in the reality of appearances to faith in their efficacy, a very different thing." *Negative Imagination,* 213. Charles Altieri, "From Expressivist Aesthetics to Expressivist Ethics," *Literature and the Question of Philosophy* ed. Anthony J. Cascerdi (Baltimore and London: Johns Hopkins University Press, 1987), 132–66, attempts in his extremely interesting article to reconcile a Kantian approach to ethics with the "social roles that can be played by aesthetic experience" (135). Altieri's project suggests some of the philosophical underpinnings that might support my own response to this novel.

39. There is an interesting parallel in the Prince's response to Poe's short story, "The Narrative of A. Gordon Pym"—his metaphoric self-blinding described through the closing of "the iron shutter of a shop" (both discussed above)—and his final words to Maggie: what it means for the Prince to see remains undecidable. For a discussion of the relationship between comedy and tragedy in James's work, see Ellen Douglass Leyburn, *Strange Alloy: The Relation of Comedy and Tragedy in the Fiction of Henry James* (Chapel Hill: University of North Carolina Press, 1968).

40. For an extremely interesting discussion of the imagery of the novel in this context, see Stephen Spender, *"The Golden Bowl"* in *The Question of Henry James,* 236–45.

41. For a discussion of the symbolism of the golden bowl and the way in which this symbolism works in the novel, see F. O. Matthiessen, *The Major Phase,* 91–104.

42. See p. 134 for explicit references to the Borgias and the poisoned cup.

Chapter 6. The Looped Garland

1. Matthiessen does note what he calls this "extraordinary passage" but misses much of its significance when he reads it exclusively as Maggie's recognition of "the pathos in Charlotte's situation." For Matthiessen it seems the piece is an expression of Charlotte's identity: she "has been brought up in Europe, [and] is 'of a corrupt generation'" *The Major Phase* (New York: Oxford University Press, 1963), 99–100.

Works Cited

Books by Henry James

A Little Tour in France. New York: Oxford University Press, 1984.

The Ambassadors. Boston: Houghton Mifflin, 1960.

The American Scene. Bloomington: Indiana University Press, 1968.

The American. Boston: Houghton Mifflin, 1962.

The Art of the Novel: Critical Prefaces. New York: Charles Scribner's Sons, 1962.

The Aspern Papers: The Spoils of Poynton. New York: Dell, 1971.

The Awkward Age. Harmondsworth: Penguin, 1976.

The Bostonians. New York: Random House, 1956.

The Complete Tales of Henry James. Ed. Leon Edel. London: Hart-Davis, 1964, 12 vols.

English Hours. Oxford: Oxford University Press, 1981.

The Europeans. Harmondsworth: Penguin, 1977.

The Future of the Novel: Essays on the Art of Fiction. Ed. Leon Edel. New York: Random House, 1956.

The Golden Bowl. Harmondsworth: Penguin, 1974.

Italian Hours. New York: Grove Press, 1979.

The Ivory Tower. London: Collins, 1917.

The Letters of Henry James. Ed. Percy Lubbock. New York: Charles Scribner's Sons, 1920, 2 vols.

Literary Reviews and Essays. Ed. Albert Mordell. New York: Grove Press, 1979.

The Notebooks of Henry James. Ed. F. O. Matthiessen and Kenneth B. Murdock. New York: Oxford University Press, 1961.

The Novels and Tales of Henry James. 'New York Edition'. New York: Charles Scribner's Sons, 1907–9. Rpt. 1962–5. 26 vols.

Parisian Sketches. New York: New York University Press, 1957.

Partial Portraits. Ann Arbor: University of Michigan Press, 1970.

The Portrait of a Lady. Boston: Houghton Mifflin, 1963.

The Princess Casamassima. New York: Harper & Row, 1964.

The Reverberator. New York: Grove Press, 1979.

Roderick Hudson. New York: Harper, 1960.

The Sacred Fount. London: Hart-Davis, 1959.

The Scenic Art. New York: Hill and Wang, 1957.

Selected Literary Criticism. Ed. Morris Shapira. Cambridge: Cambridge University Press, 1981.

176

The Sense of the Past. London: Collins, 1917.

Theory of Fiction. Ed. James E. Miller, Jr. Lincoln: University of Nebraska Press, 1972.

The Tragic Muse. Harmondsworth: Penguin, 1978.

Washington Square. New York: Bantam, 1959.

Watch and Ward. New York: Grove Press, 1979.

What Maisie Knew. Harmondsworth: Penguin, 1973.

The Wings of the Dove. Harmondsworth: Penguin, 1980.

Secondary Sources

Alberti, John. "The Economics of Love: The Production of Value in *The Golden Bowl.*" *The Henry James Review* 12, no. 1 (winter 1991): 9–19.

Allen, Elizabeth. *A Woman's Place in the Novels of Henry James.* London: Macmillan, 1984.

Altieri, Charles. "From Expressivist Aesthetics to Expressivist Ethics." In *Literature and the Question of Philosophy,* edited by Anthony J. Cascardi 132–66. Baltimore and London: Johns Hopkins University Press, 1987.

Anderson, Charles R. *Person, Place and Thing in Henry James's Novels.* Durham, NC: Duke University Press, 1977.

Anderson, Quentin. *The American Henry James.* New Brunswick, NJ: Rutgers University Press, 1957.

Anesko, Michael. *"Friction with the Market": Henry James and the Profession of Authorship.* New York and Oxford: Oxford University Press, 1986.

Armstrong, Paul. *The Challenge of Bewilderment: Understanding and Representation in James, Conrad and Ford.* Ithaca: Cornell University Press, 1987.

Barzun, Jacques. "Henry James, Melodramatist." In *The Question of Henry James,* edited by F. W. Dupee, 261–73. New York: Holt, 1945.

Beach, Joseph Warren. "The Figure in the Carpet." In *The Question of Henry James,* edited by F. W. Dupee, 107–19. New York: Holt, 1945.

———. *The Method of Henry James.* Philadelphia: Albert Saifer, 1954.

Beebe, Maurice. "The Turned Back of Henry James." In *Henry James: Modern Judgements,* edited by Tony Tanner, 71–88. London: MacMillan, 1968.

Bell, Ian F. A. *Henry James and the Past: Reading into Time.* New York: St. Martin's Press, 1991.

Bell, Millicent. *Meaning in Henry James.* Cambridge, MA, and London: Harvard University Press, 1991.

Bellringer, Alan W. *Henry James.* London: MacMillan, 1988.

Bersani, Leo. *A Future for Astyanax: Character and Desire in Literature.* Boston: Little, Brown, 1976.

Blackmur, Richard P. "The Loose and Baggy Monsters of Henry James." *Twentieth Century Interpretations of "The Ambassadors,"* edited by Albert E. Stone, Jr., 49–56. Englewood Cliffs, NJ: Prentice Hall. 1969.

Bloom, Harold, Paul de Man, Jacques Derrida, Geoffrey Hartman, J. Hillis Miller. *Deconstruction & Criticism.* New York: Continuum, 1979.

Booth, Wayne C. *The Rhetoric of Fiction.* Chicago: University of Chicago Press, 1969.

178   "A THING DIVIDED"

Bowden, Edwin T. *The Themes of Henry James: A System of Observation through the Visual Arts.* New Haven: Yale University Press, 1956.

Bradbury, Nicola. "'Nothing that is not there and the nothing that is'": The Celebration of Absence in *The Wings of the Dove.*" In *Henry James: Fiction as History,* edited by Ian F. A. Bell, 82–97. London: Vision Press and Barnes & Noble, 1985.

Brooks, Peter. *The Melodramatic Imagination: Balzac, Henry James, Melodrama, and the Mode of Excess.* New Haven: Yale University Press, 1976.

———. *Reading for the Plot: Design and Intention in Narrative.* New York: Vintage Books, 1985.

Brownstein, Rachel M. *Tragic Muse: Rachel of the Comédie-Française.* New York: Alfred A. Knopf, 1993.

Carroll, David. *The Subject in Question: The Language of Theory and the Strategies of Fiction.* Chicago: University of Chicago Press, 1982.

Cavell, Stanley. *The Claim of Reason.* Oxford: Oxford University Press, 1979.

Cohn, Dorit. *Transparent Minds: Narrative Modes for Presenting Consciousness in Fiction.* Princeton: Princeton University Press, 1978.

Crews, Frederick C. *The Tragedy of Manners: Moral Drama in the Later Novels of Henry James.* New Haven: Yale University Press, 1957.

Cross, Mary. *Henry James: The Contingencies of Style.* London: MacMillan, 1993.

Culler, Jonathan. *Saussure.* Glasgow: Fontana, 1976.

———. *The Pursuit of Signs: Semiotics, Literature, Deconstruction.* London: Routledge and Kegan Paul, 1981.

de Man, Paul. *Allegories of Reading: Figural Language in Rousseau, Nietzsche, Rilke, and Proust.* New Haven and London: Yale University Press, 1979.

Derrida, Jacques. *Speech and Phenomena and Other Essays on Husserl's Theory of Signs.* Translated by David B. Allison. Evanston: Northwestern University Press, 1973.

———. *Of Grammatology.* Translated by Gayatri Chakravorty Spivak. Baltimore: Johns Hopkins University Press, 1976.

———. *Writing and Difference.* London: Routledge and Kegan Paul, 1978.

———. *Positions.* Translated by Alan Bass. Chicago: University of Chicago Press, 1981.

Donadio, Stephen. *Nietzsche, Henry James, and the Artistic Will.* New York: Oxford University Press, 1978.

Dupee, F. W. *Henry James.* New York: Doubleday, 1956.

Eliot, T. S., "Tradition and the Individual Talent." In *Selected Essays.* New York: Harcourt, Brace and World, 1964.

Felman, Shoshana. "Turning the Screw of Interpretation." In *Literature and Psychoanalysis: The Question of Reading Otherwise,* edited by Shoshana Felman, 94–207. Baltimore: Johns Hopkins University Press, 1982.

Fogel, Daniel Mark. *Henry James and the Structure of the Romantic Imagination.* Baton Rouge: Louisiana State University Press, 1981.

Forster, E. M. *Aspects of the Novel.* London: Edward Arnold, 1958.

Foucault, Michel. "What is an Author?" In *Textual Strategies: Perspectives in*

Post-Structuralist Criticism, edited by Josué V. Harari, 141–160. London: Methuen, 1979.

Fowler, Virginia C. "Milly Theale's Malady of Self." *Novel* 14 (1980): 7–74.

Freedman, Jonathan. *Professions of Taste: Henry James, British Aestheticism, and Commodity Culture.* Stanford, CA: Stanford University Press, 1990.

Freund, Elizabeth. *The Return of the Reader: Reader-Response Criticism.* Methuen: London and New York, 1987.

Fried, Michael. *Realism, Writing, Disfiguration: On Thomas Eakins and Stephen Crane.* Chicago: University of Chicago Press, 1987.

Fussell, Edwin Sill. *The French Side of Henry James.* New York: Columbia University Press, 1990.

Gabler-Hover, Janet. "Truth and Deception: the Basis for Judgement in *The Wings of the Dove.*" *Texas Studies in Language and Literature* 29 (1987): 169–86.

Gard, Roger, ed. *Henry James: The Critical Heritage.* London: Routledge & Kegan Paul, 1968.

Gelley, Alexander. *Narrative Crossing: Theory and Pragmatics of Prose Fiction.* Baltimore: Johns Hopkins University Press, 1987.

Genette, Gerard. *Narrative Discourse.* Oxford: Basil Blackwell, 1980.

Girard, René. *Deceit, Desire, and the Novel: Self and Other in Literary Structure.* Translated by Yvonne Freccero. Baltimore: Johns Hopkins University Press, 1965.

Goetz, William R. "The Allegory of Representation in *The Tragic Muse.*" *Journal of Narrative Technique* 8 (1978): 151–64.

———. *Henry James and the Darkest Abyss of Romance.* Baton Rouge: Louisiana State University Press, 1986.

Greenblatt, Stephen J., ed. *Allegory and Representation: Selected Papers from the English Institute, 1979–80.* new series, no. 5. Baltimore and London: Johns Hopkins University Press, 1981.

Griffin, Susan M. *The Historical Eye: The Texture of the Visual in Late James.* Boston: Northeastern University Press, 1991.

Grover, Philip. *Henry James and the French Novel: A Study in Inspiration.* London: Paul Elek, 1973.

Habegger, Alfred. *Henry James and the "Woman Business."* Cambridge: Cambridge University Press, 1989.

Higgins, Joanna A. "The Ambassadorial Motif in The Ambassadors." *The Journal of Narrative Technique* 8 (1983): 165–75.

Hochman, Baruch. "The Jamesian Situation: World as Spectacle." *University of Denver Quarterly* 11 (1976): 48–66.

———. *The Test of Character: From the Victorian Novel to the Modern.* Madison, NJ: Fairleigh Dickinson University Press, 1983.

Holland, Laurence Bedwell. *The Expense of Vision.* Princeton: Princeton University Press, 1964.

Howells, William Dean. "Mr. Henry James, Jr. and his Critics." *Literary World* 13 (14 January 1882), 10.

Jacobson, Marcia. *Henry James and the Mass Market.* Tuscaloosa: University of Alabama Press, 1983.

Jolly, Roslyn. *Henry James: History, Narrative, Fiction.* Oxford: Clarendon Press, 1993.

Kappeler, Susanne. *Writing and Reading in Henry James.* New York: Columbia University Press, 1980.

Kaston, Carren. *Imagination and Desire in the Novels of Henry James.* New Brunswick, NJ: Rutgers University Press, 1984.

Kermode, Frank. *The Genesis of Secrecy: On the Interpretation of Narrative.* Cambridge, MA: Harvard University Press, 1979.

Krook, Dorothea. *The Ordeal of Consciousness in Henry James.* Cambridge: Cambridge University Press, 1967.

Lacan, Jacques. *Ecrits: A Selection.* Trans. Alan Sheridan. New York and London: W.W. Norton & Company, 1977.

———. *The Four Fundamental Concepts of Psycho-Analysis.* Translated by Alan Sheridan. Harmondsworth: Penguin, 1979.

Lacoue-Labarthe, Philippe. *The Subject of Philosophy,* edited by Thomas Trezise, translated by Thomas Trezise et al. Minneapolis and London: University of Minnesota Press, 1993.

Landau, John. *"The Ambassadors:* 'The Story of the Story.'" *Hebrew University Studies in Literature and the Arts* 12 (1984): 85–115.

Laplanche, Jean and Pontailis, Jean-Bertrand. *The Language of Psychoanalysis.* Translated by Daniel Lagache. London: Karnac Books, 1988.

Leavis, F. R. *The Great Tradition: George Eliot, Henry James, Joseph Conrad.* London: Chatto & Windus, 1962.

Lemaire, Anika. *Jacques Lacan.* Translated by David Macey. London: Routledge & Kegan Paul, 1977.

Leyburn, Ellen Douglass. *Strange Alloy: The Relation of Comedy to Tragedy in the Fiction of Henry James.* Chapel Hill: University of North Carolina Press, 1988.

Litvak, Joseph. *Caught in the Act: Theatricality in the Nineteenth-Century English Novel.* Berkeley: University of California Press, 1992.

Loesberg, Jonathan. *Aestheticism and Deconstruction.* Princeton: Princeton University Press, 1991.

Lubbock, Percy. *The Craft of Fiction.* New York: Viking Press, 1957.

Macnaughton, William R. "The New York Edition of Henry James's *The Tragic Muse.*" *The Henry James Review* 13, no. 1 (winter 1992): 19–26.

McWhirter, David. *Desire and Love in Henry James: A Study of the Late Novels.* Cambridge: Cambridge University Press, 1989.

Matthiessen, F. O. *Henry James: The Major Phase.* New York: Oxford University Press, 1963.

Matthiessen, F. O., and Kenneth B. Murdock, eds. *The Notebooks of Henry James.* New York: Oxford University Press, 1961.

Miller, James E. "The Writer and His Culture." In *Theory of Fiction: Henry James,* edited by James Miller. Lincoln: University of Nebraska Press, 1972.

Miller, J. Hillis. "The Figure in the Carpet." *Poetics Today* 1. 3 (spring 1980): 106–109.

———. "A Guest in the House: Reply to Shlomith Rimmon-Kenan's Reply." *Poetics Today* 2 (1980): 189–91.

———. *The Ethics of Reading: Kant, de Man, Eliot, Trollope, James and Benjamin*. New York: Columbia University Press, 1987.

Mitchell, Lee Clark. "The Sustaining Duplicities of *The Wings of the Dove*." *Texas Studies in Literature and Language* 29 (1987): 187–214.

Norrman, Ralf. *The Insecure World of Henry James's Fiction: Intensity and Ambiguity*. London: Macmillan, 1982.

The Norton Anthology of English Literature. vol. 2, 3rd ed. New York: Norton, 1974.

Nussbaum, Martha Craven. "Flawed Crystals: James's *The Golden Bowl* and Literature as Moral Philosophy." *New Literary History* 15, no. 4 (1983), 25–50.

———. "Finely Aware and Richly Responsible": Literature and the Moral Imagination." In *Literature and the Question of Philosophy*, edited by Anthony J. Cascardi, 169–91. Baltimore and London: Johns Hopkins University Press, 1987.

Poole, Adrian. *Henry James*. New York and London: Harvester Wheatsheaf, 1991.

Porter, Carolyn. *Seeing And Being: The Plight of the Participant Observer in Emerson, James, Adams, and Faulkner*. Middletown, CT: Wesleyan University Press, 1981.

Posnock, Ross. "Henry James, Veblen and Adorno: The Crisis of the Modern Self." *Journal of American Studies* 21 (1987): 31–54.

———. *The Trial of Curiosity: Henry James, William James, and the Challenge of Modernity*. New York and Oxford: Oxford University Press, 1991.

Pound, Ezra. *Literary Essays of Ezra Pound*. London: Faber and Faber, 1963.

Powers, Lyall H. *Henry James and the Naturalist Movement*. East Lansing: Michigan State University Press, 1971.

Przybylowicz, Donna. *Desire and Repression: The Dialectic of Self and Other in the Late Works of Henry James*. Tuscaloosa: University of Alabama Press, 1986.

Rahv, Philip. "Attitudes Toward Henry James." In *The Question of Henry James*, edited by F. W. Dupee, 280–87. New York: Holt, 1945.

Raphael, Linda. "Levels of Knowing: Development of Consciousness in *The Wings of the Dove*." *The Henry James Review* 11.1 (winter 1990): 58–71.

Reesman, Jeanne Campbell. *American Designs: The Late Novels of James and Faulkner*. Philadelphia: University of Pennsylvania Press, 1991.

Rimmon, Shlomith. *The Concept of Ambiguity: The Example of James*. Chicago: University of Chicago Press, 1977.

———. "Deconstructive Reflections on Deconstruction: In Reply to Hillis Miller." *Poetics Today* 2.1 (1980–81): 185–88.

Rivkin, Julie. "The Logic of Delegation in *The Ambassadors*." *PMLA* 101 (1986): 819–31.

Ron, Moshe. "The Restricted Abyss: Nine Problems in the Theory of *Mise en Abyme*." *Poetics Today* 8 (1987): 417–38.

Rowe, John Carlos. *Henry Adams and Henry James, The Emergence of a Modern Consciousness*. Ithaca: Cornell University Press, 1976.

———. "Structure." In *Critical Terms for Literary Study*. Edited by Frank Lentricchia and Thomas McLaughlin, 23–38. Chicago and London: University of Chicago Press, 1990.

————. *The Theoretical Dimensions of Henry James.* Madison: University of Wisconsin Press, 1984.

Salmon, Richard. "The Secret of the Spectacle: Epistemology and Commodity Display in *The Ambassadors.*" *The Henry James Review* 14.1 (winter 1993): 43–54.

Sangari, Kumkum. "*The Wings of the Dove:* 'Not Knowing, But Only Guessing.'" *The Henry James Review* 13.3 (fall 1992): 292–305.

Schneider, Daniel J. *The Crystal Cage: Adventures of the Imagination in the Fiction of Henry James.* Lawrence: Regents Press of Kansas, 1978.

Sears, Sallie. *The Narrative Imagination.* Ithaca: Cornell University Press, 1968.

Sedgwick, Eve Kosofsky. "The Beast in the Closet: James and the Writing of Homosexual Panic." In *Sex, Politics, and Science in the Nineteenth-Century Novel,* edited by Ruth Bernard Yeazell, 148–86. Baltimore and London: Johns Hopkins University Press, 1986.

————. *Tendencies.* Durham, NC: Duke University Press, 1993.

Segal, Ora. *The Lucid Reflector: The Observer in Henry James's Fiction.* New Haven: Yale University Press, 1969.

Seltzer, Mark. *Henry James and the Art of Power.* Ithaca: Cornell University Press, 1984.

Sherman, Stuart P. "The Aesthetic Idealism of Henry James." In *The Question of Henry James,* edited by F. W. Dupee, 86–106. New York: Holt, 1945.

Silverman, Kaja. "Too Early/Too Late: Subjectivity and the Primal Scene in Henry James." *Novel* 21 (1988): 147–73.

————. *Male Subjectivity at the Margins.* New York & London: Routledge, 1992.

Smith, George E. "James, Degas, and the Modern View." *Novel* 21 (1987): 56–72.

Smith, Peter. *Public and Private Value: Studies in the Nineteenth-Century Novel.* Cambridge: Cambridge University Press, 1984.

Spender, Stephen. "*The Golden Bowl.*" In *The Question of Henry James,* edited by F. W. Dupee, 236–45. New York: Holt, 1945.

Stanzel, Franz K. *A Theory of Narrative.* Translated by Charlotte Goedsche. Cambridge: Cambridge University Press, 1984.

Stevens, Hugh. "Sexuality and the Aesthetic in *The Golden Bowl.*" *The Henry James Review* 14, no. 1 (winter 1993): 55–71.

Stone, Albert, ed. *Twentieth Century Interpretations of "The Ambassadors": A Collectin of Critical Essays.* Englewood Ciffs, NJ: Prentice Hall, 1969.

Stowe, William W. *Balzac, James, and the Realistic Novel.* Princton: Princeton University Press, 1983.

Tanner, Tony. *The Reign of Wonder.* Cambridge: Cambridge University Press, 1965.

————. *Henry James: Modern Judgements.* London: MacMillan, 1968.

————. *Adultery in the Novel: Contract and Transgression.* Baltimore: Johns Hopkins University Press, 1979.

————. *Henry James: The Writer and His Work.* Amherst: University of Massachusetts Press, 1985.

————. "Proust, James and Le Dèsir de Venise," *Journal of American Studies* 21 (1987): 5–29.

Teahan, Sheila. "The Abyss of Language in *The Wings of the Dove*." *The Henry James Review* 14, (spring 1993): 204–214.

Tintner, Adenline R. "The Museum World." In *Henry James: A Collection of Critical Essays,* edited by Leon Edel, 139–155. Englewood Cliffs, NJ: Prentice Hall, 1963.

———. *Henry James and the Lust of the Eyes: Thirteen Artists in His Work.* Baton Rouge and London: Louisiana State University Press, 1993.

Todorov, Tzvetan. *The Poetics of Prose.* Translated by Richard Howard. Ithaca: Cornell University Press, 1977.

Torsney, Cheryl B. "Specula(riza)tion in *The Golden Bowl*." *The Henry James Review* 12, (spring 1991): 141–45.

Veeder, William. *Henry James—The Lessons of the Master: Popular Fiction and Personal Style in the Nineteenth Century.* Chicago: University of Chicago Press, 1975.

Walton, Priscilla L: "'A mistress of shades': Maggie as Reviser in *The Golden Bowl*." *The Henry James Review* 13, no. 2 (spring 1992): 143–53.

Ward, J. A. *The Search for Form: Studies in the Structure of James's Fiction.* Chapel Hill: University of North Carolina Press, 1967.

Watt, Ian. "The First Paragraph of *The Ambassadors:* An Explication." In *Henry James: Modern Judgements,* edited by Tony Tanner, 283–303, London: McMillan, 1968.

Wilkinson, Myler. "Henry James and the Ethical Moment." *The Henry James Review* 11.3 (fall 1990): 153-175.

Williams, Merle A. *Henry James and the Philosophical Novel.* Cambridge: Cambridge University Press, 1993.

Winnett, Susan. *Terrible Sociability: The Text of Manners in Laclos, Goethe, and James.* Stanford, CA: Stanford University Press, 1993.

Woolf, Judith. *Henry James: The Major Novels.* Cambridge: Cambridge University Press, 1991.

Yeazell, Ruth Bernard. *Language and Knowledge in the Late Novels of Henry James.* Chicago: University of Chicago Press, 1976.

Index

aesthete: ethical dimension of, 28–29, 143; figure of, 33, 35–37, 40, 139, 140
aestheticism, 39, 153 n.14
Ambassadors, The, 18, 30, 38, 56–77, 78, 79, 80, 81, 92, 109, 110, 122, 127, 138, 139, 140, 141, 142, 143, 158 n.12
America. *See* international theme
American innocent, 121, 125
American romanticism, 21, 130, 131
American, The, 21
art: as foundation of relationships, 32, 40, 130, 133, 144, 145 n.6, 152 n.6; function of, 48; and generational conflict, 35; views of, 37–38, 155 n.26
artist-audience, 19, 31–55
authorial intrusion, 59, 90, 94. *See also* narrative voice

Balzac, Honoré de, 61, 110
blank, 90, 103, 105–7
Booth, Wayne, 26
Borgias, 134
Bronzino, 101
Brooks, Peter, 17

cable, 63, 64, 123, 159 n.15
Cavell, Stanley, 16, 143
centers of consciousness, 79, 137, 138, 141, 163 n.3
Claim of Reason, The, 16
collecting, 111, 112, 134
copy, 91, 112, 143
correspondence, 60–62, 64, 66–67
Cortez, Hernan, 111, 119, 121

"Daisy Miller," 21
Derrida, Jacques, 20, 23, 24, 62, 164 n.11
differance, 24, 158 n.8, 169 n.5

dissemination, 58, 122. *See also* proliferation
double negative. *See* writing under erasure
dramatic scene, 25, 26, 29, 119, 155 n.28, 172 n.27
Dupee F. W., 25
duplicity 121, 131, 166 n.22. *See also* lie

ethics/aesthetics opposition, 28, 29, 72, 139–43, 149 n.36, 150 n.39, 174 n.38
ethics: code of, 120, 137, 139, 140–41, 148 n.26; problems of, 13, 14–15, 27–28, 115, 122, 125

feminism, 14, 174 n.37
ficelle, 37, 138
figuration, 47
"finger-posts," 22, 146 n.15
focalize, 115, 124. *See also* point of view
Forster, E. M., 58
Freedman, Jonathan, 36
French Revolution: role of, 39

garlands, 136
gaze, 129, 142, 172 n.29
Gelley, Alexander, 29, 30, 139, 141
Gloriani's garden, 70, 73, 74
Golden Bowl, The, 20, 22, 23, 24, 25, 30, 103–35, 136, 138, 139, 140, 142, 143, 144, 170 n.11

history: role of, 39, 121
Hochman, Baruch, 161 n.29
Howells, William Dean, 21
humbugging, 92, 132